TAROT

AND DIVINATION CARDS

A VISUAL ARCHIVE

Laetitia Barbier

TAROT

AND DIVINATION CARDS

A VISUAL ARCHIVE

LAETITIA BARBIER

CERNUNNOS

IN THE BEGINNING
WAS THE VOICE

n the beginning was the voice. These words woke me up in the middle of the night, not as a dream or a spoken statement, but as a kind of message waiting for me. I had spent the day and evening reading this wondrous book, thinking about its array of marvels over many centuries and many traditions, the way it gracefully dances between Renaissance classical art, folk images, alchemical and magical symbols, fashion shows, and mystically received messages, all the way to movies, television, and comic books—and especially how Laetitia moves gracefully through every part of it.

What unites it all is joy, that much is clear on every page—love, and delight for all the manifestations, all the twists and turns of cartomancy and its endless variety. Many years ago, a Greek-American teacher named Ioanna Salajan told a group of us in Amsterdam, "Nothing is learned except through joy." And then she added that many of us would not believe it. I believed it, and I wonder now if it was because the tarot had already come into my life, and even though the cards might expose pain and hard challenges, there was always joy in the discovery.

Laetitia knows this. We see her delight in every picture, every story. We feel it at the beginning, when she tells us that she and the tarot were like "the vampire sweethearts in Jim Jarmusch's movie, *Only Lovers Left Alive,*" always drawn back to each other so that the years would fall away the moment she picked up the cards again.

Notice that she does not say that she was drawn back, but that she and the tarot were pulled to each other. This is a great secret, one that Laetitia not only knows but lays bare before us, over and over—the tarot, and all the varied traditions of *les jeux divinatoires*, the "games" known collectively as cartomancy, are alive, a living being expressed in pictures and meaning.

Let me be clear. I do not refer to angels, or devils, or ghosts haunting or simply inhabiting the pictures. There are certainly many for whom the cards, tarot or others, open them to actual spoken messages from "angels and guides," as many contemporary psychics like to say. Rather, I am talking about something simpler, and perhaps stranger, or at least more direct. For many of us, the cards do not need an outside spirit to enter them. The pictures themselves, fed by centuries of artists and writers and readers devoted to them, become our teachers, our friends—our lovers. All this we find in this wonderful book, in every cluster of images, every *joyous* story.

And let us say as well, and as strongly as possible—no one has ever done anything like this before. To my knowledge, no one has even attempted anything like this, a deep and loving survey of the entire history of cartomancy. We might think of Stuart Kaplan's four-volume *Encyclopedia of Tarot.* But Kaplan's work was exhaustive rather than appreciative, a heroic attempt to include every tarot deck from the beginning to the present—an impossible goal, of course; the final volume was incomplete even before it was released. And, of course, he confined himself to tarot, rather than explore the vast "multiverse" (a comic-book term Laetitia would no doubt appreciate) of cartomancy, from the earliest days to the present.

OPPOSITE PAGE

The High Priestess, Arthur Hacker,
nineteenth century.

Laetitia too does not attempt to cover the vast range of contemporary cards, whether tarot or oracle decks. For this we will have to hope for a second volume. But she certainly explores the world of non-tarot cartomantic traditions, not just the ones many of us know, but deck after deck of obscure miracles, fascinating in their (sometimes unique) mantic systems and gorgeous in their lush art.

And, yet, with all this, there was something else in the book. And so I woke up in the middle of the night with that sentence. *In the beginning was the voice.*

Here is the first thing the book tells us: "I am a Frenchwoman writing in English." There is something special about writers who write in the "tongue," which is to say the sounds, the living voice of their adopted country. We might think of Isaac Bashevis Singer, who began in Yiddish and switched to English, or most famously, Vladimir Nabokov, who first translated his own books from the original Russian, then wrote directly in English. Both of these, Nabokov especially, sought fluency in their new language, the quality of a native speaker.

Laetitia embraces her border-crossing, the straddling of two linguistic worlds to bring a sense of play and wit. It is the Voice of Delight, and it infuses every page, even those that are mostly, sometimes entirely, pictures. For isn't the tradition of cartomancy one of images speaking to us? And here they speak across cultures, as does the author.

As I write this, the internet, that wondrous Otherworld straddling the physical and the disembodied realm of information, has given birth to a new generation of cartomantic mediums. That somewhat ponderous phrase—Laetitia no doubt would find a better one—refers to those psychic card readers mentioned above, who refer to "angels and guides." They use tarot, often multiple decks—and how can you resist, there are so many?—and, like this book, often mix tarot and oracle cards. At the same time, the messages they receive may come in images or statements. And because the internet fosters equality and access above all else, the mediums want us to know that we too have this ability. We just need to open ourselves, to trust. To listen.

For Laetitia, the angels and guides are the cards themselves. And their language, their native tongue, is images, which is to say *beauty*. Look through this book—really, begin anywhere at all and go in any direction at all, and the inescapable message, almost a physical sensation, is that the true language of divination is beauty. The cards in fact contain precise meanings (this is perhaps most true of nineteenth-century cartomancy decks, such as Lenormand), sometimes even written directly on the cards, but they truly speak to us, even the simplest ones, through the power of images.

Many writers on tarot and cartomancy, especially its history, attempt a detached, "objective" style, attempting to distill from their words the passion and curiosity that originally drove them to their subject. Laetitia knows better, for isn't cartomancy, tarot or otherwise, at its core the most subjective and personal of experiences?

Not just the historians, but many of those who write about specific decks and traditions, say, Lenormand in cartomancy, or Etteilla in tarot, give a set of instructions for how to interpret the cards. I remember looking at an Etteilla deck once and noticing that if card A came up next to card B, "you will go on a picnic but it will be rained out." Amazingly, the only time anyone ever did a reading for me with Etteilla, those two cards came out. The reader interpreted them psychologically.

Laetitia actually goes beyond the false separation of objective meaning and subject interpretation. She uses herself as the vehicle of understanding the cards and what they can mean in our lives, and her two languages as something akin to the two sphinxes, one black, one white, who pull the tarot chariot.

She points out that the word *image* becomes, in French, an anagram of the word *magie*, or, in English, "magic." The pictures, she says, "anoint themselves within us, and their beauty brush over our soul." What changes, what *moves* between the two words, is the letter *i*, from the beginning of image to almost the end of magic. In English, that letter becomes not only the I of the reader, but also, in sound (for cartomancy is spoken and heard as well as seen), the *eye* that sees the images and lets them into our soul.

Laetitia sees all this, but with the eye (I) of a poet, a dancer.

This lovely *image* of *magie* comes to us at the beginning of the book, followed quickly by the description of cartomancy as "highbrow, lowbrow, throughout the world, a pocketable museum of art history," with a spread, that is to say, a reading, as "a small-scale temporary exhibition." But of course, this momentary museum exhibit is also a portrait of a person's soul and a map of their lives.

She also tells us that the cards for her become "an Orphic artform," and a "poetic ritual," and then, dancing lightly (Laetitia's movements are never ponderous) "a *trickster* art form." As a storyteller, I *imagine*, that is, see images in the mind's I, a tale of Orpheus the singer, and Hermes, god of magicians and con artists, doing a reading together. And who might their client be? Maybe Laetitia Barbier, at the very beginning of this glorious journey—and then again, at the end.

RACHEL POLLACK

Best known as one of the world's foremost tarot experts, Rachel Pollack is the author of such classics as *Seventy-Eight Degrees of Wisdom* and *The New Tarot Handbook*. She's also the creator of The Shining Tribe Tarot and co-creator with Robert Place of The Burning Serpent Oracle and the Raziel Deck.

A prolific author, Pollack also penned over 40 books of fiction and non-fiction, many of them in the speculative or sci-fi genres, including *Unquenchable Fire*, which won the Arthur C. Clarke Award, and *Godmother Night*, which won the World Fantasy Award. A comic book writer and pioneer, Pollack's work for DC Comics' *Doom Patrol* in the 1990s is celebrated for introducing one of the world's first transgender superheroes.

Rachel's work has been translated into 16 languages, and she has taught and lectured on tarot, creative writing, gender, and innumerable other topics in the U.S. Canada, Europe, the UK, Australia, New Zealand, and China. And until her retirement, she was a senior faculty member of Goddard College's MFA in Writing program.

TABLE OF

CONTENTS

INTRODUCTION

 y name is Laetitia Barbier. I'm a French person who wears many hats. I've been nesting in Brooklyn, New York, for the past ten years following a moderately bohemian past divided between Paris and Berlin. Starting at a young age, I have had an idiosyncratic relationship with the tarot, although it would be dishonest to pretend that I was any good at tarot reading until far later in my adult life. My connection with the cards has evolved immensely over time, mimicking the passionate upheavals of love as they come in and out of my life. Like the vampire sweethearts in Jim Jarmusch's *Only Lovers Left Alive*, my first Marseille deck and I would stay apart for years, only to symbiotically fall back into one another without feeling any time had passed.

In tarot, I found a solid, comfortable, and very private relationship that merged aesthetic and spiritual pursuits and provided solace in times of crisis. The pantheon of archetypal figures within it served as role models, a group of symbolic peers who judged me fairly. They revealed bad news with a dark but witty sense of humor that made my eyes roll and my mind connects the dots. Somehow, I could rely on their presence, even if we didn't have much to say to one another. In this soundless dialogue with the tarot, my own introverted nature thrived. There was something in the beauty of these cards, first the Marseille, then the Rider-Waite-Smith deck, that spoke to my own depth in a very direct, transparent way. It's as if the arcanas had their own poetic language, articulated and clear, a musicality I could immediately comprehend and connect to. From this strange encounter, I learned to understand and map the world around me, name the emotions I would accidentally drown myself in, recognize the paradoxes of my own human nature. Throughout time, these mere pieces of paper have helped me unpack and unlearn, define who I am and who I am not.

What can we learn and who can we learn from by looking at pretty pictures? How much information can we access if we gently pull the thread of our fascination for images? Although these questions weren't really formulated in my brain as I was first experimenting with tarot, the desire to find answers to them is, by default, how I fell into the study of art history. Brought up Catholic, I was raised with a vague understanding that visual representations were capable of carrying sparks of the divine and that we could create transcendent relationships with the sacred through them, using iconography as a gateway. In French, the anagram of "image" is "magie"—magic. And that's something that I took quite literally. Like an anatomist looking for the seat of consciousness in the mechanics of the human body, I yearned to understand the talismanic qualities that images hold, what makes them icons. No matter where the magic hides, the pictures we create or surround ourselves with can animate themselves within us as their beauty brushes over our soul.

Living in Paris, museums became sorts of surrogate churches for me, especially the Musée d'Orsay and the Musée d'Art Moderne de Paris. I remember oscillating between specific paintings at key moments of my life, only to realize later, through introspective work, why I needed to gravitate to these depictions, what they came to signal, the voids they symbolically filled. I loved these artworks as cultural objects, inscribed in the grand history of civilization. Nonetheless, I saw something else in them, beyond the intention of the creator. A projection of myself, a blind spot that I wouldn't otherwise be able to reach. A part of myself appeared fixating on the canvas, laid bare. As I journeyed through the galleries, a sort of dissociation operated in me between the eye of my intellect and the eye of my soul.

My relationship to tarot evolved from this way of reading images when I understood the cards as they flickered through that double gaze and not through a formulaic system of interpretation. Whether they were intended for games or for esoteric purposes, throughout the six centuries covering their existence, these cards were always a product of their own time period, infused with spiritual, artistic, social, or political values of the era in which they appeared. These aspects included the vision of the artist who designed them, the clientele they were meant to entertain, the manufacturing techniques and economical trades they served, and in some case, the occultist who conceptualized them; all these different stratas are capable of igniting something within me as I read the cards for myself or for others. Recently, I began a tumultuous exploration in search of the cards' iconographic lineage, the genealogy of their symbolism, their cultural significance, and the history of their practice. Without surprise, I discovered a culture always in motion, growing organically, morphing through contact with different communities, simultaneously encompassing highbrow and lowbrow, throughout time, throughout the world, a curious phenomenon in which card games were hijacked to become divination or meditation tools because of their powerful imagery. What these images are ultimately about can't really be asserted in a definitive way, although many readers have tried to do so, believing they have pierced the secrets of the "true tarot," calcifying this always shifting tradition to serve a doctrine.

As we'll see, the fifteenth-century Pope of the Visconti-Sforza deck shares very little with the Hierophant of the Rider-Waite-Smith deck, yet the stories these two cards encompass are definitely worth talking about. Cards are the ultimate repository of epitomes, of hyperbolic avatars. As we playfully manipulate them, in the comfort of a simulation, these big ideas appear accessible, less ferocious, and so tiny printed on paper, in the palm of our hands. Their black mirror quality shines back at us, something about our culture, about our own intimacy. Beyond the superficial nature of what they were created for, we scry into them with the hope of meeting the strangers within us.

Within the next pages, we'll see a lot of very pretty pictures. Packs of cards are more than ludic devices—they share many connections with the realm of the arts. A tarot deck, for example, is like a pocketable museum. In essence, it presents a static collection ruled by a linear progression. The numbered Minor and Major Arcanas and their narrative sequence can be read like art history itself. The Fool's Journey is a continuum, a initiatic story, canonic and empirical, an operatic succession of low and high points. When we shuffle the cards and arrange them into a spread, they become small-scale temporary exhibitions, gracefully curated by serendipity. Keeping the integrity of their own narrative, each card is reinvented, building a new story through the contact with other cards. In this symbolic pileup, we see them paradoxically identical yet nuanced, metamorphasized. The Surrealists called this very phenomenon "objective chance"—from an unpredictable encounter (let's say, for example, an umbrella and a sewing machine on a dissection table), new ideas automatically emerge, unexpected answers arise before our eyes. A color will lose its primary sense and speak to us differently. Friction and other dynamics will carry our attention beyond what is objectively visible. Suddenly, these cards we've seen a thousand times will appear in a new light. As readers, we are meant to study what's on the cards, but also to pay attention to what exists in the interstitial cracks forming between them.

Over the years, I've learned to appreciate tarot as more of an Orphic art form than a fortune-telling tool. It is a poetic ritual in which words and images are woven into time and space to offer us comfort, grounding, or advice. It also is a trickster art form, because the cards aren't here to tell the truth. They shed light on one of many truths that needs to be heard, seen, and made real for an instant.

Although it sounds very abstract, one of the most iconic examples of that process might be found in the cult science-fiction film *The Matrix*, and its incredible Oracle scene. In the classic sequence, Neo is brought to a diviner so she can confirm that he is "the One." I've always loved that scene for how demystifying and against expectation this contemporary prophetess, played by Gloria Foster, was, redefining the idea of a sibyl in such a drastic and inspiring way. Modern and empress-like, warm and accessible. As spectators, we are meant to understand pretty quickly that she is the *real deal*: She knows Neo is going to break a vase upon arrival, and she talks about very intimate details concerning his relationship to Morpheus. Then comes the "reading" part, performed quite comically like a medical exam: She puts her glasses on, auscultating him like a physician, asking him to open his mouth, looking at the eyes and palms, amusing herself even about the theatrics of her mystical performance while she smokes cigarettes and bakes cookies. And the auguries are fatally announced: Neo is not the One. Of course, the plot will reveal later that he is. Was she wrong? Did she know but couldn't tell? Like the Matrix Oracle, the cards often need to say no for us to be able to create a yes. What would have happened if the Oracle had told Neo who he was? Maybe he would have caved in, out of fear, crushed under the responsibility of being a cyber messiah. Maybe his ego, bloated by the flattery of such an important mission, would have failed him. As the Oracle says no, she lays the first stone for him to do the initiatic process to become the One and accomplish his destiny. With the cards, we learn we have to build our path by ourselves in response to the message—with it or against it.

What is this book really about? *Tarot and Divination Cards: A Visual Archive* is about the culture of cartomancy in a broader sense: the art and practice of reading cards—all types of cards. Within these pages, we'll look at six centuries of card-making and explore where this impulse of using them for prognostic or introspective work comes from, who does it, and why. We'll try to see what these images translate about humans and our obsession with playing games, translating images into words, and creating order out of chaos. As we look through these images from the past and explore what they communicated as they evolved through time, we'll also try to get a grip on how this culture is being revived today, through new economical systems, communication tools, and the transformation of the practice of tarot reading itself. We'll see how artists, readers, scholars of all generations, genders, and races, have allowed for these card-centric practices to find a new legitimacy and democratize themselves.

Although grounded in history, it would be a wrongful assessment to believe this book is the work of a tarot historian. I can't pretend to be a prestigious scholar of the likes of Michael Dummett, Mary K. Greer, Paul Huson, Robert Place, or Andrea Vitali, who among many others, spent decades working on these topics and whose work I admire greatly. As we'll see together, the history of tarot and card practices is a rich and complex field, laced with disagreements and speculations, which is why I'm including a lengthy bibliography. Whatever this book lacks, you'll be able to find a plethora of websites, publications, books, and many other joyous rabbit holes in which you can carve your own conclusion.

With great humility, I can admit that my work will always be biased. Although I have an academic background, I am a tarot reader, and the poetic eye will always prevail over the intellectual one. For this very reason, this book isn't encyclopedic, either—doesn't pretend to show the most iconic examples nor the most historically relevant. Curated with the help of my own arbitrary sensibility, I'm showing a collection of examples that I find fascinating for their beauty, the originality of their system, or the incredible story they tell. This book was born out of my dual relationship with the cards themselves. Esoteric and exoteric, cards as both poetic auguries and cultural products. I'd love to believe this publication exists in this liminal space. A space in which curiosity is tickled. My ultimate intent was to showcase the great beauty and wealth of the cards and make them accessible to a wider audience, whether they are divination card enthusiasts or just amateurs of pretty pictures.

Laetitia Barbier

OPPOSITE PAGE
The Star, Brady Tarot, Emi Brady. 2018.

A BRIEF HISTORY
OF CARDS AND THEIR USE
AS A SPIRITED DEVICE

Diving into the history of card divination is akin to the act of inspecting of a beautiful piece of Chantilly lace: a strange, tantalizing experience, flickering through opacity and see-through perceptions, interwoven storylines and a great deal of holes and mysteries in which one is invited to imagine what hides behind hazy veils. Writing a thorough and empirical history of card divinations is a thorny, ever-shifting enterprise for a myriad of reasons. On one hand, this story exists in the shadow of other more concrete, well-documented narratives, like the development of card games, the evolution of printed media, or the accessibility of paper in late medieval Europe, for example. But whether we discuss tarot, piquet, or minchiate decks, we have to keep in mind that these packs of cards were invented for play, nothing else. The phenomenon of reading fortunes with them is a bastardization of their primary function, a sort of intuitive hijacking. The divide between card history as cultural objects and their vernacular use for magic or divination is hard to parse through. As we'll see, the earliest decks commercially released as esoteric tools date from the eighteenth century, and, to this day, historians still debate the use of cards for divination prior to that time because of the lack of tangible evidence or written documents. Yet, like many other forms of folk divination condemned by the Catholic Church, we could easily imagine why such practices would have been perilous to chronicle or advertise, so they were left to survive between the cracks of orality and clandestinity. Nonetheless it is hard to believe that cartomancy and later taromancy—products of the perennial human obsession with creating meaning out of the chaos of life—were suddenly born after centuries of card circulations, while so many other games of chance, like dice, were used in some playful scrying.

On the other hand, the inherent fragility of the cards themselves, preventing their conservation, hinders their studies to the few examples that survive the passage of time. For every pack of cards we have left, there might have been hundreds of others simultaneously in circulation, now withered away and lost forever. In the context of the tarot, the earliest example we have access to are the precious decks commissioned by the Northern Italian aristocracy in the fifteenth century, kept like treasures behind the prestigious doors of libraries. Yet these exceptional objects, designed as status symbols, only inform us about a small layer of the card culture from then on, and fail to address the *carta vulgaris*, the infra-world of popular card playing, of mass-produced decks and their hypothetical divinatory use. Never thought to be valuable, these ephemeras turned into dust, only leaving a handful of games, a minuscule fragment of each epoch's reality.

OPPOSITE PAGE

Fresco from the Casa Borromeo in Milan, Italy, showing a group of tarocchi players, unknown artists, 1440s.

In the realm of card divination scholarship, we grasp onto a small array of historical evidence, the tip of an iceberg mostly submerged by oblivion, leaving much room for speculation and romantic theories. Many occultists mythologized cards and their sacred origins, sometimes to justify a doctrine, affirm their spiritual authority, or have a definitive assessment of the white whale that is the "true tarot." An understanding of the cards' factual history began to solidify in the twentieth century as scholars began to untangle the romance from reality, carving out different narratives, distanced from the esoteric, yet always with one foot plunged in the dark. Still in the making, this history is filled with tricksters and legends. Theories can shift at any moment every time a scholar finds a missing link—a text or a card in a forgotten drawer of an institution, a piece of evidence that joins together two elements of this historical puzzle. Here, I'll try my best to break down this parceled story in a synthetic fashion, looking at what we know for fact, as well as the different satellite beliefs surrounding each era, but please be aware that I'm only brushing the surface of a history that is always in motion.

Card games arrived in Europe around the late fourteenth century. If the Chinese invented the concept of playing with pieces of printed paper, trade connections helped these games to diffuse and adapt in different ways through Persia, India, or Northern Africa. One of the most established theories knighted the so-called Mamluk deck as the legitimate ancestor of our playing cards. Originating around the thirteenth century in the Mamluk Sultanate of Egypt, this game of cards was composed of four suits (Cups, Polo Sticks, Scimitars, and Coins) as well as a group of four non-figurative courtcards (King, First Governor, Second Governor, and Helper[1]), a structure and suit system that our Western card games inherited.

Brought by merchants and sailors, these games inherited from the Muslim world were introduced to Europe by its Mediterranean gateways. Spain and Italy developed their own singular games according to a nomenclature comparable to the one developed by the Mamluk decks, adjusting the suits to Cups, Coins, Swords or Arrows, and Clubs. In the blink of an eye, card games went viral, produced en masse via woodblock printing presses and circulated, all over the rest of Europe, so much that local governments were compelled to write laws against gambling. The Church also pulled the trigger, adding card playing to the long list of sinful behaviors capable of corrupting one's soul.

In the fifteenth century, the Italians conceptualized a new type of deck, including a fifth suit, a group of allegorical cards referred to as the trionfi suit, which aimed to add some complexity to trick-taking games. More cards, more fun. Left for us to admire are the several Visconti decks commissioned by the Duchy of Milan, as well as a couple of other examples from Northern Italy. Gilded and hand-painted, these decks were prized possessions and luxury assets, often portraying cameos of the family members who commissioned them or their coats of arms. Within these next pages, we'll look at many of these early trump cards and come to appreciate their great iconographic variety; in the beginning, the trionfi cards featured an unfixed sequence of images. Like a pictorial laboratory, they present a visual matrix of the known world, ordered from the microcosmic to the macrocosmic, in which secular characters meet philosophical allegories, antique divinities, and cosmic representations. At this point in time, the choice of images on these cards evoke, if not esoteric practices, a sophisticated attitude toward the connection between images and the profound depth of their symbolic meanings.

During the sixteenth and seventeenth centuries, card culture tentacularity expanded over Europe with a profusion of new games, decks, and systems. If cards were alive and well in Italy, they became a favorite pastime in France, which developed its own suits system (Hearts, Clubs, Diamonds, and Spades), just as Germany did (Hearts, Leaves, Bells, and Acorns), both countries falling head over heels into the trionfi deck bandwagon. If "tarau" is listed as one of the two hundred games played by ogre Gargantua in Rabelais's sixteenth-century novel, the earliest examples of French tarot accessible to us are from the seventeenth century. The Vieville Tarot, the early

RIGHT
"Card Maker Costume" from *Costumes grotesque* (Fancy Trade Costumes), Nicolas de Larmessin, 1695.

Jean Noblet, or the Anonymous Parisian showcase a plural iconography, while the order of the trump cards shifts from one *maitre cartier* to another. Inspired by similar conceptual axes, each deck is visually reinterpreted according to the card maker's taste and poetic licence. All these variations will be calcified in around the eighteenth century according to one standardized pattern which will become known as the *Tarot de Marseille*. However, if the Phocean city swarms with card making artisans (François Bourlion, François Chosson, Jean François Tourcaty), other card makers in Besançon, Dijon, or Paris, but also Swiss and Belgium artisans instigate popular tarot decks with slightly different patterns.

1781—a coup de théâtre in tarot land with the publication of the eighth volume of *Le Monde Primitif* (The Primeval World), an encyclopedic behemoth by French erudite Antoine Court de Gébelin. In the last book of this ambitious, all-encompassing project, the Protestant pastor and Freemason claims for the first time that tarot is an esoteric tool and the repository of a lost hermetic knowledge, a statement that will dramatically reshape tarot's perception, setting the pack of cards into Western esotericism for the centuries to come. In his chapter dedicated to the popular card games[2], Court de Gébelin recounts the fateful episode in which this revelation came to be. One evening, invited in some private salons, a woman he identified as "Madame C. de H." persuaded him to join her party for a game of tarot. The deck puzzled him, as he admitted he had never seen anything like it before, describing the cards as "a rhapsody of bizarre and extravagante figures."[3] Yet, as he explains, it took him a dashing fifteen minutes[4] to decipher the allegories presented on the cards and declare the Egyptian origins of the tarot in a definitive way. Although based on a self-possessed revelation rather than historical evidence, Court de Gébelin's affirmation is a butterfly effect moment of the world of reading cards, reinventing tarot for the century to come. Moreover, since *Le Monde Primitif* also featured illustrations of a *Tarot de Marseille*, Court de Gébelin's text hammered the temporary hegemony of the Marseille model as the "true tarot" par excellence. The author indeed describes how the *Most Sacred Book of the Egyptian* was concealed in a vulgar vessel, a pack of cards, to avoid being destroyed, but his keen initiated eye wouldn't be fooled. This chapter also discusses early sacred numerology aspects of the cards and some fabulist etymological sources for the "tarot." The text is followed by an equally seminal and disputable essay by the Comte de Mellet (writing as the "C. de M.***") on tarot as a divination tool. He describes the narrative sequence of trumps as an allegory of the three ages—Golden Age, Silver Age, and Iron Age—inverting the sequence and starting with the World card to finish with the Bateleur. But most importantly, he'll discuss the use of playing cards for divination in more technical terms, and for the first time in history, will refer to tarot as the Book of Thoth. Although historically erroneous, the belief in the Egyptian origins of the tarot is a pure product of the eighteenth-century zeitgeist, squeezed between the early hours of disciplines like archeology but before the Champollion era, his subsequent translation of hieroglyphs, and a more rigorous approach to historical research. At that time, Ancient Egypt was embraced as an exotic and mystical civilization, its elaborate funerary rites, theriomorphic gods, and a bewildering mythology fueling the imaginations of esoteric groups trying to emulate the ancient world's mystery schools. Court de Gébelin and De Mellet's lack of historical accuracy can be interpreted as absurd to our twenty-first century practices, but they were not aberrant for that time.

The eighteenth century is one of the first golden ages of the art of reading cards, marked by many theories and publications paving the way of this culture for the century to come. Jean Baptiste Alliette, aka Etteilla, published the first books on cartonomancy in the 1770s, offering for the first time in publication a technical method with spreads and formulaic meanings to be used with a regular piquet playing card deck. The Etteilla case is fascinating, and we will dedicate a full chapter to it later as we'll look at his decks since, in the 1790s, Alliette famously tergiversated. Influenced by the work of Court de Gébelin and De Mellet, the "algebra master" will subsequently fully revisit his card mythos after reading *Le Monde Primitif*, contributing to the diffuse the idea of tarot as the esoteric legacy of the Egyptians. A keen merchant and prolific writer, Alliette created his own reading system, doubling down by publishing the first card deck published solely as a divination tool, with a set of trump cards reordered according to his own Book of Thoth interpretation.

Many aspects of his legacy allowed card readings to be accessible to a wider audience. More importantly, and along with Mademoiselle Lenormand, Alliette was instrumental in establishing the cartomancer as a public, popular archetype going from a fairground act to an educated mystic, with the attempt to legitimize the profession as a quasi-scholarly practice, if not a science. Boosting that signal to the apex of European fame, Lenormand, the first "celebrity cartomancer" and improbable French Revolution[5] icon, will become a literal household name for cartomancy. After her death, several card makers will (re)brand old games into new divination systems bearing the name and sometimes the idealized likeness of the famed Parisian sibyl to quench the growing thirst for fortune-telling games.

Throughout the nineteenth century, the divide between the popular and esoteric approach to card divination widened, sharply cleaving the diffusion of popular cartomancy against the development of the occult tarot. On one hand, card production boomed with the industrial revolution, accelerating the creation and circulation of oracular decks to a mass audience. In France, *La Sibylle des Salons*, *Le Livre du Destin*, and a plethora of other packs of cards were designed to appeal to a new market of armchair cartomancers. Without any esoteric knowledge whatsoever, these novices could just pick up these oracle games and give themselves a lighthearted reading following the simplified instruction provided or the indications and keywords conveniently inscribed directly onto the cards. In Germany and Eastern Europe, the *Petit Lenormand* or *Kipper Karten* became popular fortune-telling games, and each country, according to their own sensibility, developed a kinship for one system or another. Musing on one's future is a recreational parlor occupation. "Mariage," "Money," "Betrayal," "Birth," "Gossip," "Court Case"—the designs of these cards usually present a little nineteenth-century time capsule, displaying the fashion, architecture, or way of life of their times. Most importantly, the attributed meaning of these folk systems reflects the hopes and fears of everyday people wondering what this tumultuous era will bring to them as the century constantly shifts between political upheavals, economic developments, and the birth of new social classes. Card-based divination games were everywhere, from chocolate giveaways to newspaper stalls, and for a couple of nickels, one could purchase a humble pamphlet[6] capable of turning a regular playing card deck into a domestic fate soother.

ABOVE LEFT AND RIGHT
"Shipwreck" and "Fortune" cards from a unique, hand-colored divination deck created in France in 1791.

In response to these times ruled by materialism, technological advancements, and a growing suspicion toward conventional religion, the occult sensibility deepens and new forms of spirituality emerge, thriving on a longing to reconnect differently to the sacred. The mid- and late-nineteenth century era will see many new philosophical systems or practices bloom, regularly amalgamating ancient magical traditions with more modern views. Tarot is of course a prominent part of this story, in no small part because Eliphas Levi's work contributed greatly to make the popular card game into the esoteric vessel par excellence. Probably the most influential occult thinker of his time, the once-named Alphonse-Louis Constant was a former sub-deacon who left the Catholic Church because of a failed paramour and subsequently deep-dived into High Magic, promulgating a reconciliation between religion and science through the form of a syncretic esoteric practice. His massive *Dogme et Rituel de la Haute Magie* (Dogma and Ritual of High Magic), published in two volumes between 1854 and 1855, will exist as one of the cornerstones of French esotericism for the next century, serving as a seminal text for several generations of occultists. What makes Levi's contribution so important is that he manages to establish a coherent correspondence system between several ancient traditions within the Tarot de Marseille trump cards. Suddenly, alchemy, astrology, or hermeticism find a consistent expression within the cards onto which Levi also assigns a letter of the Hebrew alphabet, linking the tarot to the study of Kabbalah. With his acidic opinions of cartomancy, Levi will contribute to polarizing these profane practices and establish the esoteric studies of the tarot as a well of transcendence. Comprised within its twenty-two Major Arcanas, the impeccable synthesis of the rational and the metaphysical was laid bare for those who could decipher its content, a mystical portal opening toward the sacred wisdom of the past.

Dogme et Rituel de la Haute Magie set the tone for the next hundred years, and the legacy of Levi's work would have a profound influence on the work of Papus, Oswald Wirth, Falconnier, and the myriads of esoteric scholars of the French Belle Epoque. It is important to note that the occult tarot at this point is usually seen as a meditation object and a sacred book, and not really in its profane form as a pack of cards. Envisioned as a set of hieroglyphic icons, the twenty-two cards are from now on referred to as the "Majors Arcanas,"[7] usually tightly bound in a codex, to be studied progressively in its original order, the cards and their symbolic narrative guiding the allegorical process of initiation.

1886—On the other side of the Channel, a young Brooklyn-born, British-raised scholar, who had discovered Levi's work a handful of years prior, publishes for the first time a summarized version of the French magus' esoteric theories for the Anglophone world. *The Mysteries of Magic: A Digest of the Writings of Eliphas Levi*, compiled by a twenty-nine-year-old Arthur Edward Waite, greatly impacts a Great Britain culture already twirling at full speed in its own occult revival. This same year, theosophist and ceremonial magician William Wynn Westcott sketches a group of drawings guided by the interpretative descriptions of Levi's work. Apart from the chariot and its two sphinxes directly mimicking the illustrations of Levi's *Rituel de la Haute Magie*, the Westcott cards are unique and icon-like, hieratic and meticulously symbolical, but completely removed from the classic iconography of the French games. In fact, tarot isn't really played in Great Britain, and a Marseille pack would have been rather hard to find in Victorian England, which left much room to imagine the visual impact of the Major Arcanas and their magical subtext. Wescott, along with fellow occultists McGregor Mathers and Woodman later founded the Hermetic Order of the Golden Dawn, an initiatic organization whose teachings mended together esoteric philosophy and ceremonial rites, incorporating many ancient traditions and in which the study of the Major Arcanas of the tarot became central. As tarot historian Helen Farley[8] suggests, McGregor Mathers is the one who will place the study of tarot at the center of the Golden Dawn magical teachings, renovating quite a bit of the corpus of interpretations and renaming some of the cards to match a doctrinal body laced with ancient philosophy. Under his impulse, The Bateleur becomes the Magician, the Pope morphed into the Hierophant and the Popess emerges as the lunar High Priestess. Mathers will invert the Justice and the Strength cards, now respectively number XI and VIII to adjust the order of the cards to his system that corresponded to the Kabbalah.

RIGHT

"Liberal person, loyal friend," King of Hearts cartomancy card showing an elegantly dressed woman leaving money in a donation box. Produced by Chocolat du Foyer, these little cartomancy cards were given as a free gift with chocolate bars. Printed by La Lithographie Parisienne, late nineteenth century.

BOTTOM LEFT

Oswald Wirth's *Bateleur*, first card of his *Tarot des Imagiers du Moyen Âge* (The Tarot of the Magicians), associated with the Hebrew letter *Alef*.

BOTTOM RIGHT

The World, tarot sketch by William Wynn Westcott, 1886.

The Golden Dawn teachings turns into an incubator for what will later become the full-fledged Anglo-Saxon tarot tradition, conspired as we'll see by two of its former members. Riffed with internal feuds, the order slowly disbanded starting in 1899, ostracizing the Aleister Crowley - McGregor Mathers clan and forcing fractions to form satellite initiatory groups. Waite, our early Eliphas Levi translator, evolved into a preeminent occult scholar and, freed from the political battles within the Hermetic Order, initiated the conception of his first tarot deck. For the design, he sought the services of artist extraordinaire Pamela Colman Smith, herself initiated to the Golden Dawn.

Bohemian and multi-faced genius, "Pixie" Colman Smith, a Pratt Institute student, wore many hats at the time. She working as a set and costume designer for the Lyceum Theater along with Bram Stoker and Ellen Terry, while juggling a writing career, her own publishing business, and work as an illustrator, folklorist, and storyteller. A visionary artist in her own right, she developed a synesthetic approach to painting triggered by music. The experience of sounds inspired her shapes and colors, enabling her to automatically transcribe sonic tonalites into epic scenes, weaving together the whimsical and the poetic. Her bold, unique visual style, influenced by art nouveau, symbolism, and Japanese ukiyo-e, is incredibly subtle, conveying complex narrative depths with very few lines and details. If her legacy was almost forgotten during the twentieth century, her name has been reestablished within the past decades as the unsung hero of the tarot world, her artistic contribution becoming the classic template of many decks created in Great Britain and the United States.

Waite commissioned Smith's original drawings of tarot's seventy-eight cards, executed for a flat fee, between April and October 1909. If Waite might have been heavily involved in the visual conception of the Major Arcanas, he seemingly gave carte blanche to Colman Smith in order to create the minor suits according to her own vision. Inspired by the Sola Busca deck, an Italian game from the fifteenth century, she is credited for the idea of designing a set of figurative images instead of the geometric pip cards, an innovation breathing dramatic and psychological intensity in this traditionally abstract group of cards. This groundbreaking alteration, a revolution so to speak, allows any novice to intuitively connect with the evocative dimension of the cards, and ultimately to their esoteric significance. The first dynamic duo of the tarot, the Waite-Smith collaboration will turn into the cartomantic golden standard in the English-speaking world, morphing the pack of cards into an Aquarius age must-have. Indeed, in the 1970s, Stuart R. Kaplan and his freshly founded company U.S. Games Systems negotiated the copyrights of the deck with Waite's daughter Sybil to publish it on the United States territory, greatly contributing in anchoring Colman Smith's extraordinary images in the popular imagination.

As mentioned earlier, Waite wasn't the only Golden Dawn squire experimenting with tarot production, and if the Waite-Smith duet produced a canonic deck, the Thoth Tarot isn't far behind in popularity. Brainchild of trickster supreme Aleister Crowley and artist Lady Frieda Harris, the Thoth is another example in which a complex esoteric system is brought to life by the visions of a psychic artist.

The recent discovery of the Collection of Palermo in 2012 shows that Crowley was already interested in assembling his own interpretation of the tarot while he was in Cefalu, Sicily, establishing his magical utopian commune, the Abbey of Thelema. From the small group of oil paintings produced by the British magus in the 1920s, two of them openly portray tarot cards: an Egyptian-inspired Moon card showing two Anubis-like divinities facing each other in a nocturnal landscape and a self-portrait of Crowley as the Hierophant, on which the number 5, associated with the card, is clearly visible.

OPPOSITE PAGE

Sun card, Pamela Colman Smith,
Rider-Waite-Smith Tarot, 1909.

Crowley and Harris joined forces on this project from 1938 to 1944. With her modernist lines and darker palettes, the artist managed to empower Crowley's renovated tarot system, incorporating his interpretation of Kabbalah, astrology, and his own doctrinal system. Nebulous and sophisticated, the Thoth Tarot is, to many, the culmination of Crowley's work, a visual compendium synthesizing a lifetime of esoteric research. Crowley and Harris's merged talent was revealed as *The Book of Thoth*, a limited publication of two hundred copies. Though neither of them lived to see their work distilled into a deck of cards, the Thoth Tarot is nonetheless considered a quintessential esoteric tool, vying in popularity with its Waite-Smith cousin.

With the 1960s and the development of the *occulture*, tarot and card divinations adapted and transformed, forging distinctive and parallel paths, expanding as a tool for self-exploration, introspection, and a starting point for psychological reflection. Authors like Eden Gray, Rachel Pollack, Alejandro Jodorosky, and Mary K. Greer contributed to democratizing its practice while raising its integrity standard and allowing for its complexity to be accessible to a broader audience. Toward the end of the twentieth century, reading cards transformed into a normalized ritual, both sacred and profane, using a spiritual device that many feel inspired to explore and reinvent.

Starting in the 1990s, new types of decks appeared, bearing witness to the great variety of practices and practitioners coming from all sides of the spiritual spectrum and social fabric. Transformed into a political oracle, tarot slowly brews the urge for representations, showcasing the diversity of people who feel the desire to reclaim their spirituality with such a versatile tool, infusing with great inventiveness its perennial tradition with their own symbolic modalities.

Inspired by television, film franchises, comics, and pulp literature, novelty tarots mushroom in legions at bookstores and lifestyle retailers, making tarot purists roll their eyes, yet demonstrating so profoundly how our pop culture fills the void of ancient archetypes and creates new pantheons in which we can identify with. And, as with everything else, the internet will completely reshuffle the way we experience card culture, research its history, produce decks, learn how to read cards, and form guilds of interest around them.

The millennial divination culture is a real renaissance, moving forward an arcane art form with the help of micro-technological revolutions; library and museum digital collections such as Gallica/Bibliothèque nationale de France or the British Museum suddenly giving access for free to historical card decks and primary sources profoundly expanded the way we perceive and research cards. This availability of information and the ability for people to create platforms on forums or social media to share their theories stimulate a constant dialogue and contribute to keep cards practices and its research a lively, expandable field. This accessibility, one could argue, might be partly responsible for the regain of interest in historical systems. Once known by a handful of selected enthusiasts, the Lenormand system is now a popular alternative for cartomancers who have access to hundreds of new decks each years. One could wonder now if the slightly overlooked Etteilla might soon grow toward the same fate. And, thanks to digital means, historical decks from the sixteenth and seventeenth centuries are often restored as absolute labor-of-love ventures by makers longing to reconnect to tarot's glorious past, and by extension, introducing these antiquated decks to a new generation of diviners.

Within the past ten years, the development of Kickstarter completely reshaped the way card decks are financed, allowing some of them to become cult objects before even being produced. The secret architect of so many revolutionary decks, Kickstarter served as a creative midwife for a large cohort of artists and makers, allowing them to find their own audience, support their projects, and regularly create a financially sustainable life around what they hold so sacred. Unveiled in 2019 by Meredith Graves, in-house Director of Music and Many Magickal Things, Witchstarter contributed greatly in defining what would become the business model of contemporary deck-making. Through that system, a new type of cards bloomed, created by artists. More experimental, aesthetically rigorous, norm-challenging, or simply just extravagantly niche, these cards are other, freed from a commercial need to please the mainstream taste, divorced from the idea of a one-size-fits-all spiritual quest. For the first time in card history, we have a somehow cloudless, panoramic view on this practice past, present, and future. And if, as we'll see in these pages, that past is fascinating, I hope that by the end of this book, you'll believe as much as I do that its future is just as exhilarating.

LEFT

The Moon, Aleister Crowley, from the Palermo Collection, 1920–23, courtesy of the OTO.

THE MAJORS ARCANAS

THE FOOL

ohubohu—an expression commonly used by the French to describe incomprehensible noises. A loud, continuous, and often irritating sound whose origins can't be identified. The term, derived from the Hebrew phrase *Tohu wa-bohu*, which appears prominently as one of the early sentences of Genesis, as part of the ancient testament's effort to define the primordial chaos and darkness at the beginning of time, before the divine creative act.

In the narrative sequence formed by the Major Arcana cards, the Fool is the Tohu Bohu. The primitive, unshaped energy, where all things emerge from and return. Associated with the numbers zero or twenty-two, our Fool is a sort of wild card, a dynamic alpha and omega tightrope walk through the symbolic tale of the trump cards. Our Fool is the materia prima of the alchemists, the raw substance whose successive encounter with the archetypal figures of the cards will allow him to find shape and lead him to transcendence.

Like a commencement clap, a big bang, he attracts our attention, sucking us into the parade of archetypes we are about to meet. In the *Tarocchi Fine dalla Torre*, we catch him in a jig, dancing and simultaneously playing the flute while beating drums. In the Sola Busca, our Mato plays bagpipe, a musicality and enthusiasm for wind instruments that might find echos in the etymology of his name. The "Fool," a word derived from the Latin follis, used to describe bellows and empty leather bags. In this context, one can read a pejorative commentary based on the fact that the head of our protagonist is hollow, inflated with air, windy. "Empty vessels make the most noise," as some might say.

The Fool's cacophony reminds me of the Feast of Fools, a medieval tradition abolished in 1445 after the Protestant Faculty of Theology of Paris found that these obscene and pagan manifestations violated good morals.[1] One day a year, on January 1, people were allowed to transgress all the rules dictated by the church and state. A day of inversion and anarchist merriment in which one would conjure the spirit of the Fool: temporary madness, lewdness, and irreverence toward the established order. Hence in the Momus card of the *Minchiate de Poilly*, our jingling jester takes the role of the Roman god of satire and mockery, who ridicules the gods and lampoons Zeus for being a violent god, incapable of refraining from his lust toward women. His nefarious talents lead Momus to be expelled from Mount Olympus. What happens to him next? Does he become a rolling stone, wandering aimlessly as he loses his place among the Olympian divinities? Like Momus, the Fool belongs nowhere, therefore he is at home everywhere.

In the *Misero* card and the infamous Noblet card, the Fool appears as a vagabond, a destitute whose nudity isn't related to indecent behavior this time. His exposed body is an indicator of his complete *décalage* to his surroundings. The sensitive flesh of both characters is attacked by small animals, fangs and claws all out. The first does not flinch, his gaze contemplating the horizon, lost in his meditative thoughts. The other, caught in a frantic pilgrimage, keeps going, moving forward, unbothered by the bite, as if pushed by a calling. Both are disconnected from our reality, closer to a divine one. His uncanny, inherent wisdom makes him a maverick, pushing him at the edge of society. Like the animals around him, the Fool is uncollared, carefree, undomesticated. He is a feral soul.

OPPOSITE PAGE

Laughing Fool, attributed to Jacob Cornelisz van Oostsanen, sixteenth century.

In his *Tarot des Imagiers du Moyen Âge*, Oswald Wirth depicts a somehow incongruous creature to the Fool's bestiary, a crocodile,[2] hidden by an elongated pillar. The Swiss occultist describes the image using these terms: "The Lynx with piercing eyes, is pursuing the insentient Wanderer towards an upturned obelisk, behind which a crocodile lies in wait, ready to devour whatever is destined to return to chaos, that is to the primeval substance from which the ordered world was born."[3]

The Fool's crocodile lingered as a visual trope until the legendary Egyptians origins of tarot were objected to by history itself. The voracious reptile recalls Ammitt, devourer of souls, a symbol of danger, highlighting by contrast the naivete and inexperience of the Fool. One could also see it as a personification of Sobek, the Egyptian god of fertility, who somehow self-created, emerging from the primeval waters of Nun. Vigorously walking toward Sobek, the Fool could be seen as what Paul Foster Case called "the active principle of existence prior to actual manifestation."[4] Perhaps he is born to be wild. Maybe he is wild to be born. He bends the rules, mocks himself, fails, and smiles. He is connected to divine exuberance instead of instinctive fear and will never trade an occasion to stop and smell the roses.

Mato, Sola Busca Tarot, Italy, fifteenth century.

Fool card from the *Tarocchi Fine dalla Torre*, Bologna, Italy, seventeenth century.

Fool card from the so-called Gringonneur or Charles VI Tarot, Northern Italy, fifteenth century.

ABOVE LEFT
Fool card from the Vieville Tarot, France, seventeenth century.

ABOVE RIGHT
Le Fou, Noblet Tarot, France, 1659.

FOLLOWING SPREAD, LEFT
Momus card from Minchiate de Poilly, François de Poilly, published around 1712 and 1741.

FOLLOWING SPREAD, RIGHT
La fête des fous et des diacres (The Feast of Fool and Deacons), from *Paris a travers les siècles* (Paris Through the Centuries), Gourdon de Genouillac, 1881.

Momus

LA FÊTE DES FOUS ET DES DIACRES

(XVIIᵉ SIÈCLE)

Misero, so-called Mantegna Tarot,
E-series, engraved by Johann Ladenspelder,
published between 1540-1550.

LEFT

Fool card from the Visconti-Sforza Tarot,
Milan, Italy, fifteenth century.

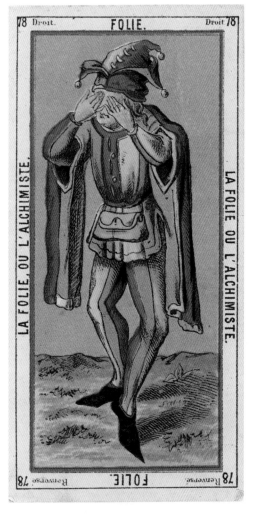

ABOVE LEFT

Le Fou, Tarot des Imagiers du Moyen Âge,
Oswald Wirth, 1889.

ABOVE RIGHT

Madness, or the Alchemist, from the *Grand
jeu de l'Oracle des Dames*, designed
by G. Regamey, France, 1890-1900.

THE MAGICIAN

ow you see it, now you don't: In this 1502 painting attributed to Hieronymous Bosch or one of his followers, a street performer has set a table in a busy area of town. The man carries a basket attached to his belt, from which an owl, symbolizing deceit in the medieval bestiary, peaks his head out. At his feet sits a jester dog, wearing a belt of bells strap around his small brown body. Quickly set up, he has disposed of a variety of objects on the table in front of him—tumblers and a conic-shaped cup, little marbles similar to the one he holds, a golden hoop, a small wand, and, as incongruous as it sounds, a minuscule frog.

The magician performs a sleight-of-hand trick and a diverse crowd of men, women, nobles, merchants, children, and a nun slowly form around his stall. As the performer rolls a marble between his thumb and index finger, a man is spontaneously struck with some abnormal reaction and regurgitates another frog. Incapacitated by this strange behavior, he doesn't realize that the man behind him is stealing his bag of coins, only leaving the elaborate key he is also carrying around his belt.

Although this painting isn't a tarot card, it was created around the same time as the Visconti-Sforza deck and draws around the same cultural tropes, all celebrating the late medieval imagination. *The Conjurer* indeed shares both the narrative and the archetypal essence of the first protagonist of our major arcana whose English denomination—the Magician—dilutes the iconographic roots and lessens the meanings of the card. Traditionally, the image comes with a more profane twist—Le Bateleur/Il Bagatto/The Artisan/The Stage Magician—a man of humble means who, by his skill set, can create beauty and a sense of wonderment, wow an audience, and conjure metamorphosis. He might be of a nomadic kind as much as the Fool is, but he stops his travels and sets up temporary shop by putting his table down. This table is a stage, a laboratory of visual experience, the focal point swallowing people's gaze like a black hole. On it, you can find the tools he used—the tools of the tarot—a reminder of each suit corresponding to the four elements: the Knife, a symbolic sword; a twig or a stick; the Wands; the magical goblets; the Cup, the balls or the coins.

The Bateleur is often associated with Mercury, god of thieves and travelers. His arm gesture, one arm pointed upward, one arm down, mimics the Roman God's gesture found in classical statuary. With such patronage, one could expect our character to have an edge and shares some of his characteristics. A trickster, he is capable of distorting appearances, challenging boundaries. He can shift realities in front of our eyes.

OPPOSITE PAGE

The Conjurer, Hieronymus Bosch or his workshop, 1502, Musée Municipal de Saint-Germain-en-Laye.

He is the tarot reader, who performs and gives meaning, hides and highlights in a ballet of gestures and words an ageless, cunning art form. He is an artist, a poet, who, like the Greek lyre player Orpheus, can travel between realms, lift the veil of realities using his standing body as a conduit, an antenna for the vibrations from other dimensions. He is both a charlatan and a prophet and his tricks don't have to be real to produce real effect. As in the Bosch image, the stage magic, a controlled simulacrum, allows for the bizarre to puncture our reality. If the trick is fake, the frogs this spectator vomits are nonetheless very real. In the Etteilla decks, showing a Magus in front of magical implements or even a puppet, the card will be associated with diseases and their cures. Performing the show impacts the spectator. In this sense, the Magician presents an allegory of tarot itself—a poetic spectacle that allows for inner transformation—an initiatic art form in which symbols are manipulated in a provocative, sometimes disquieting way that coerces vulnerability. In the Bosch painting, the man vomits frogs and gets robbed, yet that wonderful key is still there. In tarot, no matter which side of the table we stand behind, we gamble with the spiritual. In what the cards allow us to witness, we cannot lose.

Mercure, first card of the minchiate created
by François de Poilly, published between
1721 and 1742.

The Charlatan, from *l'Oracle Symbolique*
(The Symbolic Oracle), a parlor
divination game published by Watilliaux,
in Paris, 1890.

Mercurio, forty-second card of the so-called
Mantegna Tarot, E-series, engraved
by Johann Ladenspelder,
between 1540 and 1560.

ABOVE LEFT

Mercure, a knave of hearts from
the *Cartes Heroiques* playing deck,
illustrated by Victor Lange in 1847.

ABOVE RIGHT

Odéon, king of spades from a deck of
French playing cards depicting the different
theaters of Paris and the type of theatrical
entertainments they would showcase
in the early nineteenth century. Odéon,
like l'Odéon-Théâtre, renowned for the
gravitas of its performances, a theater in
which Sarah Bernhardt will later play
in Racine's *Phèdre* for the first time.
Appearing in a cloudy explosion,
this charismatic gentleman lands onstage,
leaving the spectator in awe, with
a supernatural staging reminiscent
of the smoke-and-mirrors characteristic
of the Magician archetype.

Maladie, Grand Etteilla Tarot Egyptien,
Paris, 1879–90.

ABOVE RIGHT

Le Magicien ou le Bâteleur (Maladie),
Grand Etteilla Tarot Egyptien,
Paris, 1850-90.

Tarot Della Rocca, with a double-headed and rather impish and barely sober Bagatto, raising a glass and not a wand, created in 1887 by Fratelli Armanino, Genova, Italy.

Zoroastro, a Florentine minchiate card from 1725 depicting Zoroaster, the Iranian prophet, performing a ritual.

"The False Prophet," from the Egyptian revival Grand Etteilla, published in Paris in 1875. The card, numbered fifteen, is associated with "melancholia" and "lack of foresight."

THE POPESS —
THE HIGH PRIESTESS

C an one really unsee this image of 2018, as Barbadian singer Rihanna appeared on the red carpet of the Met Gala, clad in a pope-inspired attire composed of jewel-encrusted mantle, matching miter, and a minidress revealing her legs perched on twelve-inch stilettos? If the provocative outfit unofficially won "best dress"[1] at the Catholic-themed fashion event, it also stirred the pot in a glorious controversy. Rihanna reclaimed for one night the regalias of the Roman Catholic pope, one of the most important spiritual leaders of the Western world, taking the opportunity to make her own the symbolic garments solely worn before her, and for centuries, by white men. The world of words was scandalized, enamored, and fascinated by such a powerful image, and so was I. With poise and an authoritative charisma, she strode the scarlet stairs of the museum, maintaining stoic eye contact with the cameras, magnetizing the thousand and one photographers grouped at her feet. Her sartorial fearlessness and the clamering storm that ensued was riveting and immediately brought to my mind the Tarot Popess/High Priestess axiom. The card, a favorite of many readers, weaved the exact same cultural paradox as Rihanna's taboo appearance—the explosive collision of femininity, wisdom, and power. The affirmation of the feminine mystique in the realm of a patriarchal order.

Who is this woman historically called the "Popess" in the tarot, and how did she morph into the High Priestess later on? Her identity, role, and significance have enthralled many scholars over the years, making her one of the most controversial of the Major Arcanas. She first emerged on the Italian trionfi decks in the fifteenth century, presented as a woman in religious garb, wearing the papal crown, which seems, even to our modern eye, incongruous. To this day, there is little room for women in the Vatican hierarchy, and this image feels antithetic. Patently, the feminine pontiff recalls the tantalizing myth of Pope Joan, which grew in popularity during the late medieval period in Europe. As the legend goes, in the ninth century, the learned woman successfully passed as a man and ascended one by one the steps of the eclesiastic ladder to be elected pope. Her subterfuge is said to have lasted for several years, until the day in which, during a procession, the pregnant popess gave birth to a child, to the surprise, or should we say the horror, of the cardinals around her. Copiously illustrated in medieval manuscript, the Pope Joan narrative doesn't seem to fit. Commissioned by the aristocracy of Northern Italy, it's hard to believe that these early trionfi cards would mock the validity of the Roman Catholic authority. It is more likely that our triple-tiara-wearing damsel represented a personification of "Mother Church," the protector and the nurturer of the faithful, or an allegory of Faith not uncommon to see in Italian churches. In the tarot, the Popess accoutrements knows very little variations until the nineteenth century. Always wearing the distinctive papal crown, she is typically represented with a book. A blue one, the focal point of the image in the Visconti Sforza, she holds it closed in her left hand as if to signify not only was she the guardian of knowledge, but also policed its accessibility. As the iconography consolidated in the seventeeth century through the *Tarot de Marseille* prototype, the Popess isn't just holding the book but actively reading it, the large volume spread open on her lap. As we look at her, it almost feels like we are interrupting as she reading, a perennial ritual, a gestative meditation. Her head is raised, yet she doesn't look at us. She is intimidating, impenetrable, and mysterious, and her unavailability to us makes her somehow more compelling. Deviated, subverted from both pleasure and maternity, her femininity challenged what's socially expected from her and from women in general. Engorged with the enigma of the book she reads, she became the pregnant vessel for sacred knowledge, and her intimacy is reserved for spiritual matters, the intuitive and the esoteric.

Behind her, a coiled curtain is stretched between two columns. These iconographic details, as well as the eighteenth-century idea of the Egyptian origins of tarot developed in esoteric circles, would ultimately lead the Popess to be interpreted as Isis in disguise. Slowly, her triple tiara is replaced by a crescent headdress, inspiring illumination through reflection. She becomes appreciated as a feminine figure of the liminal, a Persephone-like entity allowed, unlike her profane consort, to go back and forth between worlds and to orchestrate revelations. Not only a scholar of mystical liturgies, she becomes a gatekeeper of the sacred realms, thus connecting the human experience to the divine. The masonic tradition will claim her columns as Joachim and Boaz, the two pillars at the entrance of Solomon's Temple, making her the navel of polarities. Otherworldly, she lifts the veil. She allows perceptions to flicker between the objective and subjective. To that matter, as she finds her new symbolic identity in the nineteenth and early twentieth centuries as the High Priestess, her body and its materiality loses physical consistency. In the Rider-Waite-Smith, the lunar prophetess is a mere torso seated on a cube, rising from the cascading flow of an ectoplasmic robe. As we look at her, within the temple she guards, holding the Sacred Laws, we are confronted to an apparition, a spiritual hologram, the Shekinah that Waite describes as a the feminine expression of God[2] and the "Highest and Holiest of the Greater Arcana."[3]

The Popess, from the Visconti-Sforza Tarot, attributed to Bonifacio Bembo, c. 1450.

Who is this Popess adorning the Visconti-Sforza card? A question that has puzzled many scholars of the tarot. Through her seminal research, librarian and New Yorker Gertrude Moackley first brushed away the "Isis in disguise theory," anchoring back the image in factual history and finding in the tortuous Visconti family tree the name of Sister Maifreda di Pirovano,[4] a religious woman accused of heresy and burned at the stake for ruling over a Christian sect challenging the values of the papacy. In an incredible article,[5] Sherryl E. Smith proposes that the card isn't actually Maifreda but the subject of her subversive devotion, a thirteenth-century Cistercian nun named Guglielma of Milan, revered for her charisma and piousness as she became seen as the feminine Holy Spirit. This card is in the collection of the Morgan Library, New York.

Pope Joan giving birth. Woodcut from a German translation by Heinrich Steinhöwel of Giovanni Boccaccio's *De Mulieribus Claris* (Concerning Famous Women), printed by Johannes Zainer at Ulm, Germany, c. 1474. From the British Museum collection.

Faith: One of the theological virtues depicted in the *Tarocchi Visconti di Modrone*, along with Charity and Hope. The deck is attributed to Bonifacio Bembo and updated to the 1460s.[6] Represented as an allegorical figure, Faith sits, a king at her feet. Her golden dress almost blends with an equally solar background. In her left hand she holds a specter, and her other hand points at the heavens, as the Chalice and the Eucharist float nearby. This card in the collection of the Beinecke Rare Book and Manuscript Library, Yale University, New Haven, Connecticut.

Fides: Faith, one of the seven virtues represented by proto-Renaissance master Giotto di Bondone, from Cappella degli Scrovegni in Padua, Italy.

Lenormand card wrapper, 1868, from the Bibliothèque nationale de France collection. This Lenormand card wrapper suggests that the Cartomancer might be the symbiose of the Magician and the High Priestess. Conjuring cosmic energies and touching the cards in the iconic gesture of the first Major Arcanas, the Cartomancer is yet a woman shown standing in front of a large velvet curtain, keeping guard over the between worlds.

This Popess is unique for many reasons. Printed in 1839, she is the work of Bernardin Suzanne, a card master from Marseille. Her work is often compared to the Nicola Conver model, but her Popess presents a very unique iconographic twist: a semicircular shape behind her, colored with a dot of green ink, a detail absent from the other Marseille model. This round shape will later be interpreted by cult film director and tarot scholar Alejandro Jodorowsky as an egg and fully reproduced in the deck he created with Maison Camoin. Hidden behind the back of the Popess, who is secretly brooding, this green egg evokes the theme of gestation and invincible accumulation associated with the card.

Double-headed Italian tarot designed by Alessandro Viasonne, published in Turin, 1888.

Junon, *Tarot de Besançon*, late eighteenth century, France. During the French Revolution, as political power and authority gets shuffled, card makers erased the references to papal figures from their decks, replacing them with Roman deities: Juno for the Popess, and Jupiter for the Pope.

Le Tarot des Bohémiens, by Papus, second edition published by Durville, from 1911. The design for the card was created by Jean-Gabriel Goulinat.

The Sanctuary, second card of the Hermetic Tarot by Robert Falconnier, designed by Otto Wegener, 1896.

Queen of Cups, from *Bajara Mistica*, a Spanish playing card deck created in the late nineteenth century, showing cavorting nuns and priests.

The evanescent High Priestess from the Rider-Waite-Smith deck, conceptualized by Arthur Edward Waite and designed by Pamela Colman Smith in 1909. Extending between the two columns, the veil behind her bares pomegranates, associating the Shekinah to the myth of Persephone.

High Priestess, Ghetto Tarot, Alice Smeets and Atis Rezistans, 2015. In this stunning version of the High Priestess, paying tribute to the work of Pamela Colman Smith, the fluidic priestess, by her presence, turns everything into a veil.

OPPOSITE PAGE

The woman and her triple tiara, a figure often eroticized because it is considered inaccessible, serving as a frontispiece for *Les Bains de Bade* (The Baths of Baden), a series of sensuous short stories by decadent author René Boylesve, illustrated by Armand Rassenfosse in 1911. Image courtesy of King Baudouin Foundation/ Studio Philippe de Formanoir.

Nutrix ejus terra est.

EPIGRAMMA II.

Romulus hirta lupæ pressisse, sed ubera capræ
 Jupiter, & factis, fertur, adesse fides:
Quid mirum, teneræ SAPIENTUM viscera PROLIS
 Si ferimus TERRAM lacte nutrisse suo?
Parvula si tantas Heroas bestia pavit,
 QUANTUS, cui NUTRIX TERREUS ORBIS, erit?
C   Apud

THE EMPRESS

R omulus is said to have been nursed at the coarse udders of a wolf, But Jupiter to have been nursed by a goat, and these facts are said to be believed: Should we then wonder if we assert That the earth suckles the tender Child of the Philosophers with its milk? If an insignificant animal nursed such great heroes, Shall he not be great, who has the Terrestrial Globe as a nurse."[1]

"Nutrix Ejus Terra Est" (The earth is his nurse), says the motto above the second illustration in the *Atalanta Fugiens*, the famous book of emblems by Michael Maier that uses pictures, music, and poetry to describe the alchemical process. The hand-colored vignette shows how the materia prima, symbolized as an infant, will be metaphorically fed by suckling on the breast of earth itself in an early hour of its transformation to become the philosopher's stone. In this fantastic depiction, Nature is anthropomorphized, shown as a feminine nourishing force, an idea we'll see later reemerge as our Empress.

In the Visconti di Modrone Tarot, the Empress appears youthful and luminous, with rose petal lips and a radiant gown of pure gold. Coiffed with a crown and yielding a scepter, she sits on a throne surrounded by four young escorts. Two of them, dressed in matching red robes, are elevated and flanking her lovely visage, while the other two stand in prayer at her feet, honoring her. Are they children or servants? One of them points with insistence at the imperial black eagle cast on her shield, the heraldic marker of the Roman Empire, reminding us that her beauty and gentle attitude should not divert us. Undeniably, she is a woman of authority, and her role is clearly established as she holds the symbols of regalian powers—she's a political figure. According to the historical contexts in which this card was created, this meant she would, by her marriage, create powerful political alliances that would served to maintain peace between states. By providing a son to her imperial consort, a woman of such rank assured the continued influence of her dynasty, maintaining and cementing symbiotic bonds between political clans, bridging the past and the future of her house. From her womb, power is formed to thrive in the world. To that extent, she is a political matron, a concept hard to grasp and quite unromantic to our contemporary mindset, yet one which is very well anchored in the Northern Italy mindset of the quattrocento.

Nonetheless, in this very deck, even as the Empress is depicted as a tender and eminent matriarch, she is met with another "mother," a symbolic one, under the guise of an allegory of Charity. Her breast peeking through her flowery garment, the metaphorical figure breastfeeds a standing child, thus manifesting one of the seven theological virtues promulgated by Saint Thomas Aquinas, in which love, protection, and care for others are esteemed as a form of devotion to God.

OPPOSITE PAGE

Second emblem of *Atalanta Fugiens, hoc est Emblemata nova de secretis naturae chymica*, Michael Maier, Illustrated by Matthias Merian, published by Johann Theodor de Bry, Oppenheim, Germany, 1618, from the Bibliothèque nationale de France collection.

Throughout its iconography, the Empress and her archetypal avatars rove between these two previously described aspects of the feminine, ruled by the manifested world, against the grain of her sister the Popess, Sovereign of the Abstract. While one is mute, ethereal, and fathomable, the Empress is open, active, forward, and accessible. In the Marseille cards, we see her frontally, sitting on a throne, with a stern gaze piercing ours, in contrast to the Rider-Waite-Smith version, where she lounges, graceful and nonchalant, with colorful pillows comfortably stacked behind her back. This later sensual depiction, as noted by scholar Mary K. Greer,[2] might have been inspired by the 1338 fresco *Allegory of Peace* by Ambrogio Lorenzetti located at the Palazzo Pubblico in Siena. In this image, a woman in a translucent white robe holds a symbolically charged olive branch, the words "PAX" above her head, identifying her as a pacifier. In the Viéville Tarot, the dynamic queen trots in the rolling hills, staff solidly in hand. Whatever is her mission, she is proactively involved, baring a smile on her face. To rule well, one has to preserve concord and be a diplomat. Thus is the role of the Empress.

In the eighteenth century, a subtle iconographic shift occurred, perhaps due to the fact that several European countries revolted against their monarchies, thus the grande dame lost her symbolic hegemony. The symbolic mother appears disguised in certain decks, rubbing elbows with the Empress or just replacing her as the female lead of a set of triumph cards. Call these depictions Charity, Eve, Love, or Nature itself, they are always shown as primeval figures. Depicted in the nude, unveiling their decollétage, nursing a child, and even multibreasted, like the she-wolf and the interspecies nurses, feeding the heroes and gods populating the mythology of the Ancient World. In "La Nature," the images recall Ephesian Artemis, goddess of wilderness and fertility, worshipped to provide protection and sustenance to the people of Ephesus. Her chest composed of a myriad of mammary-shaped protuberances, whose smoothness lead archeologists to believe they might represent bull's testicles rather than breasts.[3] Gorged with seeds, the Empress, in her new emanation, contains multitudes. As a creatrix, she embodies the nurturing force of Nature, she is a wild goddess of love binding together the complex chemistry of our world to foster and give birth to all shapes and forms. At the dawn of the twentieth century, Waite and Colman combined these two expressions of the feminine, making the Empress the icon she has been striving for ever since. On one hand, she is, like her Italian ancestor, the Queen of Fair Command, a compassionate ruler and loving protector whose shield was marked with the planet Venus. On the other, she is a Demeter-like figure, the soul and source of untamable elements that compose our visible, tangible world. Her pomegranate-patterned dress, in which each seed is clearly visible, promises all of the splendor she is capable of generating—the infinite miracle of life itself.

OPPOSITE PAGE

The Empress, from the Visconti-Sforza
Tarot, attributed to Bonifacio Bembo,
c.1450.

LEFT

In the *Tarot des Imagiers du Moyen Âge*, Oswald Wirth introduces for the first time symbolical elements drawn from Catholic iconography to link his Empress to the Virgin Mary—the crown of stars, the white lily on her right side, and the lunar croissant under her foot—making her "the immaculate Virgin of the Christians, in whom the Greeks would have recognized their Venus-Urania, born shimmering in light out of the dark waves of the wild Ocean." These new iconographic elements originated from Saint John's Book of Revelation, which describes a Marial apparition, the Woman of the Apocalypse, as "a woman clothed with the sun, and the moon under her feet, and upon her head a crown of twelve stars."

ABOVE

Imperial power on the go with this jetting Empress from the *Tarot Anonyme de Paris*. Running in the hills in a carmine dress, she reminds us that the Empress is a woman of action and an initiative taker. From the *Tarot Anonyme de Paris*, c. 1650, Bibliothèque nationale de France collection.

LEFT

Figure of Peace, part of the *Allegory of Good and Bad Government*, a series of three frescoes painted by Ambrogio Lorenzetti, in 1339, in the Palazzo Pubblico of the city of Siena, Italy. Commissioned by the Council of Nine of the Republic of Siena, these images were meant to inspire civic and moral responsibilities in the members of the council and remind them what was at stake as they made important decisions for the collectivity.

Erased crown and flowery shield for this nameless card of the *Tarot de Besançon*, published in 1794, right after the French Revolution and the abolition of constitutional monarchy. Like many other decks of that era, Nobility markers were censored from figurative cards and often called *Jeu Revolutionnaire* to signal the iconographic variations. From the Bibliothèque nationale de France Collection.

The Empress and Charity cards from the Visconti di Modrone, an incomplete tarot deck colloquially referred to as the "Cary Yale," whose sixty-seven cards are now kept at the Beinecke Rare Book and Manuscript Library in Yale University. Created in the mid-fifteenth century, it is considered, along with the Visconti Sforza, to be one of the earliest decks that includes a set of trionfi cards. The Visconti di Modrone cards were presumably commissioned by Filippo Maria Visconti and painted by Italian painter and fresco artist Bonifacio Bembo, who produced numerous portraits for the Visconti family.

Holding one child by the hand as she breastfeeds the other, the woman represented in this card from the *Jeu de Poilly* shows a traditional yet tender depiction of the theological virtue of Charity. Minchiate deck created by François de Poilly, 1712–41. From the Bibliothèque nationale de France collection.

An Empress-like figure, this time referred to as "the Great Mother" in this set of cards engraved by François Isnard during the French Revolution. Stripped from her royal crown but still holding a shield, the feminine figure metamorphoses into the maternal protector of the people. From the Bibliothèque nationale de France collection.

"Smiling Impératrice," from an Italian hand-colored deck printed in Milan, Italy, c. 1860, from the Bibliothèque nationale de France collection.

Charita—another allegorical card linked to the virtue of charity, this time from the so-called Mantegna Tarot. If in this one, the feminine figure is shown, hand on heart, emptying the contents of a bag of coins in the air to testify to her generosity, the canonical "nurturing" iconography linked to this image is hidden in the bottom left corner by an image of a pelican in her piety. In this motif, frequently used in Christian iconography, the pelican mother pierces her breast with her beak to feed her young ones with her blood, at the peril of her own life, to save them from starvation. Charity, the thirty-eighth card of the Mantegna Tarot, part of the E-series, printed by Johann Landenspelder, in around the 1540s. From the Bibliothèque nationale de France collection.

Eve, in the Garden of Eden, a bucolic vision of the first woman in the Etteilla, *Grand Jeu de l'Oracle des Dames*, from the late 1890s.

Leaning on her pillowy throne, the Empress is both a mother and a guardian of peace. Standing in a field of golden wheat, she exists at the intersection of the Political Mother from the early tarots and the Symbolic Mother, emerging as a symbol of natural abundance and its ability to nurture. Empress card, from the Rider-Waite-Smith deck, commissioned by Arthur Edward Waite, designed by Pamela Colman Smith. The deck was first published in 1909.

"Wild Woman and Unicorn," a playing card from the fifteenth century, anonymous German artist, from the Metropolitan Museum of Art collection. Body covered with a soft layer of fur, leaving only her hands, feet, and breasts bare, wild women were a popular visual trope in medieval Germany, especially in heraldic coats of arms. They were regarded as the primeval spirit of the wood, often considered mischievous. Sometimes depicted breastfeeding a "wild child," as in the famous armorial shield by Martin Schongauer, they were associated with fertility.

La Nature from *Jeu Arithmétique* (Arithmetic Games), designed by Bouchard, 1820–30.

Ephesian Artemis with a shepherd boy playing pipes. Etching by P.A. Novelli, eighteenth century, from the Wellcome Collection, London. This pastoral evocation of the cult of the Ephesian Artemis shows a man playing a pan flute at the feet of an Artemis statue, while the fertility of nature is evoked through the different vignettes. The column forming her body presents various mammals, topped by two lions standing on her hand.

Animal nurses galore! A rather comical card from the *Verkehrte Welt*, a German deck from the 1840s, depicting an anthropomorphized leopard wearing a maid costume and caring for a human child set in a neoclassical bedroom.

THE EMPEROR

ig Daddy Energy! She is the Emperor, definitely the Emperor!" a student of mine once joyfully declared, while looking at an iconic portrait of disco and New Wave overlord Grace Jones photographed by her partner, Jean-Paul Goude, about forty years ago. We were all hovering over this extra-large image from an open book, in the context of a free association game I like to play in which students are invited to match an image with one or several tarot cards, according to what their own symbolic attachment to shapes, colors, objects, and the meaning these details allow to see surface. Dressed in a black blazer with shoulder pads angled with eighties gravitas, Grace Jones's outfit perfectly echoes the rectangular geometry of her haircut. She looks us in the eye, challenging us, the severity of her gaze is matched with seduction, her face slightly off and an unlit cigarette in mouth. Her figure emanates so much authority. The image is composed in a multitude of lines crossing in perfect 90-degree angles, apart from the plunging V of the jacket, revealing the curve of a breast, pulverizing gender expectations.

Can there be a more perfect connection for Grace Jones than with the Emperor card? A provocative image embracing the masculine, for a woman famous for never complying to rules but her own. This idea, celebrated in the Chief card of Courtney Alexander's extraordinary Dust II Onyx Tarot, is a reminder that in this tarot dichotomy of gender roles and attributes, things are a lot more flexible that they appear.

Holding an imperial scepter and the golden orb defining his political function, the Emperor of the so-called Charles VI Tarot also wears a somehow curious, mismatched outfit. The upper part of his body is encased in a suit of armor, while from the abdomen down, we see a blue robe flowing to the ground. Martial at the top, casual at the bottom, so to speak. A softer trait brought forth as well as the smaller character at his feet, who we could imagine as his offspring.

The idea of imperial power is synonymous with a supreme authority surpassing monarchy, a power that defines rules and territorial boundaries, which we've seen expand in history in the tremor of war, conquest, and the nefarious desire of complete hegemony. But as we'll see, in the tarot, the Emperor is quite different and should not be perceived only as a political figure abusing his dominion as a patriarchal sovereign. Although often depicted wearing an armor chest plate, he never bears any weapon and has been assimilated as a figure of protection more than a warmonger. Associated with Mars, he is sanguine yet guarded, and his beard, attesting of his age and experience, gives us clues on how experience allowed him to ground his vindictive nature. Using logic and strategy, he is reason made flesh, a leader who rules by example, aware that his role is to convey a sense of security and maintain sustainability.

OPPOSITE PAGE

The Chief, Dust II Onyx Tarot deck,
Courtney Alexander, 2018.

From one century to the other, he barely changes: in the Marseille decks, his masculine majesty is shown barely sitting, leaning on the imperial shield, ready to pounce in case of emergency. By essence, he is a man of action, postured toward his right and "active" side with an authoritative demeanor.

In the Jean Dodal Tarot, the number four of the card appears twice, as "IIII" in Roman numerals and as "4" in Arabic ones. Why such a redundant mark? We could speculate that this figure is, of course, resonating with the intersect symbolical qualities of our Emperor. In his book *The Way of Tarot*, cult filmmaker and tarologue extraordinaire Alejandro Jodorowsky read this number as "the very symbol of material security." He explains: "The four legs of a table or the altar of the church have a connection to the number 4. A 4 is incapable of falling unless there is a large revolution."[1] This number is of course accentuated by the exaggerated leg-crossing of the Emperor, often emphasized to form the number 4, a signature posture that is in its most hyperbolic manifestation in the Thoth Tarot. With one foot solidly anchored in the ground, soaking up telluric energies, giving this monolithic solidity that intimidates and reassures all at once.

In the Oswald Wirth Tarot, the Emperor's throne has been substituted by a cube, which reminds me of Johannes Kepler's study of the platonic solids. In his incredible *Mysterium Cosmographicum* (The Cosmographic Mystery), the German astronomer illustrates the Platonic associations of the regular solids with the elements. His cube, linked to the element of earth, presents on three of its facets a tree rooted in the ground, a radish, and a crossed hoe and crock, agricultural tools to work the soil. Sitting on his cubic pedestal, the Wirth Emperor reminds us he isn't an omnipotent demiurge but only presides over the limited realm of the concrete world; his dominion only serves the manifested realm of creation, not the spiritual. Austere and strong, he appears to us like a sleeping volcano, balancing his capacity to destroy with a posture of rational grounding.

ABOVE

The two Emperors from a Minchiate deck
produced in Florence, Italy, by Pietro Alligo
in 1725, and released commercially in the
twentieth century as the Etruria Minchiate
by Il Meneghello and Lo Scarabeo. Usually
referred to as the Emperor of the East and
the Emperor of the West, they evoke an
episode in the history of the Roman Empire
in which, in 289, Emperor Diocletian
divided the territory in two, promoting
Maximian as Augustus, giving him control
over the western part of the empire and
guarding the hegemony on the eastern side.

A rare Emperor in full body armor, represented standing in a field. His red cape barely conceals a sword in its scabbard. From the Anonymous Parisian Tarot, seventeenth century.

Emperor from the Marseille Tarot created by François Bourlion, c. 1760.

In the Visconti di Modrone, the Emperor card is very likely a cameo of Emperor Sigismund, depicted with his distinctive double-prong beard featured in many of his portraits, including his posthumous one by Albrecht Dürer. Sigismund received the Iron Crown of Lombardy in 1431, a detail we could see illustrated in this card, as a second crown is held by one of the young boys at his feet. Sigismund was also granted the title of Holy Emperor of Rome by Pope Eugene IV in 1347, making him the supreme head of state, and *primus inter pares*, first among equals, giving him sovereignty above other Catholic monarchs across Europe. In this card, the imperial eagle is visible, stretching its black wings above the head of the ruler.

Pink chest plate and crown for the meticulously etched Emperor of *Tarot de Besançon*, published by Pierre Isnard, 1746–60.

Emperor card from a double-headed card deck published by J. Gaudais, 1860–89.

OPPOSITE PAGE

Sigismund, Holy Roman Emperor, by Albrecht Dürer, 1511–13, from the Germanisches Nationalmuseum in Nuremburg, Germany.

Dis bildt ist kaiser Sigmunds gstalt

Sigismud⁹
Annus
·Z8·

inparanit

Der dir rat so mangin falt - vn vnder
gwunn vas genut - Das bracht er har vor offinbar
Da hau er zal fur vn zwainzig iar as Was
Al hatuns das man Iacit von svg suntus ric

TAROT DE PAPUS

ABOVE LEFT

Emperor card from the so-called Charles VI Tarot deck also often referred to as the "Gringonneur" deck. The hand-painted deck was erroneously attributed to Jacques Gringonneur, a medieval painter who royal records show was hired by King Charles VI to create several "golden packs" of cards in 1392. In fact, these unique and unfortunately incomplete sets of cards, preserved at the Bibliothèque nationale de France, are more likely to have originated from Northern Italy in the fifteenth century.[2]

ABOVE RIGHT

The Emperor from Papus's *Tarot des Bohémiens* replicated the posture of his Marseille predecessors, dressed in regal outfits drawn from ancient Egypt including the psencht, a double crown symbolizing governance of Upper and Lower Egypt. Papus described the meaning of that crown as "indicating the dominion of Divine Will" and the eagle, placed at the frontal part of the headdress as "the Universal action is Life's Creation."[3]

4 and IIII—the twice-numbered Emperor card from the Jean Dodal deck, a Marseille model, printed in Lyon, France.

The Red Emperor is in full martial regalia, sitting on a cubic structure from the Oswald Wirth Tarot, which described him as a "Worldly Prince" reigning over "the concrete and corporal things."[4]

Chinese Emperor from a card deck created for Cochinchina exportation, printed in Marseille, France, 1870.

Aging Emperor and his opulent white beard, on the elongated card of the *Torocchi Fine dalla Torre*, an Italian tarot deck created in Bologna in the seventeenth century.

Italian tarot deck with a double-headed figure, printed by Fratelli Armanino in Genova, Italy, in 1887, a variant from the Soprafino Tarot, designed by Carlo della Rocca, in which the colors were slightly changed.

THE POPE —
THE HIEROPHANT

troppo vero! È troppo vero!" (It's too true! It's too true!), gasped Pope Innocent X, so the legend says, as he examined for the first time the canvas Diego Velásquez, the Spanish court portraitist, had him sit for in 1650. Although the pontiff couldn't deny the mastery of execution, Velasquez's naturalistic audacity had somehow startled him, being such an unconventional rendering for a state portrait such as this one. Represented coiffed with a camauro and minimal papal regalia, his enthroned Eminence is shown projecting forward the "fisherman" signet ring on his relaxed hand, the sole clear memento of his authoritative status. But it's the composition of the image, the tightening around his gaze, which meets the eye of the viewer as if to scrutinize him. A striking realism, captured in some quick brushstrokes, makes this portrait so unique that it is often considered one of the best ever created. Velásquez, with his petulant sincerity of execution, diluted the prestige into the secular. Conveying more than the dignified image of God's emissary, he painted the psychologized picture of a shrewd, ambitious man, whose penetrating eyes betray an intelligence only matched by an astute awareness of his realm of influence. In this bold portrait, the "truth" painted by Velásquez that seemed so puzzling to Innocent X, is that under the attribute of his divine function, one can see him as a mortal man. In the tarot, this very duality—the human being and the intercessor of God, the teacher and the vessel of teaching, the unite and the collective—are the fundamentals of the Pope/Hierophant/High Priest card.

Serving as a governing figure of the Roman Catholic Church, the papacy is one of the oldest institutions of the Western world, and its iconography in the tarot was practically unchanged until the late nineteenth century, as the Pope slowly shifted into the Hierophant. If one can envision the trionfi cards of the Italian Renaissance as representing allegorical values and powers of the known world, the Pope, serving as a spiritual counterpart of the Emperor, was unmissable. At the time, the papacy's power was immense and undisputable, a religious authority and a political force capable of rivaling the authority of European monarchs and emperors. As such, he also wears a crown, a triple tiara, but unlike his aristocratic peers, he is at the crossroads of the material and spiritual. In several cards, we see him holding a pair of oversize skeleton keys, an indication of his role as apostolic successor of Saint Peter who, according to the Gospels, received the keys of heaven from Jesus himself. These two keys, featured in the papal emblem, grant him the power to "bind and loose"—to forbid and permit—appointing him as an earthly guarantor of the spiritual laws. To that extent, the Pope represents the "stone" on which doctrines are set, allowing traditions to be kept alive and unchanged over the centuries. In the Noblet tarot, the pontiff carries a crosier, a hooked staff resembling a shepherd's rod, as if to signify his role is not just to command but also to congregate his community, preserving their identity as a group. As we look at the Marseille prototypes, the Pope raises the index and middle finger of his right hand, a gesture often interpreted as one of blessing. This gesture is reminiscent of a similar visual trope found in Byzantine art, in which Christ or the saints are depicted raising two fingers, folding their thumb on the others. Inspired by Roman chironomy—the art and meaning of hand gestures—this hand signal is to be interpreted as meaning "I speak," and so does the Pope, voicing the sacred for us to hear, bridging through language the realm of God to ours.

OPPOSITE PAGE

Portrait of Pope Innocent X,
by Diego Velázquez, c.1650, from
the Galleria Doria Pamphilj in Rome.

As an archetype of exoteric spirituality, the image of the Pope fractured sometimes in the eighteenth century, historically changing identity as his political validity was challenged. In the Belgian Vandenborre Tarot, created in the 1780s, he was replaced by Bacchus, Roman god of ecstatic intoxication, depicted astride a barrel, suckling on a bottle of wine. During the French Revolution, a number of playing decks substituted the pontifex with the figure of Jupiter. Maybe card makers thought the vision of such a spiritual leader might kill the joy of such profane and lighthearted amusements as a game of cards? Maybe the pontiff's rigidity and fastuous pageantry felt anachronistic in the early hours of modernity? One of my favorite examples might be the nineteenth-century Soprafino Pope and its visual excess. Dressed in his lavishly embroidered vestments, he sits, like the other tarot popes, in front of an audience of monks kneeling at his feet. But one of them, dressed in blackish garbs like an ominous announcer, turns his stern face toward us, as if to signal something. I like to imagine him as a whistleblower, pointing out to us the paradox of religious eminences and the slight arrogance of papal bling. Like a Nietzschean trickster, the monk in black mourns the death of God, telling us the man in the red mantle fools himself finding holiness in such a maximalist display of wealth. Soon enough, he seems to say, the development of rational thinking and the suspicion of conventional religion will diminish his status.

As to the "Hierophant," the term was first associated with the fifth Major Arcana by Antoine Court de Gébelin,[1] who recognizes its protagonist as the "Great Priest of the Hierophants," alluding for the first time to an iconographic connection with the Eleusinian mysteries, the secret religious rites of the Hellenistic world at a time when the origins of the tarot were believed to be from the ancient world. In Ancient Greece, the hierophant was a man who would officiate the mysteries, serving as an interpreter of the symbolic content of the celebrations for people to understand. Through his chants and demonstrations, he would unfold the myth of Persephone's ravishing by Hades, the god of the underworld, and her subsequent ascent back to the land of the living. In order to become a hierophant, the man had to renounce his former identity, becoming the sacred function he served. Throughout the nineteenth century, the term, evoking a hint of fascination with the ancient world, slowly became introduced in occult cenacles and Masonic lodges, becoming associated with high-ranked officers like, for example, in the Rite of Memphis-Misraim. But it is through the impulse of McGregor Mathers, in the context of the Hermetic Order of the Golden Dawn's doctrine, that the card will find its new appellation. Quoting cartomancers Etteilla, Eliphas Levi, and Gébelin, Mathers will evacuate some of the medieval iconographic connotations to prefer an Egypto-kabbalistic reinterpretation and rename the Pope the Hierophant.[2]

OPPOSITE PAGE

Christ Pantocrator and his peculiar hand gesture, interpreted as a blessing and as a signal of speech. From the Cathedral of Cefaly, Sicily, c. 1130. Photographed and retouched by Andreas Wahra.

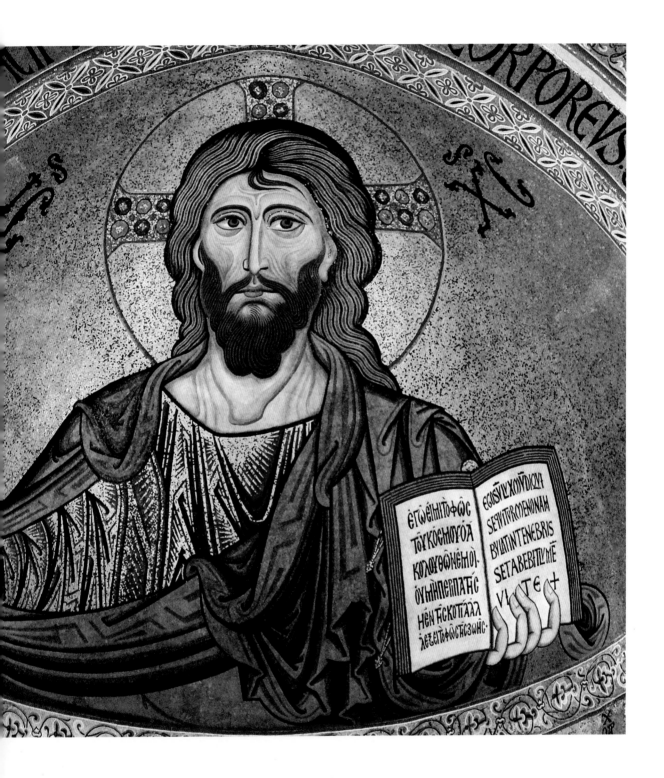

Pope from the Visconti-Sforza Tarot,
attributed to Bonifacio Bembo, created
in Milan, Italy, c. 1450–80.

ABOVE RIGHT

Colorful Pope from the so-called
Gringonneur, or Charles VI Tarot deck,
in which the central protagonist is flanked
by two cardinals dressed in red.

In several decks, including the Noblet and the Viéville Tarot, the Pope is shown holding a shepherd's rod, as if to signify his role as a congregator. At his feet, two monks with tonsure cuts are seen from the back. From the Tarot Noblet, 1659.

Pope card from the *Tarot Viéville*, published around 1650.

Tarot de Marseille of Nicolas Conver, published between 1809 and 1833. In the Conver example, and in many other decks, the Pope is wearing gloves marked with a black cross, a detail that could signify his blessing/speaking hand is of the institution he represents and not his own.

Lightning bolts in each fist, Jupiter stands on the golden wings of an eagle as colorful volutes of flowing fabrics surround his body. Numbered 5 in Roman numerals, this card from a 1820s Besançon deck came as a replacement for the traditional Pope card.

Unnumbered Pope from a *Tarocchini Mitelli*, a pastel-toned Bolognese-style deck published around 1670 in Rome, engraved by Giuseppe Maria Mitelli.

Il Papa, from an 1880s Soprafino, an Italian tarot deck published by the Avendo Brothers showing cartomantic notes handwritten at the top and bottom of the card. On the upper right, one can read "Long Life, Marriage" and on its reversed side "A deal soon settled." Image courtesy of McClosky's Antiquarian Books & Cards.

E Papa, tenth card of the so-called Mantegna Tarot, from the E-series, engraved by Johann Ladenspelder, 1540–60. Holding the keys of Saint Peter toward his heart, the Pope also carries a closed book on this right knee, a rare attribute in tarot iconography, the "law" being usually associated with the Popess, his feminine consort.

OPPOSITE PAGE

This small oil painting by occultist Aleister Crowley is from the 1920s, when he was in Cefalu, Sicily, creating his Abbey of Thelema, a utopian spiritual commune and magical school. Crowley's Sicilian period was one of his most prolific as a visual artist, and some of those images, including this one, were lost for decades before magically resurfacing in the early 2000s. In this vividly colored little wood panel, Crowley created both a self-portrait as the Hierophant and what seems to be an early study for what would become the future Thoth Tarot as indicated by the Roman numeral V visible at the top.

THE LOVER — THE LOVERS

Tucked in the lush wilderness of the Garden of Eden, Adam and Eve are caught tenderly embracing, sealing their love with a kiss. Through this image, we are reminded that the primordial couple from the Book of Genesis was once a unit. In many medieval illuminations, Eve is represented "being formed from Adam's rib," peacefully emerging from the man's side, her torso piercing his ribcage, while God, gently pulling her out, serves the role of midwife in the uncanny birth rite. Left alone at night in the heavenly jungle surrounded by parrots and rabbits, Bartolozzi represents the couple's longing for this unity, bound by an emotional pull animating them toward retrieving their past integrity. There is no guilt or shame in this image, and the devilish snake is absent. Through the expression of physical love and intimacy, Eve and Adam fuse once again, invertedly celebrating the divine act that gave them life. In the tarot, although the iconography crystallized around two prototypes—the Lover and the Lovers—the longing for this connection, whether it is introspective, romantic, or spiritual, is the palpitating heart within the image. Yet as we'll see, for the first time in the Major Arcanas narrative sequence, this card's signification finds its voice through a psychodramatic situation and not a person. This card ultimately speaks about a crisis, which once resolved, will lead to a completely different perspective.

As we look at the early Renaissance example, the cards depict allegories of Love in which union is reached through the institution of marriage. In the Visconti di Modrone, a couple face as they modestly hold hands under a brightly colored canopy in which the word "Amor" figures, barely visible, yet written in gold. Above them, a blindfolded Cupid deploys his greenish wingspan, ready to strike his arrow of love. With a closer look, one will recognize the bazons of the Visconti—the *biscione*: a blue snake devouring a man and the white cross on a red background, the coat of arms of the county of Pavia. This detail led scholars to believe the card was a marriage memorial, commissioned by Filippo Maria Visconti, duke of Milan, as a wedding for his daughter, Bianca Maria Visconti, to his successor and son-in-law, Francesco Sforza.

This visual trope of "the Lovers" exists in many decks over the centuries, usually depicted in a minimal setting: a man and a woman engaging in a close encounter, two peas magnetized together within an invisible pod. A courtship ranging from the sensual to the mystical, prefiguring a congress in which two distinct entities will blend into one another. Many see in the Lovers card a reminder of the alchemical wedding, a hermetic culmination in which opposite principles unite, represented in alchemical treatises by the symbolic union of a Solar King and his Lunar Queen. With the Lovers, what was separated reconciles, reconnects, and experiences totality.

OPPOSITE PAGE

Adam and Eve in the garden of Eden, stipple engraving by F. Bartolozzi after T. Stothard, 1792, from the Wellcome Collection, London.

Starting in the seventeenth century, and with the Marseille prototype, the sixth Major Arcana unfolds a more complex narrative, reaffirmed by the fact that the card will be often named " l'Amoureux"—the Lover, figuring the focus is on the male protagonist now flanked by one more presence. This time, winged Eros hovers around a small group. As the saying goes, two is company, three is a crowd, and the central character is sandwiched between two women both questing for his attention, while his body language expresses that he is torn by the tension. This second trope isn't about the poetic evocation of a mystical union but a dilemma, a negotiation. As he looks at the woman on his right, he blocks her body with his arm, extending his hand toward the other feminine figure. Who are these women? His mother and his bride? The Old and the New? The comfortable path of Experience against the adventurous ways of Experiment? For our hero, this dichotomic imbalance can only be resolved by a choice and not by a negotiation, a decision he has to make by himself and for himself, cutting ties with one of these two options.

In *78 Degrees to Wisdom*, Rachel Pollack described the Lover as a parable for Adolescence, the time in our lives in which we come to understand that the world is vast and goes beyond visions our elders taught us. We become ourselves, discovering what we love and why we love, an affirmation sometimes welcomed as rebellion to the ones who shaped us. Up until this point, our hero has met four archetypal figures, commanders of spiritual and material stratas, looking at them in the eyes, seeing reality through the spectrum of their knowledge. Now at a crossroad, he has to decide to stay within the limiting framework they built or cut ties and see the world through his own gaze, through firsthand experience. For me, the Lover card is a rubicon, a threshold in which one decides to step out of their comfort zone, going against the grain, toward the Self.

ABOVE LEFT

"Amor," an allegory of Love for this card from the Visconti di Modrone, also known as the Cary Yale Tarot, kept at the Beinecke Rare Book and Manuscript Library, Yale University, New Haven, Connecticut.

ABOVE RIGHT

A romantic procession for this unique card from the so-called Charles VI Tarot, dated to the fifteenth century and created in Northern Italy. Three couples march together with different levels of complicity, with the central pair, right under a swarm of cupids, kissing each other.

The Lunar Queen and the Solar King, an alchemical allegory of the conjunction of Mercury and Sulphur used by the philosophers to achieve the Great Work. This illustration was drawn from the *Splendor Solis* (The Splendor of the Sun), a magnificent alchemical treatise popularly attributed to Salomon Trismosin, reproduced many times and famous for its brightly colored hermetic illustrations. This version is dated 1582, from the British Library's manuscript Harley 3469, one of the most beautiful surviving examples.

The ambiguous sixth card of the *Tarot de Jacques Viéville*, associated with the Lover because of its number and the similarity of the composition, yet it doesn't have its name. However, in this representation, all the characters have short hair, and Cupid's bow and arrow seems to have vanished. We could speculate that this card represents a dispute rather than a romantic dilemma. This version is dated to the 1650s.

The ever saucy *Lamoureus* from an Anonymous Parisian Tarot, showing a couple sensually embracing, with madame placing her hands between his legs, seventeenth century.

"L'Amoureux," from a Marseille-style deck, published by Jean Dodal around the 1710s.

"L'Amoureux" from a Jean François Tourcaty *Tarot de Marseille*, with a cartomantic inscription handwritten in French. Although the first line is impossible to decipher, the second mentions the words "young woman," "Marriage," and "Pregnancy." The deck was published around 1740.

"L'Amoureux" from Oswald Wirth's 1899 *Tarot des Imagiers du Moyen Âge*. Although the model resembles the Marseille prototype, the Lover is shown in the center, in an introspective contemplation as he prepares himself to make a final decision. As much as his costume alternates between red and blue, so his heart sways between the two.

In the *Grand Jeu de l'Oracle des Dames*, the card numbered thirteen named "The Great Priest" represents in fact a wedding, and is the idea of union and marriage. This Etteilla-type divination deck illustrated by G. Regamey was published in France toward the 1890s.

"Marriage-Union," from *Le Petit Oracle*, a cartomancy deck published in the late nineteenth century.

Fifth card of a Florentine minchiate deck by Giovan Molinelli, published in the 1710s, showing a woman crowning her admirer, while Cupid is about to shoot a love arrow straight into his head.

Marriage card from a French cartomancy deck published in France in the 1830s.

Five of Coins from an Aluette deck,
published by Lequart in 1880.

Five of Coins from an Aluette deck,
1810–60.

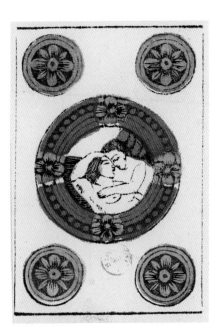

Five of Coins from an Aluette deck, 1840–50. Inspired by the Spanish naipes cards, the Aluette
deck is a type of French playing card deck used to play the *Jeu de La Vache* (Cow Game),
in which members of the same team are invited to discreetly use codified signs and gestures
to indicate information in their hands to their teammate. Its iconography is slightly different
to its Iberic counterpart, with certain pip cards having elaborate designs inviting mimics.
Hence, the Five of Coins, also known as a *Bise Dure* (The Hard Kiss) usually shows a couple,
often monarchs, kissing, embracing, or even lying naked in bed.

THE CHARIOT

F

ame, what you like is the limo, what you get is no tomorrow," sings David Bowie in 1975. Fame is also one of the six carriages parading in Petrarch's *I Trionfi* (Triumphs), a group of poems composed between 1351 and 1374 dedicated to Laura, the love of his life. In his epic vision, the Tuscan author evokes a meditation transcending his romantic sentiments into eternal bliss, under the guise of an allegorical parade inspired by the Roman *triumphus*. In antiquity, triumphal processions were equal parts military display and religious rites, sanctifying the prowess of the military commander as he returned successfully from foreign wars. High up on his chariot led by horses, the victor, accompanied by his troops, would proceed through the city's main path, while receiving ovations from the crowd. Inspired by the glorious pomp and pageantry, Petrarch imagined a procession equally exuberant, in which personified virtues mounted on floats would supplant one another. First Love, won over by Chastity, Time, Death, Fame, and eventually, Eternity.

Allegories on wheels, following one another in a conga line of archetypes. A detail which provoked the attention of Getrude Moakley, a librarian at the New York City Public Library who, in the 1950s, tried to pierce, once and for all, the genesis of the Major Arcanas. Where did the trump cards find their source? What if, Moakley proposed, the set of figurative cards came not from Ancient Egypt like the occultists proposed, but echoed the Italian Renaissance itself, and the vogue of ritual corteges and their symbolic pageantry of which Petrarch's poem is a symptom, if not one of the agents. Laying the groundwork for what would become a major contribution to tarot scholarship, and devoid of esoteric bias, Moakley imagined the Major Arcanas as carnival floats, making the Chariot a literal reminder of this symbolical caravan.

In its meaning, the Chariot is a card that speaks to forward movement, asserted pride, and the display of triumph. In the Cary-Yale example, a woman is paraded under a canopy, which could evoke the lavish procession and public festivities the family would produce to celebrate occasions such as marriage. With this card, one's drive is pushed forward in a burst of victorious enthusiasm, as if to announce a new direction, this time of one's own design. Something invisible propels the centurion into the unknown, yet he knows no fear. Is it a good sign? Yes and no. As we learned, our hero declared his independence in the Lover's card, and his risk-taking was rewarded by a boost of self-confidence, the short-lived bliss of individuality. Yet, as in the Helios card, the so-called Mantegna, as well as in the David Bowie song referenced above, the Chariot also has the capacity to express the attitude of being on your high horse, the danger of self-satisfaction, and the dramatic outcomes awaiting those who mistake winning a battle with winning the war.

OPPOSITE PAGE

"The Triumph of Fame," from Petrarch's *Triumphs*, translated by Simon Bourgouin, sixteenth century. From the Bibliothèque nationale de France's collection.

Chariot card from the Visconti di Modrone/ Cary-Yale pack, attributed to Bonifacio Bembo and painted between 1428 and 1447, from the Beinecke Library collection.

The Sun from the so-called Mantegna Tarot, E-series, printed in Ferrara, Italy, in 1465. The card shows Helios, Greek god of the sun, driving his powerful carriage along the curved sky, causing the solar light to rise and set. The card recounts a specific episode of his myth in which Phaethon, his petulant son, takes his chariot, although Helios discourages him and warns him about the danger of such an untamable ride. Stealing his dad's cool ride, the young and full-of-hubris teen will lose control under the frenetic might of the horses and fall to his demise. From the Bibliothèque nationale de France's collection.

SOL · XXXXIIII ·   44

Chariot card from the so-called Charles VI deck, created in the fifteenth century in Northern Italy, from the Bibliothèque nationale de France's collection.

"Le Chariot" from the *Tarot de Marseille* by François Bourlion, 1760s. From the Bibliothèque nationale de France's collection.

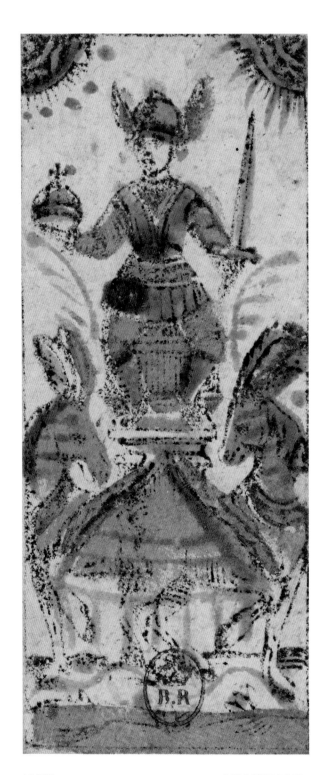

ABOVE

Chariot card from the *Tarocchi Fine Dalla Torre*, seventeenth century. From the Bibliothèque nationale de France's collection.

OPPOSITE PAGE

The Triumphal Chariot of Maximilian I, Albrecht Dürer, 1522, from the National Gallery of Art, Washington, DC.

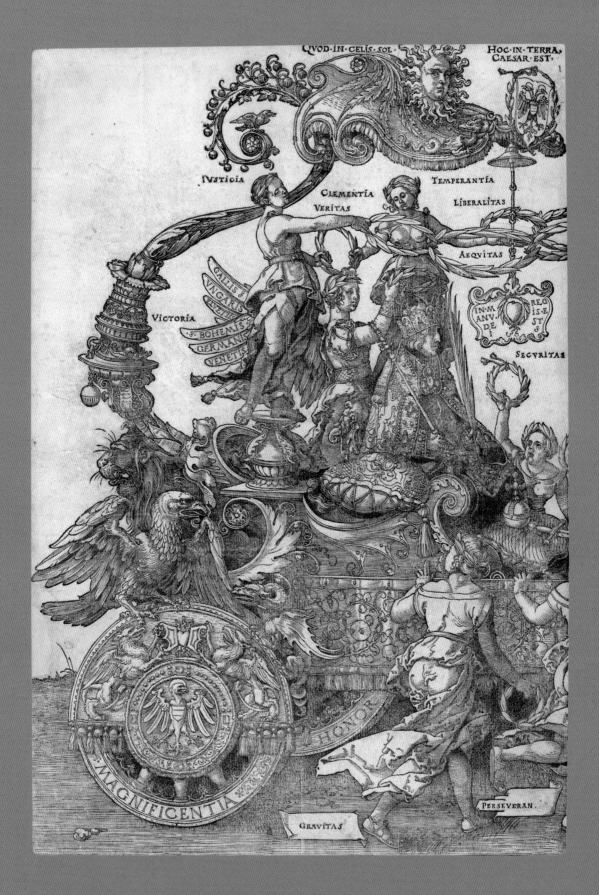

OPPOSITE PAGE
The Chariot and its heavenly canopy in Oswald Wirth's *Tarot des Imagiers du Moyen Âge*, 1899.

Chariot led by geese depicted on the seventh card of the Anonymous Parisian Tarot, early seventeenth century. On the card, the victor wears a crown of laurels.

A heavenly vehicle as the Chariot, this time, pulled by two doves instead of horses. Tarot Mitelli, seventeenth century.

"Chariot" card showing a woman in the nude pulled by two white horses. From a Florentine minchiate deck by Giovan Molinelli, 1712–16.

Nine of diamonds representing a horse-driven coach, from a cartomancy deck published in the early nineteenth century by Violet in Paris. A common trope of the divination decks, the Chariot card or its vehicular cousins signify a journey, a departure, or one's capacity to be on the move, or change.

7   LE CHARIOT

JUSTICE

ith the Justice card, we start our second group of seven Major Arcanas, unfurling a new dynamic in their overarching narrative. From the Magician to the Chariot, we followed the journey of initiation of an archaic character in the guise of the Fool, a chaotic histrion hopping from one card to the next, integrating esoteric wealth like a parched soul drinking water from a fountain in a large, slow gulp. Gradually, our protagonist starts to take shape, finding his primordial focus with the Magician. Our hero will then meet the four figures of secular and spiritual power one by one—the Popess, the Empress, the Emperor, and the Pope—who will serve as a framework for him to understand the boundaries between matter and spirit, shaping him, allowing him, through their eyes, to apprehend the world from its tangible to its most ethereal realities.

Through the Lovers card, our lead is dramatically challenged for the first time in his saga, suffering a crisis, a dilemma in which he has to choose between staying under the umbrella of these authority figures or changing direction, going toward the unknown. Will he choose to stay in the comforting but tight arms of the Mother, or will he run away with the sensuous Maiden, risking both the highs and lows of adventure for the new and the serendipitous? As we know, through the example of the Chariot, he chose to depart, reclaiming as he leaves his own individuality and power. Galvanized by his sacrifice, having cut the cord, so to speak, our hero is now liberated and driven by his own free will, ready to tackle a set of chosen perspectives.

In this new series of seven cards, bookended by the Justice and Temperance cards, our hero will have to develop his own moral compass, defining for himself his inner values, recognizing and interpreting the tensions of the material and the spiritual at play within him.

In this second sequence, the quartet of rulers, figured by the Empress and her three acolytes, are switched for another group: the Cardinal Virtues—Justice, Prudence, Fortitude, and Temperance. Evoked in Plato's *Republic*, these four virtues will later become the cornerstone of Saint Thomas Aquinas's moral philosophy in the thirteenth century. A common motif in Christian theology, the cardinal virtues will emerge as one of the moral axes of the medieval and the Renaissance mind, four fundamental pillars serving as an upstanding code for people to follow.

The Justice card, in its iconography, knows very little variation throughout the centuries, presenting the familiar allegory we associate with the institution of law, found standing in our courthouses and attorneys' offices: a feminine figure holding a sword in her right hand, a scale in the others. She is the antique goddess Themis, the Greek Titaness, and a prophetic figure who presided over the most ancient oracles, including those at Delphi. Her bronze sword was said to be able to cut through lies and allow reality to surface, thus making her the truth seeker. She was, in the antique world, associated with divine law and justice, able to parse the difference between what was right and wrong, instigating order out of chaos, and regulating ethics, which she personified.

In the tarot, the Justice card is, as we'll see, in direct correlation with the Cardinal Virtues, which, along with Temperance and Strength, are openly portrayed in the Major Arcana sequence. Lady Justice's sword, most often shown raised and impeccably vertical, is a testament to her impartiality, a tool to both defend and dismantle in complete fairness. Her scale, held in the receptive left hand, can be interpreted as her ability to maintain balance. It is, most importantly, also signaling to us that we should always measure for ourselves the impact of our actions and try to internally foresee how the consequences might affect the world. Be aware of your own butterfly wings and the future tornado you might unleash. Be ready to assume the consequences of the initiative you take and be responsible for the change you create.

Little by little, along with the normalization of the Marseille deck prototypes, comes the hieratic and frontal Justice, sitting in her throne, her challenging gaze penetrating ours in an attempt to break the fourth wall. This visual model persists in many of the esoteric tarot, the stoic figure locking our attention with her laser-like eyes to a point of slight discomfort. There is something weirdly alive in the depiction of Justice as she forces us to contemplate our capacity to abide by our own laws and practice self-governing. Are we impartial and are we fair, with ourselves and others? Is our decision-making ruled by false morality or by our own truth? The Justice card forces us to find Themis within and tune into her vibration of divine order.

IVSTICIA · XXXVII · 37

Justice card from the so-called
Gringonneur/Charles VI Tarot deck, created
in Northern Italy in the fifteenth century.

Justice, the thirty-seventh card of the
so-called Mantegna Tarot, E-series,
likely engraved and published in Ferrara,
Italy, in 1465.

Two-faced, blindfolded Justice from a French tarot deck, usually referred to as the Anonymous Parisian Tarot, seventeenth century.

Justice card, eighth card from the Jean Dodal tarot, a "Marseille-type" deck published in Lyon between 1701 and 1715.

La Justice, eighth card from the *Tarot de Besançon*, published between 1845 and 1860.

Justice card from a minchiate deck by François de Poilly, published in France between 1658 and 1693

Justice card from the *Tarocchini di Mitelli*, published in Rome, Italy, between 1660 and 1670.

"Themis as Justice" from the *Petit Oracle des Dames*, published in Paris by La Veuve Gueffier, 1807.

Justice, ninth card of this Grand Etteilla/ Egyptian Tarot, published in France in the late nineteenth century.

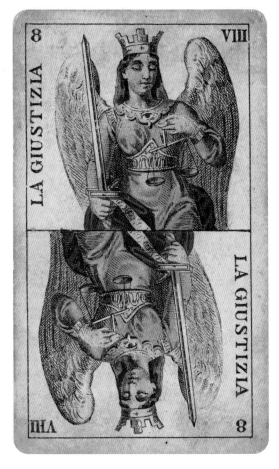

ABOVE LEFT

Ace of diamonds showing Themis, with
her sword and scale, from the *Luxus-
Spielkarte Vier-Erdteile*, published by
B. Dondorf in Frankfurt, Germany,
between 1875 and 1899.

ABOVE RIGHT

La Giustizia, Justice card from a "della
Rocca" double-headed Piedmontese tarot
published by Fratelli Armanino in Genova,
Italy, 1887.

OPPOSITE PAGE

Justice, Cthulhu Dark Arts Tarot,
illustrated by Førtifem, 2020.

VIII . Justice

In Chymicis verfanti Natura, Ratio, Experientia & lectio,
fint Dux, fcipio, perfpicilia & lampas.

EPIGRAMMA XLII.

DUx Natura tibi, túque arte pediffequus illi
 Efto lubens, erras, ni comes ipfa viæ eft.
Det ratio fcipionis opem, Experientia firmet
 Lumina, quò poffit cernere pofta procul.
Lectio fit lampas tenebris dilucida, rerum
 Verborúmque ftrues providus ut caveas.   Z   CAS-

THE HERMIT

ound by broken streams
Here I make my home
There is no need for food
I can live off air alone

The birds bring me flowers
And put them by my side
I live in another world
And that is why I hide

I am a hermit
My mind is not the same
Yes I am a hermit and ecstasy's my game
—"I am the Hermit," JONATHAN HALPER

Kenneth Anger's six-minute film *Puce Moment* presents the rapturous dressing rituals of a woman as she slowly morphs into a goddess of "Pagan Hollywood." First she selects a gown, iridescent and green like a scarab, from among many other shimmering robes. The heady perfumes she then puts on her skin blissfully intoxicate her. Her big, vampy eyes roll and flicker, the fragrant fumes provoking metaphorical and literal Baudelairian transports, as she magically swooshes in space onto a fainting couch. As in many Anger films, the music is here to underscore the esoteric message of the images we witness. The lyrics of Jonathan Halper's song " I Am a Hermit," transcribed above, are played to signal that this woman playing dress-up is in fact involved in a transfixing performance with initiatic undertones. Like the Hermit, she rises to sacred pinnacles. Ecstasy is her game, but she uses cologne and hypnotic flapper dresses instead of a lantern and a pilgrim staff. This folky, psychedelic ballad fascinated me for many years, and so did Jonathan Halper, only known from this song and the equally hermitic "Leaving My Old Life Behind," featured back to back to form the entire *Puce Moment* soundtrack. These two ethereal songs exist as the only recollection of Halper, who, like a real-life hermit, vanished from the rock 'n' roll map forever after that, these two enigmatic hymns of spiritual solitude enshrined in this very film his only legacy: Similarly, the themes of elevation, isolation, initiatic journeying, and going against the grain are all part of what makes the Hermit card a captivating one.

OPPOSITE PAGE

"Nature, Reason, Experience and Reading must be the Guide, Staff, Spectacles and Lamp to him that is employed in Chemical Affairs." A man with a lantern, goggles, and walking staff chases Sophia, a feminine allegory of Knowledge. Although he can't see her, his tools allow him to follow her footsteps. Forty-second emblem of the *Atalanta Fugiens* by Michael Maier, illustrated by Matthias Merian, and published by Johann Theodor de Bry, Oppenheim, Germany, 1618, from the collection of the Bibliothèque nationale de France.

Iconographically speaking, the Hermit wasn't always the Hermit in the early days of the tarot. Don't be fooled by the early Italian examples presenting a similar character as our wandering monk—an old bearded man, bundled up in clothing as if to signify that he is prepared for long peregrinations in the cold wilderness, sometimes outfitted with a wooden cane to help him move forward. The traditional lantern we associate with the pilgrim is, in fact, in early Renaissance tarot, an hourglass. We are not in the presence of a man, but of a pagan divinity. Indeed, these images are depictions of Kronos, the primordial god of time derived from Greek mythology, who is viewed as an all-devouring and destructive force. The hourglass is of course his attribute, and so are the crutches, as well as the knife, a reminder that he castrated his own father, Ouranos, to take his place. The so-called Mantegna example shows him gobbling up his own children, which he did out of fear of being removed from his position of power by his descendants. These early depictions of the god of time as a crippled patriarch reminds us of Gertrude Moackley's theory that the Major Arcanas might have been inspired by Petrach's *Triumph* and the symbolic procession that takes place in the Italian author's poem. Prominently featured, Time, of course, is the antepenultimate chariot, followed by Eternity. As described in Petrarch's vision, the allegorical float, led by several stags, is illustrated in manuscripts and etchings topped with the withering personification of Time modeled after Kronos, holding an hourglass in his hands.

There is no clear point or reason that led to the substitution of the Hermit instead of Kronos, but as the Marseille deck developed, the Monk-like figures became generalized on playing cards. In the Viéville deck, the pilgrim points toward the sky with one finger, an indication of the direction of his path toward spiritual elevation. In the 1775 Hooper's Conversation card game, the Contemplation card presents an aging old man meditating on his own mortality, isolated in a grotto, a human skull in one hand, a whip in the other. Gradually, the card's iconography transformed from a representation of an ascetic who chooses seclusion from the world to a seeker on a spiritual quest to achieve a connection with the divine. As the tarot began to be viewed as an esoteric tool, the Hermit archetype transmuted into a seeker of mysteries associated with metaphysical voyages in which the light of the lantern served as a guide toward transcendence, lighting the road and the heart all at once.

Is the Hermit card related to Prudence, the Cardinal Virtue officially missing from tarot's Major Arcanas sequence? Occultist Eliphas Levi believed so, and many others, such as Papus or Oswald Wirth, subsequently associated the card with this moral value, adjusting its esoteric meaning. Theologian Thomas Aquinas describes Prudence as a form of sagacity, an intellectual process in which one sees ahead the best actions to take in the pursuit of good. Prudence allegories often depict a startling Janus-headed woman looking into a mirror to "foresee" in every direction and make decisions inspired by what she perceives and what she knows. Many have seen the lantern as a symbol of this practical wisdom, illuminating one's path so we are made aware of potential dangers and find for ourselves the right direction in the darkness of the unexpected.

OPPOSITE PAGE

In the Gringonneur/Charles VI Tarot, the old man is an allegory of Time, holding an hourglass in his hands and standing at the foot of a mountain, whose rocky volume extends onto the right side of the card and upward.

Saturn, the Roman equivalent of Kronos, devouring his children. Represented as an elderly man, he stands helped by a walking staff in his right hand, in which he holds a dragon ouroboros. Forty-seventh card of the so-called Mantegna Tarot, E series, engraved by Johann Ladenspelder.

The old Time hopping on his crutches, from a Florentine minchiate published by Giovan Molinelli, 1712–16.

OPPOSITE PAGE

Time, from the Visconti-Sforza Tarot cards, attributed to Bonifacio Bembo, Milan, Italy, circa 1450–80, from the Morgan Library collection

ABOVE

Time, trampling Fame and its broken trumpets, on its chariot as he holds an hourglass in his hands. An illustration from Petrarch's *Triumph*, printed in Paris by Charles le Vigoureux, 1579–1605.

Hermit from a tarot deck published in Lyon, France, 1475–1500.

The smiling hermit of the Piedmontese Solesio Tarot, walks peaceful and content as his lantern projects its golden beams inward, reflecting in his cape, 1865.

The Hermit of the Viéville Tarot doesn't own a lantern yet, but points at his heavenly destination with his left hand, 1650.

Traitor card from a Grand Etteilla/Egyptian Tarot, from Paris, 1875–1899. In Etteilla decks, the Hanged Man is absent, and some of his old symbolical attributions, like betrayal, are related to a Hermit figure.

Prudence, ceramic rondo by Italian artist
Andrea della Robbia, 1475.

Hermit, from the Anonymous Parisian
Tarot, published between 1600 and
1650, showing our spiritual traveler
at the beginning of his journey, just
after he exits the gate of the city,
beacon light and rosary in hand.
Seventeenth century.

ABOVE LEFT AND RIGHT

Two Prudence cards from the *Grand Jeu de l'Oracle des Dames* and an Egyptian Etteilla, both from the late nineteenth
century. In the Etteilla system, the four Cardinal Virtues are represented in a way that slightly reinterprets the classic
iconography. Coiled around the mirror or the cadeuceus, the snakes are evoking hermetic wisdom. Crawling on the
floor, they invoke dangers that one might need to *prudently* avoid.

THE WHEEL
OF FORTUNE

Fortuna	O Fortune,
velut luna	like the moon
statu variabilis,	you are changeable,
semper crescis	ever waxing
aut decrescis;	ever waning;
vita detestabilis	hateful life
nunc obdurat	first oppresses
et tunc curat	and then soothes
ludo mentis aciem,	playing with mental clarity;
egestatem,	poverty
potestatem	and power
dissolvit ut glaciem.	it melts them like ice.

In 1937, composer Carl Orlf explosively transposed the thirteenth-century poem "O Fortuna" into the sung lyrics of his bombastic cantata, *Carmina Burana*. Like an anxious Greek chorus, the voices warn us of the capricious ways of Fate, "ever waxing, ever waning," using the moon and its celestial rotations as a metaphor signaling the inexorable power the goddess Fortuna has upon our lives and the arbitrary fashion in which she uses it. Fortuna has its own rhythm, and so does the dance of the planets above us and our own existence, which the medieval mind often represented by the conceptual motif of the wheel to express the abstraction of time passing, the flux and reflux of one's full-circle revolution. In the Wheel of the Ten Ages of Man, from from the psalter of Robert de Lisle, we get to witness a human lifespan. Each of the circular vignettes chronologically shows the progressive states of one man's life, from toddler to young boy to the fierce horse-riding teen and his boundless energy. Then comes the apotheosis of adulthood, in which our character, wearing royal regalia, tops the loop of his own narrative—reaching both a pinnacle and the tipping point. The one o'clock old man now walks with a cane and lifts a hand as he looks behind him bitterly, judging by his body language, at what he once was. The story goes downhill from this point—the other half of the circle will lead him to the tomb, prophetically in the opposite point of his prime. At the center, a medallion represents God as the axis of this wheel, an echo of the fact that, in the Catholic imagination, the divine clockmaker is the architect of our destiny, determining the path of our lives.

In a similar fashion, wheels were used in medieval cosmology to conceptualize infinity—the heavenly realms and their rhythmic movement. In the *Breviari d'Amour*, two angels are shown vigorously cranking the firmament to activate the rotations of stars, a macrocosmic dynamic we are caught in and cannot control. Ultimately, we are led to understand that the wheel of our lives, the ballet of the celestial sphere, and the many symbolic circles in between are all concentric, driven by the same divine energy. And so is the Wheel of Fortune in the tarot, a grandiose flow over which we are absolutely powerless.

OPPOSITE PAGE

Wheel of the Ten Ages of Man from the psalter of Robert de Lisle, produced in England, 1310.

The Wheel of Fortune motif found in the tarot is inspired by the Roman goddess Fortuna, the personification of Chance and Luck, who usually bears two attributes—one being the cornucopia, or horn of plenty, the lush symbol of her abundance. She also presides over the *Rota Fortunae*, the Wheel of Fortune, in which she desultorily decides to whom she will grant her boons. Although of antique origins, her image remained a popular allegorical trope for Fate throughout the medieval period and until the early Renaissance, which was featured on the tarot decks from that period. In the Visconti-Sforza exemple, she stands blindfolded at the center of a wheel, operating the circular device which her arms, which lie on the spokes. Four characters struggle to stay in place, ascending and descending from the circular structure. Dominating the wheel is a blond boy in regalian attire, who curiously grew a pair of donkey ears. Like the unstable zoomorphic jesters from Albrecht Dürer's *Feast of Fools*, he really has to be mindless like an ass to take his superior position for granted. Soon enough, the phantom hand of God, maneuvering the wheel from heaven, will boot him out of his transitory position of power. Whatever we do, it's not up to us, so we need to seize the best opportunity when it comes, since the shift operates quickly, pulling carpets from under our feet.

With the Marseille prototype, humans disappear from the wheel to be replaced by monkey-like creatures, mercurial and capricious like fate itself, and in the eighteenth century, the wheel topper will be interpreted as a Sphinx, through the lens of a persistent belief that the tarot presents the sacred knowledge of ancient Egypt. Like the monumental structure of Giza, the tarot's Sphinx is viewed as the guardian of the wheel, protecting its secret dynamic and commanding our fortunes.

"What goes on four feet in the morning, two feet at noon, and three feet in the evening?" the Sphinx asks Oedipus, who answers, a man, as a baby in the morning of their life, as an adult at noon, and with a cane as the sun sets on his existence. The Sphinx commands all wheels, from the microcosmic one ruling the Ages of Man to the immensity of the celestial spheres, like a skillful orchestra conductor. Our lives are like the discreet sound of a musical triangle being struck, high-pitched and almost inaudible among this otherworldly cacophony.

In a reading, the Wheel of Fortune calls to question our tense relationship between predestination and free will, allowing us to voice who controls and what creates the changes and what creates the chances that we build our lives on. Like on a celluloid strip of film, the card also tells us that reality only exists sandwiched between two other sequences. Although we might not be able to change the prospect of our storyline, we need to understand the invisible construct that caused grief or allowed us to seize an opportunity to be able to deviate our narrative from the redundancy of the loops we get caught in. We can all become Bill Murray in *Groundhog's Day*. Ultimately, the card heralds our awareness of cycles, their beginning and endings, and how we can surf on these rhythms to either find renewal or closure.

rebs lo rest de tolomeu en almagest e enaxel e au fragas dier que
asso es una cosa e tro prouen plur art e plur sacia testronomia e a
mostrar les emutats dels espays q daznir nos le dit els an este
labra equodran Saffo son algunes eschrmes abque els prouen
e mostren clarame̅t q̅ la catitat el espay quiy es del fermame̅t en̅
ala tia nequina luxaria h ia Aqsta sacia cart seguits q̅ es uer
ees sca aprouada E ncp aqstes mismes q̅ hi fa deliya e tresema̅
los uns los cote p estadis q die q̅ es art colu duna estadis pas los
altres los cote anulers los altres los cote acoltes O das tot es .i. citi
tat: Taula dels espays dell mon:

Cp commence le prologue du trsss/ Enentulo attendue la mutacion des
lateur du luure de Jehm bocacce · · · · choles et des temps et des seur.Et

OPPOSITE PAGE

Wheel of Fortune from the Visconti-Sforza
Tarot, attributed to Bonifacio Bembo,
Milan, Italy, c. 1450–80.

ABOVE

The blindfolded Double Fortune, with her colorful and shadow sides,
which signify her dual nature and are capable of granting and taking
her largeness. From *Livres des Cas des Nobles Hommes et Femmes*
(Concerning the Fates of Illustrious Men and Women), by Etienne
Colaud, France, 1530.

Wheel of Fortune, the Anonymous Parisian Tarot, France, 1600–50.

Three donkey-like jesters struggle to keep a grip on the wheel. On the top left-hand side, the divine hand comes out of the clouds to crank the apparatus in this etching by Albrecht Dürer, from *Stultifera Navis* (The Ship of Fools) by Sebastian Brandt, 1498.

Wheel of Fortune from the *Tarocchi Fine dalla Torre*, published in Bologna, Italy, in the seventeenth century.

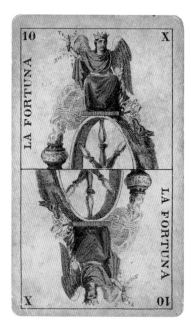

Crafty and deceitful, the fox tries to climb against the movement of the wheel, which turns clockwise, as indicated by the smoking urn and the treasure spills. From a double-headed Della Rocca/Soprafino–type tarot deck, published in Genoa, Italy, by Fratelli Armanino.

"Order" - Wheel of Fortune with cartomantic handwritten inscriptions from a Marseille deck modeled after the Tarot of Nicolas Conver, published by Maison Camoin between 1890 and 1900.

Fortuna and her wheel, spreading wealth. From the *Tarocchini di Mitelli*, published in Rome, Italy, 1660–70.

Sphinx topping the Wheel of Fortune, from the *Tarot des Imagiers du Moyen Age* by Oswald Wirth, 1889.

Omnium Dominatrix (The Ruler of Everything) a card from the Leber Rouen Tarot, an Italian deck from the sixteenth century. Courtesy of the Bibliotheque de Rouen.

STRENGTH

 et's begin by looking at this curious tarot trump as an introduction to this chapter on Strength. The gorgeous figurative card shown here, numbered 15, belongs to a double-headed German tarot deck. An object of intrigue to me, since maybe by pure coincidence, it sums up many reflections I have found articulated at the core of the Strength Major Arcana. As we look with closer attention, we see two images mirroring each other: one of Saint Blandina, represented in a pious attitude, surrounded by incongruously docile lions. On its reverse side, we are presented with the disturbing spectacle of a matador administering the coup de grâce to a helpless bull during a tauromachy event. Defeated, the animal collapses from the impact of the sword.

In both illustrations, the focus is centered on the relationship connecting a human and a fierce, impulsive animal. Contrasted polar opposites are on display, in one version to express concord, in the other, mortal confrontation. Two sides of a coin. If the first drawing evokes the lore of Saint Blandina, it might be important to remind ourselves of the legend associated with the Catholic martyr. Persecuted by the Romans in the second century, she was thrown into the arena, along with a group of other early Christians, to be eaten alive by the lions. As the story goes, her faith, her chastity, and rectitude were so grand that the feline predators meekly sat at her feet, refusing to eat her. Somehow, these inner qualities actively and invisibly tamed the ferocity of the beasts.

In the tarot, the Strength card is associated with Fortitude, the second Cardinal Virtue summoned in the Major Arcana sequence. The plurality of iconographic variations depicted on this card is astonishing. It is worth taking the time to unpack the splendor and variety of this card and recount the startling stories associated with it. The overarching concept of Fortitude is fragmented into two parallel visual tropes that existed simultaneously during the fifteenth century. Maidens, holding broken columns together or coiling their arms around perfectly vertical ones, or masculine heroes assailing lions with their hands or with the help of a club. As with the Justice card, the Fortitude motif reprises a lot of the allegorical depictions already circulating during the medieval period. The trope of the maiden and the column reminds us of how Saint Thomas Aquinas described Fortitude: a moral courage to take on or to refuse suffering for the benefit of reason. Fortitude evokes our capacity to stand up firmly, like a column, for the pursuit of good, even if we get roughed up. The column is, we can speculate, a visual rendition of this moral rectitude, immovable and consistent, even as fear looms, we don't let ourselves be intimidated.

In the so-called Mantegna exemple, the allegorical figure wears an extravagant lion pelt as a headdress while the live beast hides behind her. Queen of nonchalance, she holds together a falling-apart column with only one hand. Smashed pillars and ferocious cats—with this image and in many others instances of the Strength card, we are invited to connect to Fortitude by meditating on the story of Samson, the old testament proto-superman whose tale weaves together baffling fits of physical prowess with devotion to God. In one epic tale, on his way to Timnah to ask for the hand of a Philistine in marriage, Samson is attacked by a lion and, in some strange turn of events, God bestows miraculous physical power upon him, allowing him to not only kill the animal, but rip it apart without a weapon. Copiously represented in art, the violent account reached an apex of brutality in Cranach's version. Samson, with one foot on the back of the lion who is contorted in pain,

OPPOSITE PAGE

15th Card of a German tarot deck
published in Frankfurt around 1840.

pulls open the jaws with his bare hands. In a last, fatal episode, Samson also punished the Philistines for their idolatry in worshiping Dagon by grasping the columns of their temple until the pillars collapsed, causing the destruction of the building and our hero's own demise. In this case, the virtue of Fortitude is expressed through the transformation of Samson's faith in God, which is sublimated into physical strength. An inner, spiritual experience becomes the fuel of his capacity for action.

Another iconographic nuance also exists in the Visconti-Sforza Tarot and a few others, which depicts a man charging the lion with a wooden club in hand. It is no one else but Heracles, the ancient Greek champion and poster boy of bravery, as he defeated the Nemean lion, the first of his twelve labors. In this case, Fortitude is invoked as a commentary on pure heroism and viril might, without echoing inner experience.

The emblematic Maiden and the Lion is the most familiar theme. Stabilizing in the *Tarot de Marseille* in the eighteenth century and broadly established in the nineteenth and twentieth centuries, this incarnates the symbolic prototype of Strength. The image may be found in the Visconti di Modrone Tarot, in as early as the fifteenth century. If, at first glance, the image resembles the Samson representation, the brutishness of the confrontation has been eliminated. As we look closely, we see that the woman is seated on the back of the lion, whose tail is carefully wrapped around his feet. Her contained attitude is calm and regal, and her body language expresses nothing but softness with absolutely no physical tension. As she puts her hands in the lion's mouth, revealing its sharp fangs that emphasize the danger of such an act, we can only discern the slow gentleness of this intimate physical account. In order to sit so closely to the beast and pursue this rather invasive gesture of opening the mouth of the lion, we could surmise that she had established a relationship of trust with the animal. The Maiden isn't looking for supremacy by projecting her dominion on the lion through aggression and mortal combat. Something more subtle is at play in this image, a subduing in which the beast keeps its integrity, an encounter where the energy is derived from negotiation, not strife.

We could imagine that the Maiden and the Lion trope prevailed over time because it revealed something more profound than the moral rectitude of the unshattered pillar metaphor, or the ritualistic bashing and diminishing of the enemy. Fortitude, as Thomas Aquinas described it, is an inner strength in which we courageously go toward what we fear, what might hurt us, in order to preserve the good. This strength, unlike physical abilities, comes from infinite sources, which is why many tarot scholars have interpreted the hat of the Maiden of the Marseille decks as forming a lemniscate, the symbol of boundless energy. We can tap into that well of strength without ever knowing thirst. The fact is, often the lion comes to represent a facet of ourselves, the unleashed animality, both noble and voracious, destructive and fierce. The Strength card establishes that the paradoxical nature of this animal needs to be appraised in order to be managed. Strong mastery means establishing a connection, not using suppression in order to gain power.

ABOVE LEFT

A feminine allegorical figure holds the broken pillar with her arms, trying to preserve its integrity. Fortitude card from the so-called Gringonneur/Charles VI, Northern Italy, 1475–1500.

ABOVE RIGHT

One of my favorite "Force" cards, from the Minchiate of François de Poilly, casually carries the column on her shoulder like an amazon. Published in France in 1658–93.

Forteza, thirty-sixth card of the so-called Mantegna Tarot, from the E series, engraved by Johann Ladenspelder, 1540–60.

The Maiden and the unbroken column, as an allegory of Fortitude, from a double-headed tarocchino deck, published in 1850.

An allegory of Fortitide, showing both Samson destroying the lion of Timnah, in parallel with a classic representation of the Cardival Virtue, as a woman in armor clinging onto the shattered pieces of pillar. Drawn by Jos Murer, 1545-1580.

"Strength/Ennui - Disgust." eighth card of the *Petit Oracle des Dames*, published by La Veuve Gueffier, in Paris, 1807.

Manly strength wrapped in a lion pelt from *the Tarot Hieroglyphique*, by Madame Dulora de la Haye, published in Paris, 1897.

Strength card from the Jean Noblet Tarot, published in Paris, 1659.

Strength card from the Tarot of Jacques Viéville, Paris, 1650.

Strength card from the Arnoux and Amphoux Tarot, published in Marseille in 1801.

OPPOSITE PAGE

Samson's Fight with the Lion, Lucas Cranach the Elder, Germany, 1525.

THE HANGED MAN

Many winters ago, I found myself browsing through the shelves of the C.G. Jung Institute's library in New York City, trying to unearth serendipitous new rabbit holes to explore, as one does in such an institution. Scanning the book-filled horizon with squinting eyes, my gaze got caught on the bluish spine of a book—*The Hanged Man*—what a surprise! A familiar name surfacing in an ocean of psychoanalysis treaties. I pulled out the volume immediately, revealing a front cover adorned with a pale rendition of Pamela Colman Smith's Hanged Man. This serendipitous find, written by the prominent psychotherapist Sheldon Kopp, bore a title as provocative as a malefic grimoire—*The Hanged Man: Psychotherapy and the Forces of Darkness*. A promising read, indeed! Once back home, it took me a couple of seconds to track down a copy of this tome for sale and, to my bewilderment, I also found this rather curious customer report as part of the description. "Random Factoid: This book appears in the cell of Dr. Hannibal Lecter in the 2002 movie *Red Dragon*, based on the Thomas Harris novel of the same name. I have not read it, so I cannot offer a review."

Although I rewatched the thriller trilogy several times since, I've never found that to be true, yet I'd love to be wrong about it. In contemplating the prospect of an iconographic study of the Hanged Man of the tarot, Hannibal Lecter—psychoanalyst of the elite, cruelty connoisseur, Italian Renaissance enthusiast who believed himself to be a descendant of the Visconti family—is a bizarre but shrewd candidate to chaperon us through the disquieting visions of this specific Major Arcana. One of the peculiar reasons is that Dr. Lecter gives a presentation on this very topic in the 2001 film *Hannibal*. Filmed in Florence, Italy, a city in which our fictional anthropophagite gentleman choose to exile himself incognito. Having recently "removed" the librarian of the Capponi Library, Lecter misappropriated his place and began to live his longtime dream of being a Renaissance man, fully emerging himself in fourteenth- and fifteenth-century Italian art, poetry, and correspondence describing political power plays and theatrical death sentences. In one scene, Hannibal the Cannibal gives a highly romanticized art history lecture of the visual depictions of the Hanged Man, an iconography, he explains, that is associated with the crime of betrayal. To support his arguments, Dr. Lecter presents to a captivated audience illustrations drawn from Dante's *Inferno*, in which the poet finds, in the Forest of "Self-Murderers," the disgraced jurist Pietro della Vigna and Judas Iscariot, who sold Christ to the Romans, after they both committed suicide by hanging.[1]

A long introduction and a very deep digression to lead us here: The Hanged Man card and the history of its iconography are paradoxically hard to stomach, yet it's one of the most fascinating cards in the tarot. It exemplifies perfectly an image that has known very few pictorial modifications, yet what it means to represent has changed over time. The way we interpret the Hanged Man, whether it is from a cultural or esoteric standpoint, is informed by societal evolution, and in this case, we could speculate that the association with traitors faded when the death penalty as moral spectacle was slowly eliminated from Europe in the nineteenth century.

From the fifteenth century to its most recent version, the card depicts nearly the same visual apparatus. A wooden gallow, created from two tree trunks with a horizontal piece of wood laid across them; a man, attached to the structure by one leg, the other folding in a more natural angle, depending on the version. The protagonist is sometimes seen carrying bags, their heaviness pulling him down and meant to augment his pain. From one card to another, his facial expression goes from a painful grimace to what I call the "resting martyr face," emotionless. If today we tend to assimilate the Hanged Man as a model of acceptance and serenity toward climactic suffering, the gesticulation of the man in the Gringonneur deck or his struggling in the Soprafino deck makes us feel almost queasy. A clear reminder that originally, the card's iconography belonged in the field of capital punishment. In fifteenth-century Italy and across Europe, the severity of public executions varied depending on the crime and the social status of the criminal. Organized to be witnessed by an audience, executions functioned as moral spectacles that involving torture, the atrocity serving as a cautionary display to the spectators. It is important to note that physical suffering in the Catholic imagination was also believed to offer a redemptive effect. Pain endured was seen as a way to connect to Christ and his own suffering during the Crucifixion.

Death by hanging was stigmatizing, reserved for the lower classes. By one foot, the act was even more painful and degrading, a humiliation reserved for traitors and people involved in corruption or fraud, especially those driven by greed. In the tympanum of the Abbey of Sainte-Foy in Conques, France, Avarice is personified by a hanged man with a hefty sack of gold attached to his neck, his desire for material goods becoming part of his condemnation, the materialization of what "brought him down." Maybe here lies one of the symbolic explanations of these bags held by the upside-down sufferer, a parody of one's sinful behavior.

The motif also recalls the Italian phenomenon of *pitture infamanti*—the shame paintings commissioned by the governments of city-states to symbolically punish certain citizens who committed ugly deeds. Placed in the streets for all to see, the images would depict them hanging by one foot, thereby punishing them by tarnishing their reputation. In the Italian Renaissance, still ruled by feudal codes of honor, disgrace and character assasination were meant to be a social death. In the same way, the idea of betrayal and hanging can be seen through the example of Judas, seen as the twice-traitor. The corrupted disciple delivered Christ to the Romans against a sum of money, and later committed suicide out of guilt, an act condemn by the Catholic doctrine as a betrayal of faith.

In the eigheenth century, as Antoine Court de Gébelin drafted his often ill-informed esoteric conclusions on the tarot, he mistakenly looked at the Hanged Man in reverse. Seeing a man standing with one leg up, caught in a jig, his other foot roped to the ground, the learned Protestant pastor associated the card with Prudence, solving with this error the puzzle of the Cardinal Virtue. Some playing decks do present a standing hanged man, a surrealist vision to say the least.

OPPOSITE PAGE

Two preparatory sketches for a *pittura infamante* by Andrea del Sarto, meant to be placarded in the Palazzo Pubblico in Florence, Italy, 1529-30.

The shift of interpretation unfolds in the nineteenth century, also the rush hour of the occult tarot. By this time, the *Tarot de Marseille*'s iconography is well established, and the Hanged Man is back up, swinging in the air. But it's not the only thing that changed. In France, for example, after the French Revolution, the death penalty was reformed, and use of the guillotine became standardized, a quick procedure seen as more humane at the time. Torture practices were pathologized and executions ceased little by little to be public spectacle, regressing to the modesty of prison courtyards. The Hanged Man and his humiliating treatment lost their primary meaning, and the traitor vanished to become a martyr, a character who we are meant to empathize with. Occultist Eliphas Levi, aware of Gébelin's misreading, describes him in 1856 as a symbol of sacrificial culmination, his physical transcending as an accomplishment.[2] With Oswald Wirth, or in the Waite-Smith deck, the Hanged Man is crowned with a glowing halo, the attribute of sainthood. Pointing to the heavenly spheres with a leg as if to indicate his focus, the Hanged Man has transcended physical pain, he is removed from corporeality, falling upward into his initiation. Don't confuse his lack of facial expression for apathy. We are witnessing a man in a state of peaceful abandon. Although his faith is on trial, his conscience is somewhere else, already elevated, surrendering to spirit. The angular body posture echoes the shape of a skeleton key, puncturing open the dimensions above. Ignoring everything about his destination, yet accepting his lack of control, the Hanged Man is suspended in a threshold, soon to be meeting Death.

OPPOSITE PAGE

L'Appeso, the Hanged Man from the Italian Soprafino deck, late nineteenth century, from the McClosky's Antiquarian Books and Cards collection. Courtesy of McClosky Rare Books and Antiques.

RIGHT

The Suicide of Judas, a grotesque detail from the fresco created by Giovanni Canavesio in the Chapelle Notre-Dame des Fontaines in La Brigue, France, 1492. Judas is shown having hanged himself from a berry tree, his abdomen opened and inner organs spilling out. On the right side, an anthropomorphized demon is pictured reclaming Judas's soul.

Drawing of Bernardo di Bandini Baroncelli, hanged, by Leonardo Da Vinci, 1479. After Instigating a complot against the Medici, Baroncelli was caught in Constantinople, arrested, and brought back to Florence, where he was executed for betrayal and hanged in the Palazzo del Bargello. The text, hand-written by Da Vinci in his iconic mirror writing, translates in a rather stoic way, listing the hues of the colors of his clothes.

One large drop of ink on his mouth and this accidentally expressive Hanged Man appears to almost comically lose his traditional peaceful attitude. From a Jean Noblet Tarot, a Marseille-type deck published in Paris, late seventeenth century.

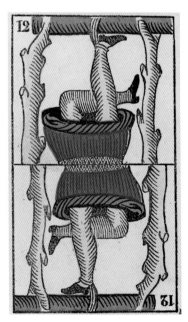

A tragic fate for the Hanged Man of this double-headed Marseille deck, who also lost his head in the process. Published by B.P. Grimaud between 1860 and 1899.

Defying gravity, this upside-down Hanged Man looks like he is dancing. From the Viéville Tarot, 1650.

Hanged Man from the Anonymous Parisian Tarot, 1600–50.

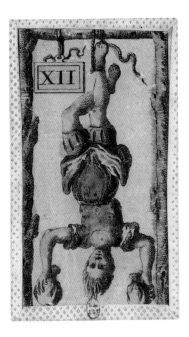

Hanged Man from a minchiate deck, printed on silk, by Giovan Molinelli, Florence, 1712–16.

"Expiation," "Torments," "Speech," "Angst," "Sacrifice"—a few of the divinatory inscriptions handwritten on this Hanged Man from a *Tarot de Marseille*, modeled after Arnoult's deck, published by B.P. Grimaud, Paris, 1891.

Le Supplice, "Torture,"—a Saint Sebastian–inspired Hanged Man, in which the martyr receives arrows in the chest like the Catholic saint. From the *Tarot Hiéroglyphique de Mme de Dulora de La Haye*, 1897.

In Oswald Wirth's *Tarot des Imagiers du Moyen Age*, 1899, pieces of gold are seen falling out of the bags that are tucked in the Hang Man's immobilized arms to form a golden halo around his face.

DEATH

uring the COVID-19 quarantine, I concocted a tarot class called Death and Resurrection as Muse, in which my students and I explored the narrative sequence of the Major Arcanas through the lens of art, history, and creative practice. The goal of this workshop was to invite students to reflect on metaphors of life, death, and rebirth silently emanating from the tarot and explore how to use these discoveries to reignite their own creativity in times of crisis. At the end of our four-week journey together, students had to create a tarot card of their own invention or redesign one they felt spontaneously drawn toward. Inspired by the iconic nameless card from a nineteenth-century Lequart *Tarot de Marseille*, this beautiful embroidery was the final assignment created by seamstress extraordinaire Vickie Ess. She accompanied her work with this little text:

> As a quilter I have sometimes reproduced a quilt pattern made by my grandmother or great grandmother, foremost to honor them. But also, in the process, my fingers repeat the actions taken decades ago by their fingers and a connection is made between the living and the dead. I thought of this process in the making of this Death card, bearing witness to an artist and an image from the nineteenth century. I chose to use embroidery, which for me is slow, elongating the action of learning and remembering the image. I chose to feminize the image with the bright pink and purple of the skirt. The flower at her waist and the plants on the ground signify the rebirth promised even as she wields her scythe.

Vickie's work is particularly moving to me for the profound and unpretentious way it articulates complex ideas about our finite existence, how we connect to the past rituals of our ancestors, and the way in which a humble craft practice like embroidery or sewing can morph into a meditative process empowering us to meet grief, memorialize, and celebrate what was before us. This embroidered death, as poetically described by Vickie, weaves together several storylines, past, present, and future, through a timeless choreography of fingers, needle, and thread. Once that narrative has been completed, a knot is done, the floss cut short, and this image exists as a keepsake of these stories outside of us, to be passed on to future generations.

With the Death card, something similar happens. In the overarching tale of the Major Arcanas, up until the Death card, we are meant to believe that life is like this thread. A linear and tight continuum, weaving one story, tensed between a beginning and an end. However, the way tarot unfolds, the Death card is a rubicon instead of a termination, performing as an intimate apocalypse, a revelation. It's the "End of the World as We Know It," like the REM song that regained a bittersweet popularity in the charts during the pandemic. Once the long string of experience is interrupted, something transforms in a definitive, radical way, and we are met with open perspectives that we can't comprehend nor articulate. If this metamorphosis is welcomed with much emotional discomfort and fear, in the iconography of the tarot, the allegories of our demise tend to promote a revised, more optimistic idea of death, a pivotal point rather than an epilogue. As we look at this skeletal figure, we are passing a threshold leading us to a long stretch of esoteric adventures. Our epic journey is far from over, and might actually just be about to begin.

OPPOSITE PAGE
Embroidered Death card,
Vickie Ess, 2020.

Whether it has been called Death or presented as the nameless card, this Tarot trump is invariably associated with the number 13—a loaded number that we superstitiously associate with bad luck. The number evokes the thirteen lunations associated with a full calendar year, implying that as we reach this point, we complete a full cycle, closing a chapter to open another. Iconography-wise, the card moves according to two main variations, both already present in cards in the fifteenth century and informed by the visual culture of their time: The first one we'll call "Death the Invader" and the second "Death the Alter Ego."

With a cruel demeanor, Death the Invader is perched high on a horse and is at times presented in a suit of armor. In the Charles VI card, a grinning figure destroys and kills everything in the path of its mount, trampling the pope and cardinals alike with the same vigor. This martial attitude and thirst for rampage summons visions of the Apocalypse emerging visually in Europe during the plague in the fourteenth century. Death the Invader is associated with the Pale Horseman from the Book of Revelation, a brutal archetype spanning from Bruegel the Elder's *Triumph of Death* to the *Evil Dead*'s *Army of Darkness*—the exuberant and horrific paradox of Death being both the corpse commander and its macabre legions, united to besiege life itself. In these images, the end of our timeline echoes the end of the world, together perceived as a violation, an invasive and destructive force systemically annihilating everything under its boots. Death and its army are invincible opponents because already dead, they sack lives without mercy, forcing us to surrender, powerless under their collective might.

On the other hand, the second main visual trope, and maybe the most prominent, is Death as the Alter Ego. From the Visconti-Sforza example to the many Marseille-type variations, Death is once more anthropomorphized, this time shown simply standing, a basic but meaningful detail, and holding a scythe. Walking at our level, presenting itself on the same familiar ground we share, Death appears less intimidating, more humane, the totality of its deliquescent body on display, mirroring ours. This vision of Death is frightening and different but accessible, available for us to contemplate, as if it's saying, "As I am, so will you."

This sinister doppelgänger reminds me of the Dance of Death, a late medieval motif that also appeared during the plague. In these images, a jovial cadaver is paired with a stock character—a pope, a knight, a vagabond, a nun, a hermit . . . and many others sharing similarities with the ones we find in the tarot. Grabbing them by the hand, the skeletons are psychopomps, inviting them to a procession equally ominous and ecstatic, a final dance leading to the afterlife. The full spectrum of the social hierarchy is represented in this strange dance, as if to imply the universality of such an experience. Whether poor or rich, powerful or invisible, what was accumulated or lost in this life doesn't matter any longer, because soon we'll be disembarrassed from everything. Contrary to our first example, the macabre farandole presents an interpersonal connection with Death; as we meet our sepulchral chaperon, we reflect on what we leave behind.

One of the culminations of the Major Arcana sequence, the Death card marks a point of fracture in our story and the beginning of a rite of passage. With this arcana, we go from coping with the transitory nature of time to a first sublime glimpse into infinity. Often dreaded by people, this card describes in fact our own capacity to welcome change or to live it as an invasion, which like death itself, is a universal experience. From where we stand, clinging to what we know, everything after this card feels out of our comfort zone, unreachable or terrifying. With its gentle grin and the intimidating scythe, this grim reaper guide slashes an entrance between the realm of the living and the realm of the dead, carefully guiding our fragile souls from one bank to the other.

Death card from the so-called Gringonneur/Charles VI Tarot, Northern Italy, fifteenth century.

Death riding a horse, from the *Tarocchi Fine dalla Torre*, published in Bologna, Italy, in the seventeenth century.

Death card from a minchiate deck, printed on silk, by Giovan Molinelli, Florence, Italy, 1712–16.

Death card from the Visconti-Sforza, attributed to Bonifacio Bembo, Milan, Italy, fifteenth century.

RIGHT
Triumph of Death, unknown artist, from the Palazzo Abatellis in Palermo, 1446.

Son Fine—"I am the End," says Death, disguised as a cardinal, attributed to Antonio di Cicognara, Italy, 1490s. From the Victoria and Albert Museum, London.

"Death and the Abbess," part of the *Dance of Death* series attributed to Jacques-Antony Chovin, created in the eighteenth century. I'm particularly fond of this image from Chovin's *Dance of Death*. The half-decomposed skeleton bows down to caress the fabric of the abbess' religious habit with his gaunt fingers, on which a bit of skin feels the soft texture of the tunic. The skeleton's body translates so well the delight and surprise of this tactile encounter. The sensation provoked a vivid memory, a *madeleine de Proust*—as if he was thinking, "I remember this, I remember how it feels to feel." Lost in this memory of a past life, the skeleton forgets its duty to lead the abbess in the Dance of Death. Caught in a sensation, he is reminded that once, he was us.

Death card, Marseille Tarot deck, Stefano Vergnano, northern Italy, 1827.

Death card, *Tarot de Marseille*, published by B.P. Grimaud, 1890.

Death card from *Tarot Viéville*, published c. 1650.

Four of Clubs from a deck designed by Charlotte von Jennison-Walworth and published in 1808.

Death emerging from a tomb, holding a scythe and a winged hourglass, a reference to the Latin motto *tempus fugit*—"time flies." From an Egyptian-styled Grand Etteilla, published in France, 1850–75.

The dance of a gesticulating Death is almost comical. Shrouded in a sanguine and fluid veil, far removed from the idea of a termination, this card is an antithetical symbol of vitality. From the *Grand Jeu de l'Oracle des Dames*, designed by G. Regamey and published in Paris in the late nineteenth century.

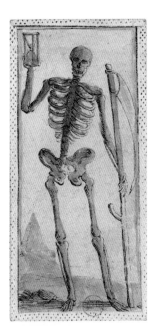

Death card from the *Tarocchini di Mitelli*, published in Rome, Italy, between 1660 and 1670.

"Mortality" and "Sorrow, Grief." Death lurks in the cemetery, while on the reverse side, a widow weeps over a loved one, holding the urn on their tomb. From *Le Petit Oracle des Dames*, published in Paris by La Veuve Gueffier, 1807.

Death as a physician, pouring medicine into the spoon of a sickened man lying in bed. A snake is coiled behind his back. From the *Verkehrte Welt*, a German tarot deck from the 1840s.

TEMPERANCE

he Temperance card summons the acknowledgement of excess, a purging process and the ultimate restoration of balance. In this reproduction of a Brygos red-figure ceramic, we see a sick man vomiting, his head gently held by a woman, often described as a hetaira, a learned courtesan. As he stands, a long string of liquid substance spews from his mouth to the floor, but thanks to the gesture of his feminine acolyte who holds his head, he doesn't soil himself. A prosaic depiction, almost amusing to us, ironically depicted inside a terra-cotta drinking vessel, that we could spontaneously interpret as a cautionary illustration: "Beware! Your self-indulgence could lead you to be like him!"

Our image of the Ancient Greeks is often distorted by Hollywood movies and images of toga parties. We tend to imagine them as a complete riot, decadent and orgy-loving. In reality, they were extremely sensitive to profligacy, and intoxication was frowned upon, only to be allowed in the context of religious rites of ecstatic release, like the drunken kommos processions or Dionysian rites, which might be the subject of this vessel's illustration. In fact, outside of the context of sacred inebriety, the Greeks were particularly vigilant about the over-consumption of alcohol, and diluted their wine with water (1 part wine to 3 parts water). They were also rather opinionated about the surrounding populations who didn't abstain, and considered excessive wine drinking a barbaric behavior.

The concept of temperance originated in Ancient Greece. The last of the Cardinal Virtues presented in the Major Arcanas, the Temperance card is often associated with moderation and self-restraint. This metaphor of diluting wine was chosen as its iconographic representation prior to and beyond its use in the tarot. Like a sacred mixologist, a feminine personification of Temperance uses a hydra, the denominated vessel containing water, to pour liquid into the krater, the wine-mixing bowl. Sometimes a small jar and a kylix, or drinking cup, will be used.

As they diluted the wine, they moderated themselves, and one could imagine how the almost transparent liquid would have allowed them to see the vomiting man depicted inside the cup. Imagine that image in your own wine glasses as a clever and dissuasive reminder that excess, which might make you sick, is only one sip away.

Another important cultural specificity of the antique world was the purification power they attributed to water and its capacity to enable hallowed sanitary circulation. Many of our modern hygiene rituals and systems were inherited from the Greeks and the Romans. They invented sewage systems, public baths, proto-showers, and public fountains. We tend to forget that our modern "spa" culture is inherited from the ancients; the twentieth-century balneary tourism and hygienist phenomenon decided to use that word as an acronym for the Latin motto *sanis per aquam*: "health through water."

OPPOSITE PAGE

A woman holding the head of a man who is vomiting, a gouache reproduction of a motif depicted on an Attic cup signed by Brygos, early fifth century, BCE, part of the Würzburg collection in Germany. The gouache is in the Wellcome Collection, London.

How to interpret this card in the context of the narrative sequence of the Major Arcanas? Temperance harvests us right after death, welcoming us into the afterlife like an ambassador, a guide, the Virgil of Dante's *Inferno*. Its radiant beauty contrasts with the cadaver-like figure of its predecessor, Death, and we could imagine that's intentional. In several decks, including most Marseille and Rider-Waite-Smith Tarots, Temperance is shown as an angel, a supernatural being whose reassuring presence also communicates the idea that we left our old world to enter a dimension we cannot yet understand fully. In the Thoth Tarot, the Temperance equivalent, named "Art," shows a bicephalous creature mixing fire and water in a crucible. Behind this ubiquitous character, an orange halo bares a famous alchemical motto drawn from Basile Valentine's fifteenth-century *L'Azoth des Philosophes: Visita interiora terrae rectificando invenies occultum lapidem*, or "Visit the interior of the Earth and rectified, you'll find the hidden stone."

Indeed, with the following cards, the Devil and the Tower, we will visit the abyss, the interior of the Earth. With two communicating vessels, Temperance's iconic gesture is to be understood as a guesture of hospitality and purification. Like the biblical foot baths, this ablution ritual owns sacred qualities which signify that we shouldn't fear this unfamiliar place (yet) and help to prepare us, purge us, from the residues of the before times. Like the hetaira on the vessel, Temperance metaphorically holds our heads so we can throw up what doesn't serve us any longer, giving us the opportunity to reboot. With her water, she performs a cleanse that will prepare us for the vertiginous descent we are about to undertake.

OPPOSITE PAGE

Temperance, Piero del Pollaiolo, 1470, Uffizi Gallery, Florence, Italy.

OPPOSITE PAGE

Temperance from the Visconti-Sforza Tarot, attributed to Antonio Cicognara, Milan, Italy, 1480–1500.

Temperance, from the so-called Gringonneur/Charles VI Tarot, Northern Italy, fifteenth century.

Temperance, from a minchiate deck, printed on silk, Giovan Molinelli, Florence, 1712–16.

Temperance, from a minchiate deck, published in Florence, Italy, by A. Baragioli, 1860–90.

Temperance, from a minchiate deck, published by Gaetano in Bologna, Italy, 1763.

Temperance as an angel from a Marseille-type deck, published in Marseille, France, by Arnoux and Amphoux, 1801.

"Combinations–Changes," Temperance card with handwritten cartomantic meanings, from the *Tarot de Marseille* published by B.P. Grimaud, Paris, 1890.

"Temperance–Night," from the *Petit Oracle des Dames*, published in Paris at La Veuve Gueffier, 1807.

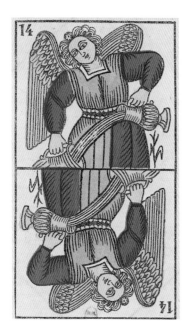

Temperance from a double-headed tarot deck, published in Paris by B.P. Grimaud, 1880.

Temperance from Oswald Wirth's *Tarot des Imagiers du Moyen Age*, Paris, 1889.

OPPOSITE PAGE

"Art," Temperance card from the Thoth Tarot, by Aleister Crowley and Lady Frieda Harris, 1944.

THE DEVIL

With his revolting anatomical configuration, the Devil of Giovanni di Modena's *Inferno*, is, to me, one of the most fascinating images ever created. Hard to look at, profoundly repulsive, yet it's impossible not to be magnetized by this image. This aberrant vision with a genital-like facial orifice is equally obscene and comical in its monstrosity. What unspeakable fate awaits these people being swallowed by the master of the underworld? The devils on the label of our hot sauce bottles pale in comparison to this spectacularly ominous figure. His bluish skin, a verdigris of decay, is like that of a putrefied cadaver. The volutes of swirling fur translate his animalistic behavior. His tall, massive stature equates to his hunger for souls, which he devours using both extremities of his being, which includes a second "mouth," technically called a gastrocephalic hole. This bizarre feature, visible in many depictions of medieval demons, visually translates his voracious appetite and how the seat of his intelligence serves lower instincts. As we look at this terrifying image, we understand that his body is as labyrinthic as hell itself, distorted and multiple. The devil is both the tormentor and the place of torment. Somehow as we contemplate his body, we are meant to believe he himself is the gateway to the chthonian realms, the hellmouth leading to the center of the Earth. Everything about this journey downward equates to a digestion, a counter-initiation into the bowels of darkness.

Besides, this demon is interesting because it was conceived early in the fifteenth century, around the same time as the tarot was created. An important detail, because none of the Renaissance cards presenting the Devil have survived over the years. Why? We don't know. They might have been lost or, as some believe, destroyed to avoid more ill-fated activities. Tarot scholar Mary K. Greer wondered the same thing in one of her blog entries, and speculated that these early cards could have been used to cast spells. She cites an article by Andrea Vitali, who quoted a sixteenth-century transcript of an Inquisition trial in Venice. The text describes a court case in which a woman was accused of witchcraft, having tried to attract the romantic favor of a man by doing a ritual prayer to the souls of purgatory, which utilized a Devil tarot card as an altarpiece.

I'd like to imagine that the early Devil cards resembled the abominable figure painted by Giovanni di Modena. In seventeenth-century France, some *Tarot de Marseille* cards did feature gastrocephalic faces in their illustrations, as if in a continuity with this ogreish figure. His furry appearance is also accounted for here, evoking the depiction of the Wild Man, a popular motif in medieval Europe. Covered with a thick layer of hair, the wild man is a primitive woodland creature, living away from civilization, animated by an atavic drive. Our Major Arcana devils are not so distant cousins, sharing lineage with the libidinous satyrs, as well as Pan, the Greek god of nature's vitality.

OPPOSITE PAGE

The Devil from Giovanni di Modena's *Inferno*, a fresco finished in 1410 in the Basilica of San Petronio, Bologna, Italy.

As it is represented in the tarot, the Devil is always an ambivalent, liminal character. A chimera, he is part man, part goat, part falcon sometimes. In the *Tarot de Marseille*, he often bears sexual attributes of both genders, which one could read through a Christian lens as a symbol of his unquenchable sexual appetite. Perched on his pedestal, the king of hell is a temptator and an enabler, and the two minions chained at his feet are ambiguously both his slaves and escorts. The rope attaching them to the column reminds us of numerous allegories of idolatry. In the *Allegory of Infidelity* created by Giotto in the Scrovegni Chapel, the character is held on a leash by the statue he wrongfully worships. His eyes are closed to signify his denial as he is commanded by the subject of his devotion. As with the Devil's submissive acolytes, he is both willingly blind and trapped.

In the nineteenth century, the cultural status of the Devil shifts from an ignoble monster to a romantic antihero. In Milton's epic poem *Paradise Lost*, written in the seventeenth century, Satan is presented as a rebellious figure fighting against a demiurgic God. His defiance will make him a symbol of insubordination and emancipation for the generation to come, inspiring artists and occultists alike, in a general climate of rational disenchantment and suspicion toward the Catholic Church and political authorities. Lucifer, etymologically "the light bringer," supplants Satan, "the adversary." A radical change of perspective takes him away from his identity as an idol of perversity to an enlightening figure of discontent. In the tarot, the Devil's iconography and meanings will often be inspired by Eliphas Levi's study of Baphomet, the goat-headed figure allegedly worshipped by the knight templars. In his chapter called "The Sabbath of the Witches," he participated as well in this rehabilitation by describing the horned deity as a pantheistc figure of balance through which opposite polarities find a harmonious restoration.[1] It is important to note that Levi's work was translated into English by none other than Arthur Edward Waite, instigator and co-creator of the Rider-Waite-Smith tarot. Although he doesn't share the French occultist views about Baphomet, his Devil card finds inspiration, like many others after him, in the sulfurous prototype drawn by Levi himself.

In contemporary tarot practices, the Devil isn't seen as the nefarious card it used to be. If it still presents our capacity to fall into self-inflicted traps and patterns such as addictive behaviors or codependency, the card is often appreciated as an invitation to explore our dark or repressed desires, going against the grain of social norms. Regularly, the Devil is assimilated as the shadow figure of the Pope card. Beyond the simple similarity of composition, the Pope creates the moral structure that the Devil inverts and abolishes, inviting us to be aware of our own blind spots and hypocrisy, and revealing to us the path to authentic self in the exact place where light and shadow intersect.

ABOVE LEFT

The gastrocephalic *Diable* of the
Anonymous Parisian Tarot, a chimeric
monster sporting bat wings, falcon legs,
and a goat head, 1600–50.

ABOVE RIGHT

Polychromatic devil and his acolytes,
from a Jean Noblet Tarot, a Marseille
model published in Paris in the late
seventeenth century.

153

Devil card from *Tarot Viéville*, published c. 1650.

"Idolatry." A man kneels in submission as he worships the statue of a "false god" shown on a pedestal. From the *Minchiate Istoriche*, published in Florence, Italy, 1725.

Hairy devils from the *Tarot de Besançon* engraved by Pierre Isnard, 1746–60.

Preditorum Raptor, the Ravisher of the Souls—from the Leber-Rouen Tarot, a sixteenth-century deck created in Italy. Striking in its originality, this card is inspired by Greek mythology, presenting an episode from the myth of Hades, the Greek god of the underworld, in which he abducted Persephone, daughter of Demeter, to make her his wife and consort in the realm of the dead. This journey into the abyss depicted in the Major Arcanas is here presented as a forceful descent in which the victim is often seen naked and vulnerable to the will of her ravisher.

Wild man holding a shield with a greyhound, illustrated by Martin Schongauer, 1435–91.

Eliphas Levi's famous Baphomet,
which served as a frontispiece
for the 1856 edition of his *Rituel
de la Haute Magie*.

Italian tarot published by Ferdinando Gumppenberg in Milan, Italy, 1830–45.

Devilish King of Spades from a playing card deck designed by Célestin Nanteuil, France, c. 1838.

OPPOSITE PAGE

Lucifer und Kleine Teufel (Lucifer and Small Devils) from the *Wilder Mann* (Wild Man) series by Charles Fréger, Austria, 2010.

In his fascinating book *Mystical Origins of the Tarot: From Ancient Roots to Modern Usage*, tarot scholar Paul Huson links the "shaggy wolf and calfskin pants"[2] worn by actors to impersonate the devils during medieval mystery plays and the strange depictions on some of the Devil cards, like the one of the Rosenwald, seemingly wearing a fur pelt rather than being completely chimeric. Although these medieval plays aren't accessible to us, they might find echoes in the costumed traditions kept alive for centuries all around Europe celebrating the wildest aspect of nature, and which photographer Charles Freger documented for many years in his project *Wilder Mann*.

Charming devil, gently patting the head of his minion, a card from a double-headed tarot published by J. Gaudais, 1860–89.

Asmodeus, prince of demons in Judeo-Islamic lore, often associated with lust, as a king of pomegranate in this Judaic-inspired playing deck illustrated by Ze'ev Raban in 1920.

Genesis am rix capitel

Da lies der herr schwefel vnnd feüer regnen von dem herren von hiemel herab auff Sodama Gomora vnnd keret die stet vmb die ganzen gegene vnnd alle einwoner der stete vnnd was auff dem lande gewachsen war vnnd sein weib sahe hinder sich vnd war zu einer salz seüle

THE TOWER

"T"he Lighting-Struck Tower," "The House of God," "The Thunderbolt," "Fire," "The House of the Devil," "Inferno": a short list of the numerous and often antithetical appellations for the inhospitable card we commonly refer to as the Tower. Visible in several trionfi games from the fifteenth century on, simultaneously and all across Europe, the design usually (but not invariably) presents the destruction of a tall, fortress-like construction caused by fiery phenomenon directly striking the Tower from heaven. Multiple names and as many visual renditions, all composed around a common axis of understanding: Something viewed as solid and impenetrable collapses under the impact of a celestial discharge. Contrasting climatic gravitas and literal explosion, this Major Arcana is, compared to its most static counterparts, always surprising for its nefarious dynamics. Something bombastic is happening, but what exactly? What is this building, and why is it being destroyed? Who are the people often seen falling or escaping from this chaotic landscape? Who causes this destruction? As we'll see, with the Tower, we enter a domain where Manichean ideas of annihilation and liberation are intertwined.

Sulfuric rains and apocalyptic horizons, the motif of the card itself is a reminder of the Old Testament and the trope of divine retribution. The image that opens this chapter comes from the Augsburg Book of Miracles, an incredible illuminated manuscript dealing with two of my favorite topics: monsters and strange sky manifestations, all presented in this sixteenth-entury Protestant storybook as clear prophetic signs of godly discontent. This book predicts that things such as a comet sighting or multiple dancings orbs floating in the sky will be followed by disasters, wars, or famine. Indeed, many of these gorgeous gouache vignettes highlight how, in decisive times, the firmament above us serves as God's wrathful bulletin board. According to the Old Testament, when mankind misbehaves, God the almighty unleashes fire and brimstone on us, as in the baleful episode of Sodom and Gomorrah depicted here, in which the azure skies turned blood red and rains of calamity are seen setting the city ablaze. In the tarot, and many other decks, this idea is visually reenacted—arrows of fire, thunderbolts that punitively zap buildings and people alike, decrowning towers in some Marseille or the Rider-Waite-Smith examples, as if to punish mankind for its defiance, lack of humility, or self-proclaimed authority.

OPPOSITE PAGE

Lot and his daughters, visible in the bottom-right corner, escaped the ruins of Sodom and Gomorrah, from the Augsburg Book of Miracles, 1552.

In the minchiate cards, a panicked nude woman is seen rushing away from the fortress as flames chase her vulnerable body out of the gate. In the Anonymous Parisian Tarot, we see a flock of demons melting through volutes of yellow flames. What if the Tower was in fact hell itself? Its proximity to the Devil card gives us a hint. The hostile architecture, reminiscent of late medieval depictions of the underworld as a fiery fort, might be another clue. In this case, the divine intervention shifts from destruction to an attempt at salvation. Several scholars have referred to these minchiate nude escapists as possibly connected to the iconography of the "Harrowing of Hell." In the Catholic tradition, this episode follows the descent of Christ into hell on Holy Saturday, after he died on the cross. In this rather incredible story, Jesus triumphantly bursts the gate of Hades open, releasing the innocent captives, including Adam and Eve, depicted as naked souls.

This ambivalence between destruction and liberation is what makes this card such a climactic one in the narrative sequence of the Major Arcanas and the high point of the "Devil-Tower-Star" triad, which throughout the centuries, even when the order of the cards changed quite a bit, has been pretty fixed. With the Tower, the carpet is pulled from under our feet, something is destroyed, and what seemed fundamental and solid dissolves against our will. In his *Way of Tarot*, Alejandro Jodorowsky talks about an "uncorking" as he evokes the Arcana XVI. I've always loved this image, having opened my fair share of champagne bottles, which can sometimes be tricky. With the Tower, accumulated pressure is released at last. Sometimes it foams and drips all over the floor. Sometimes the projected cork accidentally breaks a window. With the Tower, you lose some foundational parts of yourself at the least expected time, but once you're past the surprise, there is great wisdom to be found.

ABOVE LEFT

Thunder striking the fortress and zigzagging between the broken stones. One of the oldest examples of a Tower card from the so-called Gringonneur/Charles VI Tarot, Northern Italy, fifteenth century.

ABOVE RIGHT

Celestial explosion and a rain of sparkles igniting the tree, surprising the shepherd, scaring his sheep. From the Viéville Tarot, published c. 1650.

Arrow-shaped thunderbolt striking a man without warning. From the *Tarocchini di Mitelli*, published in Rome, Italy, between 1660 and 1670.

Two men falling from a building ablaze, from the *Tarocchi Fine Dalla Torre*, published in Bologna, Italy, seventeenth century.

From a Florentine minchiate deck by Giovanni Molinelli, 1712–16.

La Foudre—sixteenth card of the Anonymous Parisian Tarot, showing demons battling against pure yellow light, 1600-50.

OPPOSITE PAGE

Christ leads the patriarchs from hell to paradise; Methuselah, Solomon, the Queen of Sheba, and Adam and Eve lead the procession of the righteous behind Christ. Painting by Bartolomeo Bertejo, tempera on wood, 1480, found at the Center for Hispanic Art, Barcelona, Spain.

Le Feu du Ciel—skyfire from Oswald Wirth's *Tarot des Imagiers du Moyen Age*, 1899.

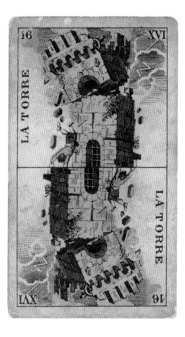

La Torre—sixteenth card from a double-headed Soprafino Tarot deck, published by Fratelli Armanino in Genova, Italy, 1887.

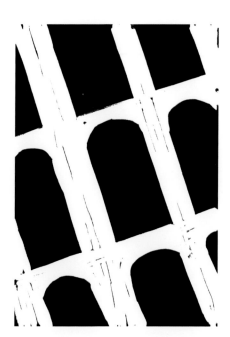

OPPOSITE PAGE

Hellmouth and the flaming Fortress of Hell. From the Hours of Catherine of Cleves, in a Latin illuminated manuscript by the Master of Catherine of Cleves, Utrecht, the Netherlands, 1440.

Tower card from Paul Vogeler's Stars Over Me Tarot. This contemporary perspective is so interesting to me: We see the building as if we were falling from it. Such a minimalist yet vertiginous take. Paul's tarot, as he explains it, was born from the cathartic process that carried him through the grief for his father, Edwin Biggs Vogeler Sr.

STAR

I n *Der Morgen*, German romantic painter Philipp Otto Runge creates an allegory of the morning, which so perfectly translates the mystical depth of the symbolic transition from darkness to light that we casually experience every day. Gradually, the tenebrosity of night is chased away by the early rays of sun rising above the skyline, guided by the Morning Star, visible as a humble white dot at the summit of the image. Surrounded by three cherub heads, this spark of pure light leads the totality of the ethereal ballet of twilight, portrayed in this painting as a complete apotheosis, a resurrection.

In the tarot, the Star is an equally spectacular card and is often seen as one of the most important in the narrative sequence of the Major Arcanas. Following the most tumultuous episodes composed by the Devil and the Tower cards, the Star leads us out of the abyssal pit we were projected into as we meet Death and Temperance. Extracted back to the surface after a cathartic descent, we slowly reemerge to light, with renewed hopes and perspectives.

In the *Tarot d'Este*, we encounter two men pointing at a large golden star hovering above them as they study the heavens. In a similar manner, in the Viéville example and many other tarot decks, the star card features astronomers surrounded by books and compasses, in the great outdoors or in their studio. Noses up in the air, their focus is on piercing the starry night's poetic language. These cards elicits the idea that until the seventeenth century, astronomy and astrology were seen as the same scholarly tradition. Observing the constellations would allow one to understand God's poetic plan, the sacred geometry of time and space, and how it concretely impacts our existence. In the medieval and Renaissance mind, the stars hid the secret blueprint of the Great Architect, so scrutinizing their celestial movements made one closer to the Divine. To this day, the Vatican, the stronghold of the Roman Catholic world, maintains an astronomical research center an hour away from Rome, as well as a telescope located in Arizona. Stargazing is a form of communion with the creator.

What is this unique star that we find in so many cards, shining brighter than the others? It is Venus, of course, named after the Roman goddess of love and beauty and which, along with the Moon and the Sun, is the most luminous celestial body visible to our naked eye. This wonderful star goes by many names, and its legendary luminosity has often served as a guide. It is Lucifer, the light bringer, son of Aurora, the goddess of dawn in the Roman tradition. We also know it as the Shepherd Star, leading the Three Magi toward the infant Christ during the Nativity tale. Like the colloquial "light at the end of the tunnel," this incandescent nugget is enough to inspire our trust, give us direction, and provide safety as we return from our darkest voyage from the night of nights.

Among the various iconographic versions of the card, the most widespread one shows a nymph kneeling in a nocturnal landscape, emptying the content of two vessels, one on the land and the other in the adjacent body of water. Is it Venus herself, caught in a fertility rite, nurturing the ground to prepare it for new growth? Although it is unclear who this character might be, she can be interpreted as an agent of regeneration and restored peace.

For me, the figures in the Temperance and Star cards are intimately connected, if not the same person, seen in their profane and sacred forms, an enigmatic character I've nicknamed the "Death and Resurrection Muse." A spectral and reassuring presence, this entity welcomes us to the other side, after the Death card, under the benevolent guise of an angel. She performs a ritual cleanse with the water in her jars and dissolves the bitterness of our previous existence, preparing us for an initiatic journey to "visit the center of the Earth." After this tormenting adventure, she serves as a guide to extract us from that *noirceur*, or darkness, allowing us to see her in her most natural form. As we see her naked, so are we, bare souls, transfigured. Bookending our descent, she teaches us that death allows for fertile grounds.

Stargazers and astronomers from the d'Este
Tarot, created around 1450 in Italy, from
the Cary Yale collection.

Raising his compass, the astronomer
studies the heavenly bodies above him.
From the Viéville Tarot, France, 1650.

The Three Magi following the Bethlehem Star, from the *Tarocchi Fine dalla Torre*, published in Bologna, Italy, seventeenth century.

"Shining Stars" and the Eight of Hearts from *Le Petit Oracle des Dames*, published in Paris by La Veuve Gueffier, 1807.

OPPOSITE PAGE

Melchior, one of the Three Wise Men, points at the Shepherd Star, which led them to the infant Christ. *The Adoration of the Magi*, Georges Trubert, Provence, France, c. 1480–90, Tempera colors, gold leaf, gold and silver paint, and ink on parchment.

Les Etoiles from the Minchiate of François de Poilly, published in France between 1658 and 1693.

Inclitum Sydus, or the Eminent Star, from the Leber-Rouen, an Italian deck thought to have been created in the sixteenth century. In this very unique card, the star is once again the guide, associated specifically with the Polar star, which is used for celestial navigation at sea. The image also evokes the Stella Maris, or Star of the Sea, associated with the veneration of the Virgin Mary, herself envisioned as a spiritual guide helping us to find direction when lost. From the Bibliothèque de Rouen, France.

EVS·IN·ADIVTORIV·MEN·INTENDE·BNE

L'Etoile, from the Tarot de Besançon, 1845–60.

How many stars do you count in this card? Eight, like in most Marseille-type decks? Make sure to add the one hidden in the belly button of the central figure. From the *Tarot Noblet*, France, 1659.

"Immortality," a Star card with handwritten cartomantic meanings, from a Marseille deck, modeled after the Nicolas Conver Tarot, published by Maison Camoin in Marseille, 1890–1900.

Star card from the Oswald Wirth *Tarot des Imagiers du Moyen Âge*, 1899. Are the angel and nymph from the Temperance (p.148) and the Star of the Wirth Tarot the same person? The two cards count many similarities: the blonde hair, the two jars, and this red flower, seen dying in the Temperance card and brought back to life, in full bloom, with the Star card.

Star card from a Petit Lenormand deck, associated with the Six of Hearts. Published by Daveluy in Bruges, Belgium, 1875–80.

Les Etoiles, a card linked with peace from an Egyptian-styled Grand Etteilla, published in France, 1850–75.

Star card from a Petit Lenormand-type deck, published by Ensslin and Laiblin, Reutlingen, Germany, 1875–99.

The Star, from an Antique Soprafino Lombard, by Fratelli Avondo, 1874-79, courtesy of McClosky's Books and Antiques,

THE MOON

hat does the Moon dream of, eyes closed, in this Hans Thomas painting? Well bundled in vaporous layers of clouds, the waning orb floats in air, metaphorically lost in Morpheus's arms. Does this Moon know that, even sound asleep, its silvery glow brightens our nights, pushing some animal species to reproduce, wolves to howl, humans to lose their temper or superstitiously get haircuts. Is the satellite aware that, even if caught in an hypnagogic state, it allows for colossal volumes of water to move, its magnetic influence causing these displacements? Does it realize, in its slumber, the circular dance it does around our planet?

With the Moon card, we meet in the dark once again, yet it's a far different hue from the dystopian, onyx-like *noirceur* ruled by the Devil and the Tower. All of a sudden, it's midnight in the tarot and we enter the uncanny dimension of the night, familiar yet absurdly different, a place in which elements we take for granted have been upturned, inverted. We are on the other side of Alice's looking glass, the Upside-Down in *Stranger Things*, a location that reminds me of what Michel Foucault called a heterotopia. In his book *Les Mots et les Choses* (The Order of Things), the French philosopher describes locations or discursive places that are *other*. Real yet contradictory because they are their own worlds within our world. The Night and the Moon who govern this ambiguous territory subject us to their own bizarre directives, a set of laws going against the grain of the rational. In this environment, inarticulate visions of the subconscious are allowed to emanate, resurfacing like the crustacea crawling out of the pond in the Marseille examples. Made visible to us in the dark, they are not what they appear to be.

In the manner of the early Star cards, the Gringonneur/Charles VI Tarot and several other decks feature the Astronomer, nose up toward the sky, observing the large lunar crescent over his head. This time, he is not studying the grand design of God nor the mechanics of the spheres, but the moon itself as a celestial generator of flux and reflux, the enigmatic mistress of tidal energy, cyclical powers, and nature's most feminine expression. The Moon is heaven's metronome, revealing to us the rhythm of time passing. To our naked eye, the lunar phases form concrete milestones, giving us indication of the macrocosmic dynamics we are caught in. In the Molinelli deck, the scientist holds a compass in one hand while his other reposes on a needleless clock dial. The transformations of the Moon are the visual tempo that allow the reader to grasp the infinite abstraction of time, leading us to invent calendars and clocks.

Its propensity to shapeshift every night made the moon mysterious and often associated it with foolishness and inconsistency. To this day, we use terms like "lunatic" to pejoratively describe someone who we believe has lost touch with reason, and some folks believe that exposure to full moonlight might affect one's mental health. Traditionally in the tarot, the Moon card is often associated with delusional behavior, smoke and mirrors, psychological projection, and how we build our own illusions.

A handful of examples depict Diana as the graceful goddess of the hunt, of the wild, and of the lunar, for she was revered in Ancient Roman times as *diva triformis*, a triple goddess with early associations to the Greek goddess Hekate. This threefold expression of her connection to the celestial, terrestrial, and chthonian realms aligns with her ever-shifting, waxing and waning presence. The dogs she surrounds herself with are both hunting dog and psychopomps, a detail echoed in the classical depiction of the card that features a landscape under the moonlight with two Canidae, a wolf and a dog, a feral animal and a domesticated one, both seen howling and serving the divine lunar presence.

What lesson should we learn from this card in the context of the Major Arcana sequence? The answer might be found in a quote attributed to Mahatma Gandhi: "Each night, when I go to sleep, I die. And the next morning, when I wake up, I am reborn." The Moon's darkness doesn't appear to us as dramatic as the Devil and its Tower because at this point in the story, we are meant to understand that death isn't a mere ending but a transformation. Without the fear of the end, we can easily transition into the nocturnal because we have faith that we'll see the light of day. The Moon card speaks about something the Wheel of Fortune introduced: Our perception of time as a linear continuum is an illusion, an abstraction that doesn't exist in nature, in which everything is cyclical. After we meet Death itself in the Arcana XIII, our story continues from circles to circles as we wait to be reunited with the cosmic totality. Every night, we lose consciousness as we go to sleep, and we do it without fear because we know we will wake up. The Moon card is a temporary moment of darkness that we meet casually, understanding from here on that we can trust the dawn will rise again.

ABOVE LEFT

Moon gazers from the so-called
Gringonneur/Charles VI Tarot,
Northern Italy, fifteenth century.

ABOVE RIGHT

The astronomer is featured in the *Tarot
d'Este*, drawing perfect circles under the
moonlight, Italy, 1450.

Moon card of a Florentine minchiate deck by Giovan Molinelli, published in the 1710s, showing a man pointing at the celestial body with a compass, while his other arm holds the round dial of a clock, symbol of the cyclical passage of time.

Diane, the divine huntress, and her dog. Moon card from the *Tarocchini Mitelli*, a Bolognese-style deck published in Rome, Italy, c. 1670, engraved by Giuseppe Maria Mitelli.

Moon card showing a woman with a distaff. One could imagine this card representing Clotho, one of the three Moiras, a unique allegory of the passing of time in the Vieville Tarot, France, 1650s.

Diane, Roman goddess of the moon and the hunt, holding bows and arrows. From the Minchiate of François de Poilly, published in France between 1658 and 1693.

OPPOSITE PAGE

Clock watch with calendars and a dial indicating the phases of the moon, made by master clockmaker Jean Vallier in Lyon, France, 1630.

ABOVE

Diana as Personification of the Night by
Anton Raphael Mengs, c. 1765.

La Lune card from a tarot deck published by Bernardin Suzanne in Marseille, France, 1816–68.

La Lune from the Jean Dodal Tarot, published in Lyon, France, 1701–15.

Moon card depicting dogs with lolling tongues, from a double-headed deck published in the 1880s.

Double-headed Della Rocca-style tarot, published by Fratelli Armanino, Genoa, Italy, c.1887.

THE SUN

à, tout n'est qu'ordre et beauté,
Luxe, calme et volupté.

There all is order and beauty,
Luxury, peace, and pleasure.

—Charles Baudelaire, "Invitation au Voyage"
in *Les Fleurs du Mal* (The Flowers of Evil), 1957

At last, we have risen! After endless peregrinations into somber labyrinths, we are welcomed back to golden radiant light and, thankfully, far more hospitable lands. I've always associated the Sun card with a sort of apogaic return from the land of the dead because of a connection I read about between this arcana and the breathtaking Resurrection panel from the *Isenheim Altarpiece*, painted by Grünewald in 1515. In this spectacular image, a radiant Christ springs up in triumph from the tomb that held his dead body "for three days and three nights in the heart of the earth." Floating in the air, open armed with hand stigmatas in full view, Christ's face expands, dematerializing into a massive orb of solar light. Everything in this image evokes a supernatural victory, the end tail of a mystical transformation in which the once-very-human Jesus is transmuted, reborn into a deity, a Christian version of Apollo. As his body dissolves into an ethereal fireball, we can see him gently smiling back at us. Through this luminescent image, whether we are Christian or not, we are meant to understand the Resurrection for the paradoxical metaphor it is, an explosion of restored peace, a joyous disintegration, a singular and collective experience of light, awe, and ecstasy.

Much like Christ, we were entombed in the chthonian spheres of the Devil and Tower cards. Guided by the Star, and cradled by the velvety darkness of the Moon, we have now ascended back to a majestic place filled with an emotional warmth. A simple, vast, and unchallenging territory miles away from the conundrum we just left. With the Sun card, the rational clock has gone backward. We are being projected back into a golden age, a childlike era, unburdened by fear. This motif is illustrated in so many Sun cards by the presence of a light-hearted youth, the *puer* Helios in the so-called Mantegna Deck, or the solar ephebe in *Tarot Hiéroglyphique*, to name a few. The card inspires so much regained dynamism, often graphically communicated by the color red, the color of blood, as the life force flows back into us. In the iconic Viéville card, a child gallops on a horse harnessed in scarlet breast straps, their dashing speed making the flag the boy holds flap horizontally in the air.

Who are the two figures depicted face-to-face in the Sun cards of the Marseille models and beyond? Nobody seems to agree, and, for a good reason, the iconography shifts, as we'll see, from card to card. Adam and Eve, Abel and Cain, a pair of lovers, even devilish figures according to Alexandro Jodorowsky. Two naked infants or young boys featured on some cards lead many to believe they were in fact Castor and Pollux. Sons of Jupiter, the two brothers are assimilated into the Gemini zodiac sign—an interesting interpretation considering the celestial twins were believed to be excellent cavaliers and commonly represented with horses, an animal visible on several Sun cards.

My favorite Sun arcana might be the one from the *Tarot d'Este*, a fifteenth-century deck kept at the Beinecke Library, which I appreciate for its unique design and the story it tells. A man sits in a circular container, stretching an open hand high up toward an elegantly dressed character who stands in a dandy contrapposto in front of him. The first man is none other than Diogenes of Sinope, a Greek thinker who was one of the founders of the philosophy of Cynicism, whose colorful existence is tainted with so many bizarre tales. He is said to have lived as a vagabond, obeying the laws of nature and having great disdain for the wealth of this world. The legend says he lived and slept in a large clay barrel and is often depicted sitting in it, surrounded by dogs, who shared in his strange habit of doing as his instinct drove him to do. A well-known philosopher, but a controversial one, Diogenes is infamous for his obscene stunts, such as urinating on guests at banquets, and for disregarding honor and power, instead using his wit to provoke tradition.

This card, associated with the Sun, depicts the most famous story about the Cynical thinker, when he was visited by Alexander the Great, who came to offer his financial help to the philosopher. "Ask me for any boons," says the Lord of Asia.

As the legend goes, Diogenes, who was lying on the ground enjoying the morning light, replied to Alexander: "Stand away from my Sun." Chasing him with a hand move like you'd swish flies off French pastry, Diogenes indicates his disregard for anything that Alexander could offer him. Solar light is for him the true gold of nature, and with the Sun card, we are led to bask in it fully, embracing its pure joy and abundance.

Solar cavalcade for the young boy riding his horse in the red harness, from the Viéville Tarot, France, seventeenth century.

Iliaco, the young Sun god Helios, holds the solar orb in his hand in the thirty-first card of the so-called Mantegna Tarot, series B, printed by Johann Ladenspelder, sixteenth century.

Apollo, Roman Sun god, and his lyre, for the *Tarocchini di Giuseppe Maria Mitelli* deck, published in Rome, Italy, 1660–70.

Sun Card from the *Tarot de Besançon*, 1845–60.

Sun card modeled after the Arnoult Tarot, published by B.P Grimaud in Paris, 1891.

Sun card from a minchiate deck, created in the seventeenth century in Florence, Italy.

Sun Card of a Florentine minchiate deck by Giovan Molinelli, published in the 1710s.

Sun card showing a man dressed in a multicolor costume and a topless woman, from the Noblet Tarot, 1659.

All dressed up! Sun card from a Marseille-style tarot published in Geneva, Switzerland, by Gassmann, 1850–70.

Diogenes in his barrel scoffing at Alexander the Great, from the *Tarot d'Este*, Italy, 1450.

Diogenes, Jean-Léon Gérôme, 1860,
Walters Art Museum, Baltimore, Maryland.

Sun card associated with Cesar, King of Diamonds, from a pedagogical playing card deck with an astronomy and geography motif.

Adam and Eve in the Garden of Eden under the blazing sun, from a double-headed tarot designed by J. Gaudais, published in Paris, 1860–89.

As of Sun from the planetary-themed divination deck named *Sorcier du XIXᵉ Siècle Tarot Parisien*, conceptualized by A. de Para d'Hermes, published in Paris in 1867.

Sun card from Oswald Wirth *Tarot des Imagiers du Moyen Age*, 1899.

LE JUGEMENT DERNIER.

Les 12 Apôtres.

St. Jean-Baptiste.

Les Patriarches et les Prop

La Sainte Vierge.

Arc-en-ciel.

St. Michel.

Allez, maudits, au feu éternel

St. Ignace.

St. Vincent de Paule.

Levez-vous, Morts, et   venez au Jugement.

À ÉPINAL, CHEZ PELLERIN, IMPRIMEUR-LIBRAIRE

JUDGEMENT

R ise up, Dead and come to your Judgement!" says the small printed text, the menacing words wrapped around the skull and crossbones at the bottom of this *image d'Epinal*. Above, a disquieting scene presents itself to us. We see God, materialized in our own sky, holding the Divine Law in his hand, symbol of his omnipotent authority. The bearded Lord is flanked by Jesus Christ his son, the Virgin Mary, John the Baptist, a profusion of biblical patriarchs and other cast members, including the apostles, serving as Grand Jury in this heavenly court. A flamboyant tribunal resting on puffy clouds, looking down at us. This trial is indeed a very public affair. On land, Chaos reigns. The dead are back to life, awakened by the clamor of angelic trumpets. Confused, these naked souls run amok, jetting out of their grave, galloping in the fields before being caught by angels or demons. Like shepherds gathering packs of senseless sheeps, these strange emissaries divided the crowd in two groups, sometimes against their will, according to their ultimate destination. Heaven or Hell.

In the center of this depiction, Saint Michael is simultaneously subduing the forces of Evil and serving as a protector for the vulnerable ones being judged. The archangel is equipped with a sword and a scale, two attributes reminiscent of the one of Justice, symbolizing equity and impartiality. His role, in this intense spectacle, is to weigh souls, count good deeds against bad ones and secure a safe passage to the candidates granted access to the Kingdom of Heaven.

In the tarot, the Judgement card is clearly inspired by the iconography of the Last Judgement, a motif directly borrowed from Christian eschatology and the sinister visions of what is supposed to happen to us at the end of time. Amply represented during the medieval era and the Renaissance, the Last Judgement depictions are visible in a plethora of churches and altar pieces, their great number and somber quality granting them the ominous title of " Doom paintings." Like any artistic trope, they follow a set of visual rules, and the most transparent one is that we are not witnessing a happy ending. Terror is palpable, translated in the supplicative gesticulations of the herd of souls as they are to be either damned or saved. In the Stephan Lochner exemple, we see allegories of heaven and hell, shown respectively as an immaculate cathedral and a fortress in flames. As we look at these terrifying depictions, we are meant to internalize the moral perils of disobeying the divine laws.

Nevertheless, the images we encounter in the tarot are suddenly different, the visual convention of Doom paintings have been somehow evacuated. Reframed to one specific narrative line, the Judgement cards do not share their frantic heaviness, nor many of their disturbing tropes. Visions of God as a wrathful authority are absent and the focus is mostly on the Angels trumpeting, the wake-up call. Most cards represent people emerging from their tombs, but their body language transcribes a peaceful attitude toward the event. Some are caught, hands joined in a solemn prayer, others are seen ecstatic, raising their arms toward the ethereal musician. The souls depicted are peaceful, they've been waiting for this, some of them can't hide their excitement. Most importantly, these images never show hell, nor demons which might explain why the souls on the Judgement cards are never frightened. In a strange way, we've already crossed paths with infernal territories, we've already been to hell and back. In the narrative of the Major Arcanas, demonic manifestations and associated mistreatments are, as we saw, the domain of the Devil and the Tower cards, places we've been through and survived.

OPPOSITE PAGE

The Last Judgement, published in Épinal, France, by Pellerin, 1876. From the Bibliothèque nationale de France.

In its unique way, the Judgement card is the last echo of an allegory of life, death, and rebirth articulated in the tarot. Against expectation, the card deploys a happy ending, announcing the climactic epilogue of the World card. As this chapter slowly ends, we now understand that what we frightfully called Death is a mere passage leading to many other cards, many other stories. The Judgement card is a Death card experienced without fear, a moment in which we accept transformation in a very frontal way. Nothing has changed but our perspective toward this transition. We embrace it candidly, with grace and courage, even though we don't know what awaits us outside of our comfort zone.

Rise Up! The many resurrected dead of the Gringonneur/Charles VI Judgement card springing out of their graves at the sound of the angels' trumpet.

Judgement card from the *Tarot Anonyme Parisien*, published in Paris, 1600–50.

OPPOSITE PAGE

A rare example of a Judgement card featuring the presence of God, towering above the action. From the Visconti-Sforza Tarot, attributed to Bonifacio Bembo, Milan, Italy, c. 1480–1500.

Judgement card from a Nicolas Conver Marseille deck, published between 1809 and 1833.

A peculiar hand-drawn deck modeled after the Arnoult Tarot, created between 1850 and 1900.

Judgement card from a double-headed
tarot deck, published by J. Gaudais,
1860–89.

Judgement from a tarot deck by Stefano
Vergnano, Northern Italy, 1827.

Judgement card from a *Tarot de Besançon*,
published by J. Jerger, 1820–45.

Last Judgement card from a Grand Etteilla/
Tarot Egyptien, published in Paris, 1876–80.

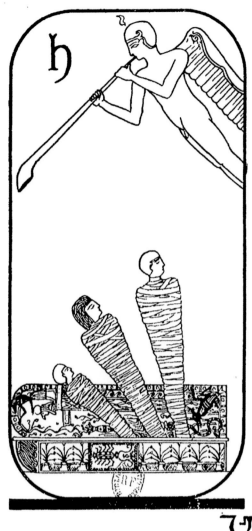

ABOVE LEFT

Last Judgement card from a Grand Etteilla/
Tarot Egyptien, published in Paris, 1850–75.

ABOVE RIGHT

Mummies rising out of their sarcophagi
by Otto Wegener, an illustration for
*Les XXII Lames Hermétiques du tarot
Divinatoire* (The XXII Hermetic Blades of
the Divinatory Tarot), in which Robert
Falconnier, the author, attempts to restore
(or imagine, rather) what the images of the
Book of Thoth might have looked like.

THE WORLD

danced myself out of the womb
I danced myself out of the womb
Is it strange to dance so soon?
I danced myself into the tomb
But then again
Once more
I danced myself out of the womb
—"Cosmic Dancer," MARC BOLAN, 1971

In his 1971 ethereal ballad "Cosmic Dancer," Marc Bolan, the sexually ambiguous imp and glittery lead singer of the legendary band T. Rex, gave us tarot readers something delightful to ponder as we try to decipher the World, our ultimate Major Arcana. Using the first person in his whimsical parable, Bolan's trippy lyrics describe existence itself as a fluidic dance of energy coming from the cosmos and descending to animate our body to life through harmonious, flowing movements. This uninterrupted cycle, whispers Bolan in his glam rock classic, nonchalantly leads him from the womb to the tomb back to the womb. A tender and psychedelic hymn from my youth, this song resurfaced while I've been trying to unpack the World card, the final picture of our cinematic journey, or so it seems.

In fact, the World is the alpha and omega of the tarot. Although the twenty-first card brings the narrative sequence of the Major Arcanas to an end, this epilogue hides the infancy of a new cycle, a climactic ending and a gestative rest. As we'll see in the historical examples, we are all walking on a tightrope extended between contradictory poles, gracefully making our way in these seemingly contradictory states of being both mature and renewed, masculine and feminine, everything and nothing. In the most elegant of ways, the "Cosmic Dancer" of the Major Arcanas undulates between opposites like the character in Bolan's song. Nothing is impossible for this person, who reconciles and balances everything. They are innocent and omniscient, reuniting impossible realities with ease and poise.

The motif of the card shifted so interestingly through time before fixating around the dancer. In the earliest examples, the World card presented to us the city, the profane world, set like a jewel in a circular medallion. In the Cary Yale example, we can observe the bustling life of a Northern Italian seaport in which ships attest to active trades and the circulation of wealth. This secular landscape is frequently shown on these cards, either held or topped by auspicious deities or allegorical figures, granting them protection. Our world is presented as contained in the world of the divine. Like in the Wheel of Fortune, our reality is shown as a microcosmic land comprising a larger sacred macrocosm, a singular, minuscule place within many concentric circles ruled by a spiritual force and powerful deities.

OPPOSITE PAGE
Roman relief of Phanes emerging from his egg, surrounded by the zodiac, second century CE. From the Gallerie Estensi, Modena, Italy.

The iconography we tend to associate with the World card seems to have appeared in around the seventeenth century. Encased in a laurel wreath, the central character holds a scepter, sometimes two, surrounded by a lion, an ox, an eagle, and an angel in niches in each corner of the card. Yet, if our contemporary eyes are accustomed to a feminine figure in the center of the verdant crown, the early long-haired dancers are far more androgynous than their twentieth-century counterparts. We could imagine them, akin to the T. Rex song, returning to their cosmic sexual indetermination, unlabeled by their incarnation.

In the Viéville Tarot example, the character standing in his wreath is crowned by a golden halo, an attribute of sainthood that reframes the card in a Christian context. Could this be Christ? In its quadripartite composition, the image visually quotes the iconography of Christ in Majesty, a design which appeared in the very early hours of Christianity, in which Jesus sits on a throne. Raising his hand in a gesture of blessing, the Son of God is contained in a mandorla, or almond-shaped aureola, surrounded by the four creatures of Ezekiel, who are the symbolic substitutes for the four evangelists: Saint Mark as the Lion, Saint John as the Eagle, Saint Luke as the Ox, and Saint Matthew as the Angel.

Many believe that the visual configuration of Christ in Majesty was in fact borrowed by artists from earlier depictions of the Roman divinity Phanes, who was still worshipped in the context of Orphic traditions in the early hours of Christianity. Hatched out a silver egg, Phanes is a primeval deity of creation and fertility, and is usually represented springing out of a broken shell, with a coiled snake around his body, holding thunder in one hand, a scepter in the other. His body is contained in yet another egg world, a zodiac on which the fours faces of the wind blow, allowing for infinite movement. Although he is depicted with masculine attribute, golden-winged Phanes is described in Orphic hymns as being hermaphroditic and a creatrix, both male and female, containing the "seeds of all gods" and capable of breathing souls into inanimate realities.

In some strange twist of fate, it seems that Phanes is connected to our androgynous "Cosmic Dancer," who likewise knots together ends and beginnings, bringing contrarian forces to perfect balance.

The emergence of the feminine figure in the World card could be, we could speculate, to take away Christic reference from the card games. Her femininity modestly covered by a scarf that floats around her, she is, like Phanes, contained in the wreath made of laurel, a symbol of victory doubling as sanctified, womb-like territory. This is the triumphal ending of the Major Arcana, a positive paradox that contrasts ending and beginning, totality and gestation, eternity, yet a moment of climax. Through this journey, we have reached a state of grace, biting our own tails and closing the loop as we float in the amniotic fluid of a beatific vision.

OPPOSITE PAGE

Knights and sailors, towers and ships crossing the sea. Visions of a busy northern Italian metropolis as the World, from the Visconti di Modrone/Cary Yale pack, attributed to Bonifacio Bembo and painted between 1428 and 1447, from the Beinecke Library collection.

The secular world of fortified cities and rolling hills, suspended in bluish clouds in the kingdom of heaven. From the so-called Charles VI/Gringonneur Tarot deck, Northern Italy, late fifteenth century.

The World, lost in the infinity of Time, symbolized by a cherub holding an hourglass. From the *Minchiate de Poilly*, by François de Poilly, published in Paris, 1712–41.

World card from the Al Leone Tarot, published in the late seventeenth century by Francesco Berti and bound as a small book at the British Museum, London.

Christ-like figure for the Viéville Tarot, published in France in or around the 1650s.

Hermes/Mercury standing on a laurel medallion in which we can see, like we'd do through a porthole, a vision of the four elements. Water and air on the top, fire and earth, symbolizing the towers of a city, on the bottom. From the *Tarocchi Fine dalla Torre*, seventeenth century.

Le Monde, from the Jean Dodal Tarot, published in Lyon, France, 1701–15.

Le Monde, Jean Payen Tarot, published in Avignon, France, 1743.

A rotating sphere on which four cherubs are blowing serves as a pedestal for a Cupid-like angel. The World card from a Florentine minchiate deck published by Giovan Molinelli in 1712–16.

Christ in Majesty, enclosed in a mandorla surrounded by the four creatures of Ezekiel. From the *Codex Bruchsal*, a medieval illuminated manuscript from 1220.

Le Monde, from the *Tarot de Besançon*, 1793–99.

World card from an Arnoux and Amphoux Tarot, 1801.

Artemis-like goddess with her lunar crescent crown, from a double-headed Piedmontese tarot published by Vacca Giacunto, 1875–80.

Voyage–Earth: First card of the *Petit Oracle* deck, an Etteilla-inspired pack of divination cards, published in 1890.

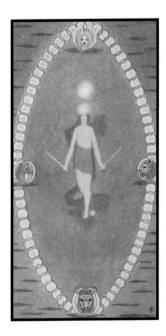

Man and the Quadrupedes–Voyage–Earth: Fifth card of the *Grand Jeu de L'Oracle des Dames*, another Etteilla derivative designed by G. Regamey and published in Paris toward the end of the nineteenth century.

World card from the *Album of the Great Symbols of the Paths; Illustrations to the Ritual of the Most Holy Order of the Rosy and Golden Cross*, commissioned by Arthur Edward Waite to artists Wilfried Pippet and John B. Trinick, and often considered Waite's second tarot deck.

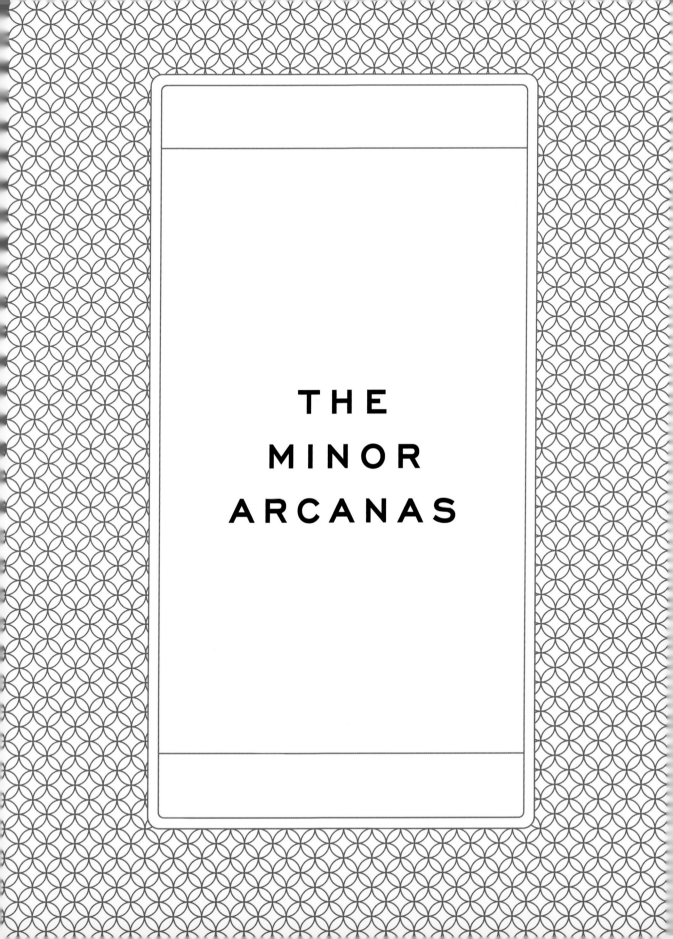

THE
MINOR
ARCANAS

I f the Major Arcanas are the allegorical jewels crowning the occult tarot, the fifty-six Minor Arcanas are no less important elements, forming a solid symbolic network through an overarching fourfold narrative deployed in suits—Cups, Clubs, Coins, and Sword. The quatuor of everyday life objects comprises ten numeral cards each, also called "pips cards," and a four-level hierarchy of court figures—Page, Knight, Queen, and King. Historically, these numbered and court cards predate the trionfi cards of the tarot, forming the core of many card games developing in fourteenth-century Mediterranean Europe and quickly spreading to the rest of the land. Where do these metaphorical artifacts come from? One of the most solid hypotheses, developed by several scholars, including Michael Dummett, is that they might have found their origins in an Arabic card game played during the Mamluk empire of Egypt, as early as the thirteen century. According this theory, the Moorish game would have entered the Western world through sultanate's trades with Italy and Muslim Spain. Although we don't have any remnants of these early examples, an incomplete fifteenth-century pack was famously unearthed by archaeologist Leo Mayer in the archives of the Topkapi Palace Museum of Istanbul in the forties. Hand-painted in cobalt blue, gold, red, and green, the lavishly ornate Mamluk deck features four suits as well—Cups, Coins, Polo Sticks, and Scimitars, the curved sabers used in the medieval Islamic world. As we look as these cards, we can easily understand why they are believed to have spawned the geometric prototype of the pip cards found in Spanish Naipes games or Marseille-style tarot, for example.

In his *Encyclopedia of Tarot*, Stuart Kaplan suggests that in the early days of the twentieth century, artist and poetic trailblazer Pamela Colman Smith, then commissioned by occultist Arthur Edward Waite to draw an esoteric tarot deck, was able to see reproductions of the Sola Busca deck, preserved at the British Museum. This fifteenth-century Italian card game appears to be, prior to the 1909 Rider-Waite-Smith cards, the only known example of a fully figurative set of pip cards, adorned with colorful figures of the Roman empire and its sacred pantheon of gods, posed in lively action, a Ferrarese landscape as a backdrop. Some cards, like the Queen of Cups or the iconic pierced heart of the Three of Swords, really speak to this influence. If occultist Arthur Edward Waite meticulously conceptualized the esoteric content of Major Arcanas, he didn't write much about the Minor Arcanas in his *Pictorial Key to the Tarot* and was to all appearances less interested in their design. It is possible that he gave very little to no directions to Smith, who gave herself the poetic license to transform the abstract pip cards into her own pre-Raphaelite visual parables. With spirited grace and artistic virtuosity, she succeeded in breathing life into the overlooked suit system, conveying powerful stories with her concise line work. Through her work, crowds of noninitiates could get a comprehensive understanding of the cards, enabling them to access the depth of their symbolic significance. In doing so, Pixie Smith completely revolutionized the practice of reading cards for the next generation to come, her work contributing immensely to making the Rider-Waite-Smith deck the now-century-old commercial success it has been, and giving permission to many tarot artists after her to visually experiment with the Minor Arcanas. "In one stroke," Rachel Polack says, "Pamela Smith created a new tradition."[1]

OPPOSITE PAGE
Sheet showing the uncut version of eight pip cards featuring the Sword Suit, the Ace, Page, and King of Wands, and the Ace of Cups from the Vandenborre deck, a Belgian set of cards created between 1790 and 1850.

FOLLOWING SPREAD, FROM LEFT TO RIGHT
Third Deputy of Polosticks, Seven of Cups, Five of Scimitars, and King of Coins from the restored Mamluk deck created by Ulrich Kaltenborn/Trzes-Art" in 2019.

Traditionally, in divinatory tarot, each suit emanates a specific energy, commending upon the symbolic a field of their own. Like the four cardinal points on the quadrant of a compass, the four suits each indicate one clear direction on an infinite spectrum of possibilities. From one to ten, the full sequence of the Minor Arcanas captures ten moments of a flowing narrative, tensed between rise and fall, push and pulls, shaping or directing us. Comparable to the monomyth template theorized by anthropologist Joseph Campbell, they tell a story with a departure, an encounter, a passage through a liminal space, and a series of obstacles that will shape the protagonist as he or she learns lessons along the way before a return to the status quo. In contemporary tarot practices, these numbered cards are thought to be mirroring our daily experience, inside and out. Through the Minor Arcanas, our profane yet very tangible lives unfold, with its cohorts of obstacles and joys, hopes and fears, the versatility of happenstance and our capacity of actions to confront situations.

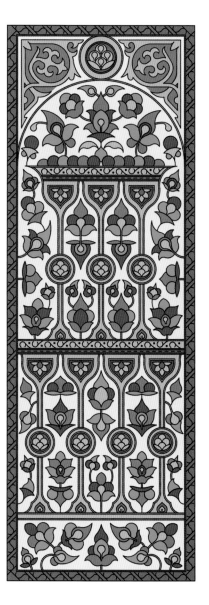

Correspondingly, the Page, Knight, Queen, and King are ruled by their suits and the specific sensibility they hold. In contemporary practice, they are often associated, but not exclusively, to psychologized figures, personality types, whether to signify fragments of our personalities or social groups, institutions, and the people that gravitate to us.

In the following page, we'll explore the four suits, the fourteen cards under their umbrella and the archetypal forces they represent, illustrating these views by beautiful examples of cards belonging to the realm of game and divination alike, all bearing the Hispano-Italian suit system. There are many ways to interpret cards and over the centuries. Traditions such as astrology, numerology, alchemy, the Kabbalah, or Christian mysticism have served as a grid to understand and unpack their symbolic significance. Convinced of the fact that there are as many ways to read cards as there are tarot readers, the following interpretations should only serve as a starting point for personal reflection and don't pretend by any means to be definitive or doctrinal.

DIES ℞10½

OCTVBER

THE SUIT OF COINS

n one of my classes, I do a free association game in which I invite my students to pair the Aces of the Minor Arcanas with one of the four seasons according to what they know of the card and what they sense intuitively. Often enough, and although multiple ideas can come up, they will spontaneously associate the Ace of Coins with fall, inspired by its connection to the element of earth and the connection they make with the harvest season. Traditionally associated with labor and financial concerns, the coins also rule over anything tangible or practical, the human body as a sensual territory, our relationship to nature and its cycles, and physical experiences on a larger scale. Many readers feel drawn to use agricultural metaphors to understand and communicate what is at play in this suit, and some decks, like the Rider-Waite-Smith or the Fyodor Pavlov Tarot, address these ideas very directly using agrarian allegories, people working the land or appreciating the abundance it creates. As we look through the entire sequence of coins, we should ask ourselves: What have you sowed and what do you reap? How do you tend to your own grounds? How many projects, ideas did you leave unattended that are now withering? Who enjoys the fruit of your hard work? Is it time to rewild the land and let an archaic side of yourself take over to restore? Contemplating the disks of gold on the cards, we meditate on the process of manifestation and its slow maturation; we patiently learn that realization takes time and effort to produce value in the concrete world.

The Suit of Coins also represents our desire to absorb, indulge, and digest, and helps us explore how this process can feed different parts of ourselves. Of course, the shadow of a materialist indigestion or the hyperacidity of greed looms over everyone, but one should keep in mind that it goes both ways, and tending to our needs is a necessity. After all, we are tactile beings of flesh, driven by a universal need for nurturing, safety, and pleasure, the rest in a quiet pursuit of balancing consuming without being consumed.

And last, I like to think that these shimmering pieces of pressed metal speak about the cultural value we symbolically attach to objects or material, and how these function as expressions of status. They could be interpreted as our inherant need to belong to a group rather than another. The other side of that coin evokes, of course, the fear we have to be ostracized, cast out from these circles because we can't achieve or generate what is socially expected from us. In this sense, the Suit of Coins invites us to define what prosperity means to us personally, and what energy and means are necessary to bring forth such an intimate idea.

OPPOSITE PAGE

October, the tenth month of the year, showing a character throwing large hips of seeds to sow his land. One of the twelve terra-cotta roundels created around 1450 by Italian ceramist Master Luca Della Rocca to adorn the studiolo of florentine banker Piero di Cosimo de' Medici. Courtesy of the Victoria and Albert Museum, London.

ACE OF COINS Like a solar disk filling up a large portion of space with light, the golden sphere of the coin irradiates the card with a glowing optimism. Like all the other Aces, it promises new beginnings and shows us the fertile ground on which a new wealth of possibilities can rise. Visually and metaphorically, the Ace of Coins is like a seed, a small, dense speck of matter which, lost in the damp obscurity of the earth, slowly gorges itself on its nutritious surroundings. One day, its shell will burst and life will branch out. Tentacular roots will anchor this new and evermore complexifying being deeper into the soil, piercing shoots breaching the surface of the land, emerging into daylight. To such a degree, the card heralds the serendipitous and often invisible process in which material opportunity—a new career path, a gain, a new relationship, a million-dollar idea—can land on our lap at any moment. Yet, as fecund as these seeds of happenstance can be, it is one's responsibility to feed them, carry them through as we ground ourselves and define our vision so they can slowly emerge and become tangible realities.

TWO OF COINS One and one makes two, and with the number two, there is the commencement of a relationship between divided entities through accumulation. In that sense, the Two of Coins speaks as much of these two opposite options and the flow underlining them. Items and their rhythmic intervals. The Rider-Waite-Smith card, as well as this even earlier Naipes card, represents a juggler throwing coins or tambourines in a syncopated dance in which imbalance and accident add adrenaline to the rhythm. Sometimes this card appears to speak about a dilemma, a choice of one over another. Sometimes it is about a negotiation to be engaged with, in which the dual forces partly fuse in concord while keeping their integrity. To be able to dance to that unpredictable beat, one has to be adaptable, aware of one's priorities, and like a Japanese butoh dancer, gracefully battling one's own rigidity.

THREE OF COINS In numerology, the number three represents creation and initial completion. The time of hidden gestation is over, our buried seed is now well anchored in the ground and sprouts out toward the sky! Traditionally, the Three of Pentacles concludes a first phase of fulfillment, making one's effort, sacrifice, and work show their effect in broad light. From an idea and a blueprint, the house now starts to elevate its structure from the ground, taking space and needing more attention than ever not to collapse. The energy of the Three of Coins feels both enormous and fragile, necessitating more than one person's expertise to consolidate it, forcing us to rely on other experiences or to foster new skills. A gasp of wind might unroot the shoots, so does the fear of asking for help or mingling our talents with others. The Three of Coins is the epitome of synergy, in which combining elements creates more than the sum of their part.

FOUR OF COINS Stability and security are proclaimed by the Four of Coins, a solid equilibrium expressed through the rationality of the square. Always ruled by tight design, this card shows what's accomplished when things fall into place. When we finally find the right piece to complete a puzzle we've scratched our heads over to solve, we derive a natural sense of satisfaction. This feeling can be what is at play in the card; our desire for ultimate perfection can paralyze us and ultimately be detrimental to our course of action. Done is always better than perfect. If we fail to find the missing piece, maybe it's because the missing piece has to find us. Obsessing over what we don't have can prevent us from solving problems. MacGyver, the eighties mullet-sporting super genius and master troubleshooter was a doer, not a purist. Give the man a toothbrush and a rubber band and he'll find a sloppy but efficient way out of a labyrinth.

Another meaning can be found in the fact that each metal coin is perfectly locked in its own corner, occupying its own space following the geometry of the card itself. In that sense, the Four of Coins often comes to speak about the territory we inhabited and the boundaries we created around it. Within the four corners of this metaphorical frame, the card asks us to question what we surround ourselves with and what we claim as our own, controlling how porous these borders are to generosity or possessivity, tightrope walking from protection to inflexibility.

FIVE OF COINS And with the five comes the struggle and adversity. Like a crooked fifth wheel, this card announces an interruption of the natural flow of energy, a blockage leading to the fear of scarcity and famine. A bad winter surprised the crops, freezing the ground and potentially causing the spoiling of all our effort. What did we do to deserve this? In the card before this one, we learn that we own a part of a larger whole, that we are naturally driven to save and secure. The card also teaches us that in Aesop's Fables, the Ant's solo feast is plentiful but joyless, and if we never develop generous attitudes or an awareness of the needs of others in times of wealth, we'll dine alone with our own reflection in a mirror as sole company. In the Five of Coins, a gasp of wind blew everything we owned away and shattered that mirror. Through this card, we learn that if we cannot fight against nature's unfair ways, we haven't lost everything if we have each other. Compassion and care can feel warmer than any mink coat in dire times.

SIX OF COINS "Give a man a fish, you'll feed him for one day. Teach a man how to fish and you'll feed him for a lifetime." Traditionally, the number six is associated with realization, and, in the Six of Pentacles, speaks about the natural equalizing of means and knowledge. Like in the communicating vessels phenomenon, the volumes are horizontally level, leaving no room for hierarchical perceptions. With the Six of Coins, there is visible value in concepts and ideas as much as in tangible reality. A skill doesn't decrease in value if taught to someone else.

Seven of Coins Seven, the alchemical number of excellence, speaks about a transformation, and, in such a manner, this card evokes the transmutation of elbow grease into juicy fruits. Suddenly the effort and energy we put toward an abstract goal pays dividends, and these results are fully manifested. Heavily bended, the branches lean down under the weight of the apples. The eyes focus on the work accomplished. Like in the Genesis myth, we rest on the seventh day and contemplate the incredible wealth of our creation, to acknowledge how, through our will, the visible emerged from the invisible.

Eight of Coins Arranged to form two squares and two columns, the coins of the eight cards speak about the perennial framework that allows for traditions and skills to be established long term. The century-old savoir faire that allows a corporation to thrive and make a name for itself, carefully crafting artifacts whose beauty is matched by their solidity. Through the process of this card, the apprentice is now well-rounded, understands the process from A to Z, and is not only able to succeed in creating, but can also transmit his knowledge, the secrets of his trade. He can aspire to the title of master. To be, this card defines what a labor of love truly is, the high point at which discipline and passion intersect.

Nine of Coins As we reach the pinnacle of our material suit, the nine is a card representative of success and abundance. In the Marseille-type decks, the odd-numbered coin stands between the two squares formed by the other golden medals. I like to call this one the "heart within the balance." If this card speaks about abundance and riches, it also speaks about the awareness of the work that came into it, the tears and sweat, the risk taken. The seed of fervor has bloomed, beautiful, and echos with our confidence as creators, humble in our triumph as we collaborate with nature.

Ten of Coins And with this maximalist card, we close the suit of coins. The ten radiant orbs now fill the space of the card, a golden hue to signify enlightened achievement and joyful abundance. Contemporary alchemist Patrick Burensteinas often says, "The alchemist looking for gold won't find it. The alchemist who knows how to make gold won't need it." Which to me expresses perfectly the message of the Ten of Coins. The pursuit of wealth without a spiritual backbone will never satisfy. A subtlety presented in the Waite-Smith deck, on which we see an aging man, contemplating what he established in a lifetime: a house, a name signified by the heraldic plate above him, and several generations bustling in the riches he created. The ten pentacles, disposed over the image as to recreate the shape of the sephirothic tree, can be interpreted as symbolizing the ascension, both social and spiritual, that the man engaged in in the process of his life.

Page of Pentacles In the Court cards world, Pages are usually considered a strong energy source with few boundaries and little maturity. The Page of Coins is no exception. Ambitious and capable of seeing a trillions pathways of execution, the Page is an enthusiastic doer seemingly unafraid (or unaware) of challenges. Beginning a project is always so! Yet when things start to be demanding and one needs discipline to push through, the Page will have to harness all his initial energy and find focus. The Page of Coins is also the "King who left that project on the back burner," leaving ventures in a hiatus for the thrill of a new pursuit. A receptive figure, he will learn best by direct experiences how to commit and tend to his own needs.

Knight of Coins If the Knights are usually on the go, this one is absorbed by the weight of his coins. Traditionally, the Knight of Coins denotes a reliable personality type who takes time to appraise a situation before making his move, especially when there are financial concerns. Patient and methodic, he loves to set plans according to his own ways and is easily frazzled by serendipity. If some might find his nature monotonous, he reminds me of Ravel's *Boléro*, a normalized yet complex melody repeated to infinity, growing in intensity. Considered loyal and trustworthy, he is an algorithm that never bugs, a safe, grounded mind digging deep.

Queen of Coins In modern tarot books, the Queen of Coins is traditionally associated with the "working mom," who holds a job from nine to five while making sure her household is cozy and welcoming, that the children have their lunch, and that the cat got his medicine. The Queen of Coins is a feminine force who is both pragmatic and loving, tender and fair. She is this magical entity who spontaneously invited you over that night you felt down and made a five-course meal from scratch out of what was left in her fridge. Many herbalists and healers have found a patron figure in her ways. She knows how matter can heal the ailments of the soul. In institutions and communities, she represents that pivotal figure, the fertile ground allowing disbanded groups to congregate and foster bonds once again.

King of Coins The King of Coins is aware of his wealth and power, as much in his traditional role as a provider as in his role as a decision maker. Generous and kind, he is also savvy and practical, mentally visualizing every step of the process leading to complete fruition of a project and appraising all the possible challenges ahead to find preemptive solutions. As a ruler, he is solid and predictable, embracing his function with poise but not necessarily bling. If the King of Coins had a car, he'd prefer a Mercedes to a Corvette, a well-engineered luxury car with great longevity.

ACE OF COINS

LEFT

Ace of Coins, *Tarot de Besançon*, 1878–91.

RIGHT

Ace of Disc, numbered seventy-seven, from the *Grand Jeu de l'Oracle des Dames*, an Etteilla-type deck, illustrated by G. Regamey and published by Delarue Editeur in 1865.

TWO OF COINS

LEFT

A Clown throwing two tambourines in the air as the Two of Coins. The card belongs to a Spanish Naipes deck published as an ad for Joseph Bardou & Fils cigarette papers in Manila, Philippines, 1880.

RIGHT

"Letter. Embarrassment."
Two of Disks, the seventy-six card from a Grand Etteilla Egyptian Tarot, published by B.P. Grimaud in the 1870s.

THREE OF COINS

LEFT

Three of Coins from a Marseille deck
created by Suzanne Bernardin in 1839.
Or is it Bernardin Suzanne? The gender
ambiguity of this card maker, Suzanne
being a feminine name, has puzzled many
scholars. Experts like the Maison Camoin
believed that the Maitre Cartier was a
maitresse, "a woman, which was rare since
the quasi-totality of card makers had [a]
masculine name." A quick genealogical
dive established by the Bibliothèque nationale
de France allowed them to establish that
he was born in 1790 in Aubagne, the son
of Françoise Verdier and Jean-Baptiste
Suzanne, himself a game publisher.

RIGHT

Three of Coins from an Aluette deck,
created in the first part of the nineteenth
century.

FOUR OF COINS

LEFT

Four of Coins and its majestic ruby-and-
gold sea unicorn floating at the surface of an
untroubled sea. From a Naipes Finos deck,
published in Spain c. 1850.

RIGHT

Four of Coins from the Anonymous
Parisian Tarot with an iconic
checkered frame, published
in the early seventeenth century.

FIVE OF COINS

LEFT

Spanish Naipes, published in Madrid by Jose D. Martinez, 1810.

RIGHT

Mid-seventeenth-century Marseille tarot deck by Jean-François Tourcaty, baring what seem to be cartomancy meanings from a previous owner. The number seventy-eight could possibly be an erroneous equivalence to the Etteilla system (the Five of Coins in seventy-three). The handwritten inscription reads "To not splurge."

SIX OF COINS

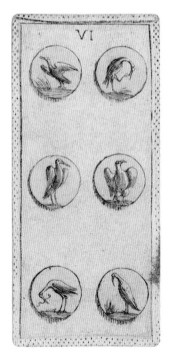

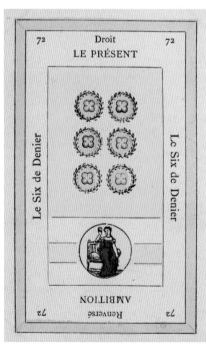

LEFT

Six of Coins from a tarocchini deck, created around 1860 in Rome, Italy, by Giuseppe Maria Mitelli.

RIGHT

"Present Times. Ambition."
Six of Disks, seventy-second card from a Grand Etteilla Egyptian Tarot, published in the 1850s.

SEVEN OF COINS

EIGHT OF COINS

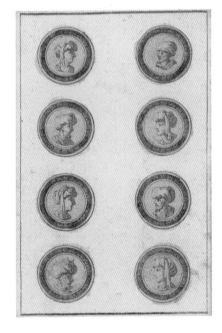

NINE OF COINS

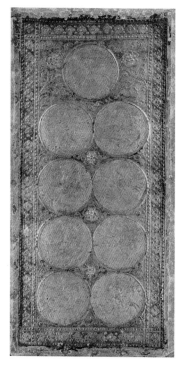

TEN OF COINS

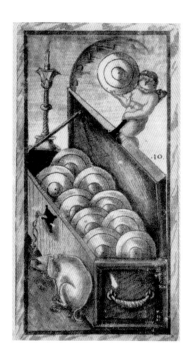

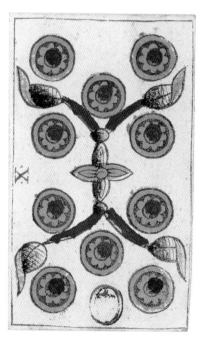

PAGE OF PENTACLES

LEFT

Page of Coins from a Nicolas Conver
Marseille deck, published by Camoin,
late nineteenth century.

RIGHT

Knave of Pentacle from a tarot deck
formerly attributed to Antonio
Cicognara, 1490s, courtesy of Croft-
Lyons Bequest/Victoria and Albert
Museum, London.

KNIGHT OF COINS

LEFT

"Centaur" as a Knight of Pentacle from
a minchiate deck published by A. Baragioli
in Florence, Italy, c. 1860–90.

RIGHT

Knight of Coins from an 1830s tarot deck
published by Fernandino Gumppenberg.

QUEEN OF COINS

Queen of Coins, numbered sixty-five, from the *Grand Jeu de l'Oracle des Dames*, an Etteilla-type deck, illustrated by G. Regamey and published by Delarue Editeur in 1865.

Queen of Coins from an Piedmontese-type tarot published by B.P. Grimaud, early twentieth century.

KING OF COINS

King of Coins from *Tarot Viéville*, created in France in or around the 1650s.

King of Coins as Sesostris Rhames the Great, from a Grand Etteilla Egyptian Tarot, published in France in the late nineteenth century.

Sésostris (Rhamsès Meïamoun le Grand).   64

VICTOIRE.

LE SEPTRE DE MILICE.

L. Gaultier fecit.

DUTUIT

Apres l'honneur des Martiaux Combats   Garder les bons et punir les Cautelles
Faire Iustice et trancher les Debats   Des Plaidereaux, Sont vertus immortelles.

THE SUIT OF SWORDS

hat is a better prologue than the Greek myth of the Gordian Knot to start dissecting the suit of swords? Made of twisted ropes, solidly entangled around two wooden beams, this legendary tie kept what was once the ox cart of Gordius together. According to the antique legend, the oracle foretold the people of Phrygia that their new commander would enter the city in a wagon, putting an end to political discords in the area. Gordius, a humble peasant, serendipitously did just that, riding his ox cart into the public square of the city. He was ultimately proclaimed king and, to express his gratitude to the gods, his son, Midas, bestowed the prophetic vehicle to Sabazios, sky god of the physicians, as a votive offering. The yoke and beams of the cart were tied with an impossible knot, described as having no beginning nor end. Loops over loops over loops of rope, intertwined into another sibylline tale: Whoever untied this complex knot would become the ruler of all Asia.

And in the popular imagination, Alexander the Great succeeded in doing so, and later gave substance to the prophecy when he extended his empire as far as the Indus River, which flowed from Pakistan into Nepal. When the young, impetuous Alexander entered the city of Gordium in the fourth century BCE, the Gordian Knot was still in the Acropolis, and its legend very much alive. Powerless to unravel the strains of rope off the wood with his bare hands, the Macedonian conqueror took a different approach. What if the matter was not to untie the knot per se, but to solve the problem in a different, more practical way? If the agility of his fingers failed him, his reason and his sword, the two greatest tools he had, wouldn't. Alexander brandished his blade in the air and in one swing, cut the knot in two. No knot, no problem. Is it cheating or is it winning? Somehow, using ruse and thinking outside the box still granted him favors from the gods, who recognized him as victorious in his conquest and made him one of the most important rulers of the antique world.

And this is, to me, where lies the spirit of the Suit of Swords, traditionally seen as the active principle of the intellect tainted with audacity, a strong capacity to solve problems, strategize, and bring abstraction into action. I like to imagine the sword suit as the left side of our brain, ruling over verbal communication, critical thinking, methodology, and reasoning. Like in Alexander the Great's evocative story, the sword is a metaphor for the type of thinking he brought forth. Sharp and incisive, it allowed him to reframe the problem in order to solve it, reimagining the situation under a different set of parameters.

Through a darker perspective, one could argue that the power that can destroy the Gordian knot is also the force that created it as well. And so it is with the Suit of Swords, with its double edge, its inherent paradoxical nature. Infamous for the disquieting iconography of its cards, a single arcana can evoke nobility and corruption, eloquence and manipulation, introspection and paranoia all at once. Ideas and their extremes, cohabitating. Misused, the capacity of our mind to fabricate, (over) analyze, and conceptualize can turn against us, mimicking the knotting of the rope: Tied up in our own head, with no beginning nor end, we cannot escape. Air is the element often associated with the Suit of Swords, a testament to the swiftness of the thought process, the valiance of a spirited mind. Yet the same air we breathe to ground ourselves in our mindful meditation, these same molecules, can unroot trees and swipe away rooftops during the storm season.

Ace of Swords Many moons ago, somewhere in the public baths of Syracuse, a man undresses to slowly enter a small basin filled with water. Oh, the joy and pleasures of ablutions! Progressively sinking in, he notices the level of the liquid rising around him in sync with his own descent. Suddenly, he has an idea. Wires connect in his brain, so to speak, and the electricity creates a spark illuminating his mind. "Eureka!" he shouts, "Eureka!" Leaping out of his bathtub, entranced by his revelation, he runs frantically into the streets of his Greek town, without realizing that, to the amusement of the passersby, he forgot to dress himself. "Any object, totally or partially immersed in a fluid or liquid, is buoyed up by a force equal to the weight of the fluid displaced by the object," said the nude Archimedes. Out of breath from his galloping, he had just formulated the physics principle that would later bear his name. The Ace of Swords energy is very similar to a eureka moment, the light bulb igniting over one's head in comic books. The moment in which the fog of our mind dissipates so we can enjoy the horizons with clarity. It can be a piercing word, an inspired sentence, a potent breakthrough resonating in one's ear, opening completely new perspectives. Traditionally, the Ace of Swords will also be associated with the quest for truth and justice, the power to fight and defend our own values, and our ability to change the world for the better by inventing the future. Like Durendal, Charlemagne's legendary sword, a good idea is indestructible and can pulverize the boulder-like obstacles leading to progress and change.

Two of Swords En garde! Can you hear the clanking noises of the dueling mind? With the Two of Swords, the polarities expressed are confrontational and transcribe an invisible struggle. If triggered emotions and confusions are internalized, the card speaks of how we can be our own nemesis, combating the phantoms of indecision, dodging the blade of self-doubt. Like every second Minor Arcana in the tarot, this card is about a relationship and demands a shift in perspective from combat to diplomacy. Ultimately, the Two of Swords points out our tendancy to use as much mental energy to foster hostilities as to establish an armistice.

Three of Swords When I think about the Three of Swords, I think about the *Oath of the Horatii*, painted by Jacques-Louis David in 1784, a painting residing in the Louvres that portrays the alliance of three brothers who promise to avenge their family name and destroy the Curiatii household. If you are not familiar with this Roman legend, it could be compared to a ferocious version of Shakespeare's *Romeo and Juliet*, only not from the perspective of the lovers but through the eyes of Tybalt, the vindictive brother. A tragedy fueled with the most poisonous essence of lex talionis—the law of retribution in kind. In David's masterpiece, the Horatii triad is seen swearing, right arms extended in a salute toward their three swords, held by their father. As the legend goes, they will duel the Curiatii triplets and all will be killed but for Publius Horatius, who brings home a vengeful victory. The David painting is famous for the hyperbolic composition of this image, which focuses in tightly on the swords in a perspective funnel. But on the right side of the image, in its periphery, we see two women weeping—the mother, who sees her sons go to battle and fears for their lives, and, Camilla, the Horatio sister, engaged to one of the Curiatius, knowing her brothers will undoubtedly kill the man she loves. Focused on the oath, the painting summons the grief of Camilla who later, in this tragic tale, collapses in sadness after her betrothed was assassinated by Publius. In an even more tragic epilogue, she will be slain by her own brother, who could not bear her mournful sentiment toward the loathed enemy. The Three of Swords is fragmented by the different points of tensions visible in this painting. The fervor of oaths made and broken, the ambiguity of betrayal, the fear and sorrow of losing what we love, and how torment can make us lose reason.

Four of Swords The number four is by essence the unyielding emblem of stability, and for the first time in the suit of swords, we find ourselves in a rather quiet place. The quatuor of blades are now immobile, as if planted in the ground, at the four cardinals' direction. Their ferocity equalizes, diffusing gently their fever in the chthonian stratas of the Earth. We are at rest, protected in a sanctified territory in which meditative interiority prevails, the mental chatterbox has finally been hushed. For the first and maybe the only time in this suit, we take time to reflect, repose, and reinhabit our mind, brushing unnecessary thought processes away.

Five of Swords In the tarot, the number five often announces a challenging episode in which the narrative takes a sour turn, often provoked by external factors impacting one's stability to the core. The protagonist, the querent, the reader, or the situation at play finds itself challenged, enduring tests of will. As we visit this number in the sword suit, we learn how our mental strength and steadiness can lose its equilibrium through the contact of others—how we recede into our own depths when individuals or groups use their charisma to dominate the room, to intimidate and silence us. In my imagination, the Five of Swords is an intense feeling of discomfort, oscillating between timidity and interiorized humiliation, seeded in power plays, in which we are left speechless, robbed of our dignity.

Six of Swords In the Rider-Waite-Smith deck, the Six of Swords depicts a woman and her child, bundled in clothing, being taken by boat on a sorrowful journey that seems more of a departure than a homecoming. Many readers have discussed this card as the "immigrant card"—it's a striking rendition of the loss of what's known to us, which once constituted our metaphorical homeland. More traditionally, the Six of Swords indicates a transition, a new direction ambiguously hopeful and unknown. Like the other number six cards in the tarot, this one speaks about harmony momentarily restored to a form of balance, but the optimism is muted by the heaviness of the emotion.

Seven of Swords Do the ends justify the means? This is one of the questions traditionally raised by the

Seven of Swords, the most active cards of the odd-numbered ones. As much as the fives, its numerical cousin, the seven speaks about a conflict, but this time, the battle isn't against a charismatic opponent but within ourselves, a discord rooted in principles of virtue and their subversions. Can we be above the law? Was Robin Hood a criminal or a hero? Is using ingenuity for cunning and mischief an insult to our intelligence? With the Seven of Swords, our moral compass goes twelve ways to Sunday before we find our own answers.

EIGHT OF SWORDS The psychological noose tightens one more notch with the Eight of Swords, the large numbers of weapons disposed geometrically on the card of the Marseille decks suggesting claustrophobic tensions and a suffocative energy. Too many blades, not enough air. Eight is 2 x 4, mathematically speaking, and figurally doubles down on the original meaning of the card. From the meditative qualities of the solitary Four of Swords, we have slowly declined to self-imposed social schism, lived like a punishment from which we feel victimized. Alienated by our own means, we can't swim back to the surface unless we manage to find within ourselves the will to extirpate from our own mind traps. Sometimes one word resonating from our vocal cords out into the world can allow us to reconnect.

NINE OF SWORDS The acerbic Nine of Swords thrusts its blade so deep that we cannot feel but from mental anguish. The bodily senses have been completely numbed, even sight has been replaced by the fog of anxiety and despair. The pain, the guilt, the agony blinds us, our intellect is birdlimed like a seagull in an oil slick. When this card turns up, we have to do the impossible task of imagining a hopeful future, and use our capacity to create to open ourselves up for reinvention instead of using this energy against ourselves.

TEN OF SWORDS The crescendo of desolation in our swords suit finds its pinnacle in the tenth card. With this last Minor Arcana, we are haunted by our own shadow, paralyzed, overwhelmed, and frozen in fear like the bull in a tauromachy arena. There is something operatic in the pathos triggered by this card, an excess of pain that swallows everything around it like a black hole. I have a fascinated attachment to this card; I find something Faustian and quite intriguing about it, with the trope of an evil doppelganger being revealed as our persecutor. It reminds me of Maupassant's short story, "The Horla." Is the man the victim of a ghost? Or is it in his mind? Does he slowly drift into insanity, his haunted house becoming the labyrinth of his mind? The card pinpoints the darkest part of ourselves as it takes the wheel and plays scary tricks on us to let the nightmare linger a little longer.

PAGE OF SWORDS In my mind, I see the Page of Swords as reminiscent of Holden Caulfield, the hero of J.D. Salinger's *The Catcher in the Rye*—a smart yet green and bungling person, stuck between two phases of their life, preferring to be on the periphery of the bustling world, wondering if they belong and how to behave "naturally." Like Holden, the Page of Swords is an opinionated person with a sharp mind who doesn't cease to have an inner dialogue, always analyzing and absorbing the energies around him, but not always digesting them properly. Impulsive, Pages often forget to turn their tongues seven times in their mouth before speaking, so they are prone to blurt and hurt. Yet they make loyal friends, with their awkward and endearing personalities. We all know and love at least one Page of Swords, maybe two. They are not really gift-givers but are always there, motivated to help you solve problems, start planning a project, or advocate for you to others even though they are often too shy to do it in front of you.

KNIGHT OF SWORDS By essence, the intrepid Knight is the court card of action and movement, often seen as a messenger or an emissary, and this one is fast and furious, plowing through life without an ounce of fear. On a good day, he would amaze us by his confidence, on another, the Knight just feels reckless and out of touch with reality. He is always ready to argue, to defend, to transform abstraction into eloquent discourse. His clever speech and quick ideas travel as fast as his horse. Yet he isn't the best team player, often incapable of exchanging, listening, or even adapting to approaches other than his own.

QUEEN OF SWORDS Characterized by her receptive, composed nature, the Queen of Swords is often believed to be a stern authority figure who treats people fairly by paying careful attention to everyone's needs and narratives. An empathic diplomat, she can "feel" people and is a good judge of character, but nonetheless rises above her own emotions to make impartial decisions. Practical and rigorous, she can easily compartmentalize how she feels about a situation and what should be done to move forward. A fine strategist, she is wicked smart, and, like a chess player calculating his adversary's game, she foresees other's moves and anticipates obstacles and traps. Brutally honest, the Queen of Swords also defines a person or a type of situation in which telling the truth prevails over politeness or leniency. She oscillates bravely between incredible wit and verbal abrasiveness with the class and poise of Dorothy Parker.

KING OF SWORDS The King of Swords is the symbol of mental clarity, bringing forth an immense power of intellect put toward action. He is often considered the guarantor of reason in the public eye, not only using his logical and rhetorical skills for his own benefit but for the profit of the collective. With his great power comes great responsibility, impassioned decision-making, articulate rhetorical addresses, and the commemoration of how knowledge, past, present, and future is being kept alive and accessible.

ACE OF SWORDS

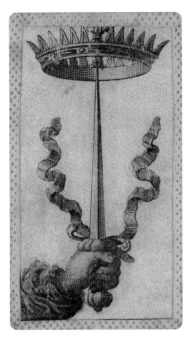

TWO OF SWORDS

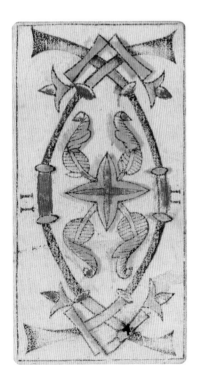

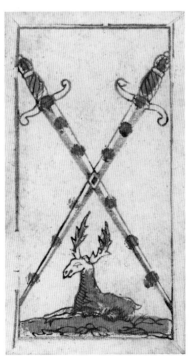

THREE OF SWORDS

TOP LEFT

The iconic Three of Swords of the Sola Busca Tarot, created in the late fifteenth century in Northern Italy. Along with several other cards like the Queen of Cups and the Ten of Swords, this one likely served as a reference to Arthur Edward Waite and Pamela Colman Smith as they conceptualized their now-classic tarot deck. Indeed, as Stuart Kaplan suggests, they might have seen the series of uncolored photographic plates representing the seventy-eight cards of the Sola Busca that was donated by the Busca Serbelloni family to the British Museum in 1907, two years prior to the publication of the Rider-Waite-Smith Tarot.

TOP RIGHT

Spanish playing card deck, engraved by J. Fonsecalas, modeled after a design by J. Ruiz and J. Atarriba. The deck was published in Madrid, Spain, by D. Felipe Ocejo between 1810 and 1820.

BOTTOM

Oath of the Horatii, Jacques-Louis David, 1784, housed in the Louvres Museum, Paris.

FOUR OF SWORDS

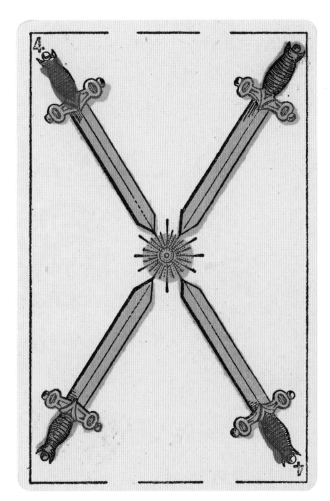

ABOVE LEFT

Playing card game published by French
card maker B.P. Grimaud for exportation
to Italy and Spain, 1858–90.

ABOVE RIGHT

Four of Swords from a Piedmontese
tarot deck, created in 1830, in Italy.

FIVE OF SWORDS

Playing card deck with Spanish suit system, printed in Madrid, Spain, by Real Fabrica in 1801.

Five of Swords from an Italian minchiate deck printed on silk, showing Reynard the Fox preaching to the chicken behind a makeshift podium. This deck was created by Giovan Molinelli, c. 1712–16.

SIX OF SWORDS

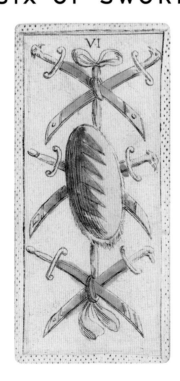

Six of Swords from a Bolognese tarot modeled after the *Tarocchini di Mitelli*, published in 1660–70.

Six of Swords showing Don Quixote on a horse jousting another man, from a Spanish playing card deck inspired by Cervantes's classic novel, created as a promotional gift by Angelical Chocolates and designed by E. Pastor, 1900.

SEVEN OF SWORDS

EIGHT OF SWORDS

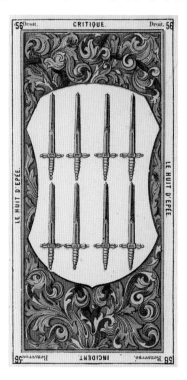

NINE OF SWORDS

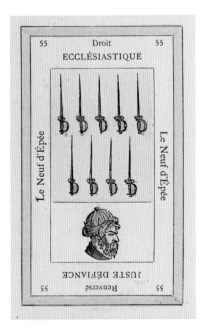

LEFT

"Eclesiatic Law—Righteous Defiance."
Nine of Swords from an Etteilla/Egyptian-
style tarot deck published c. 1890.

RIGHT

French double-headed tarot deck
published in Paris by J. Gaudais, 1860–89.

TEN OF SWORDS

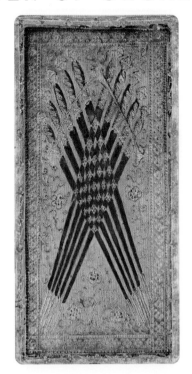
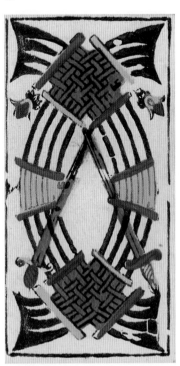

LEFT

Ten of Swords from the Visconti di
Modrone/Cary Yale Tarot deck, attributed
to Bonifacio Bembo, created in Milan, Italy,
in the mid-to-late fifteenth century.

RIGHT

Ten of Swords from a Tarot of Marseille
modeled after Nicolas Conver's Tarot,
published by Camoin in Marseille,
France, 1890.

PAGE OF SWORDS

LEFT

Page of Swords from the so-called Charles VI/Gringonneur Tarot deck, created in Northern Italy at the end of the fifteenth century.

RIGHT

Page of Swords from the *Tarocchini dalla Torre*, published in Italy in the seventeenth century.

KNIGHT OF SWORDS

LEFT

"Lady Knight" from the Visconti di Modrone/Cary Yale Tarot deck, which has the distinction of featuring knights and knaves of both genders, which might indicated the deck was created to be played by the female members of the Milanese court. Attributed to Bonifacio Bembo and created in Milan, Italy, in the mid-to-late fifteenth century.

RIGHT

Cavalier with a scimitar, from a Persian As-Nas deck published in Iran between 1750 and 1850.

QUEEN OF SWORDS

Judith holding the severed head of
Holofernes, as the Queen of Menorah in
this Judaic-inspired playing deck illustrated
by Ze'ev Raban in 1920.

Reyne de Baatons. The gentle Queen
of Swords of the Besançon Tarot deck,
created between 1878–91.

KING OF SWORDS

The mighty King of Swords from the Jean
Noble Tarot, published in France in 1659.

King of Swords from an Aluette playing
card deck, published in France between
1810 and 1860.

THE SUIT OF CUPS

ater does not resist. Water flows. When you plunge your hand into it, all you feel is a caress. Water is not a solid wall; it will not stop you. But water always goes where it wants to go, and nothing in the end can stand against it. Water is patient. Dripping water wears away a stone. Remember that, my child. Remember you are half water. If you can't go through an obstacle, go around it. Water does." An excerpt from Margaret Artwood's *Penelopiad*, which I've always found profoundly "cup-like," as it defines for me the metaphorical motion implicated by the Suit of Cups and its traditional association with water. A slow-paced elemental force that can enrapt us with comfort, nourish us, yet peacefully annihilate everything in its way over thousands of years. The flowing substance is, unlike earth, air, and fire, an intimate part of ourselves, present in our body, forming the tender flesh, circulating in tidal plasmatic waves in our veins.

Traditionally in tarot, the Cups comment on the emotional realm and imagination, our capacity to create, to love, to bond and build with affection, and the magical ways we can turn anything into fertile ground with its flowing energy. Functioning in flux and reflux, many Cups cards address the way we need to equalize these inner narratives, which like Hokusai's *The Great Wave*, growing in their intensity, can become a colossal threat and carry us away. Like water, we learn with the Suit of Cups, the power of fluidity, how being adaptable and conscious of what shapes us can help us decide where we want to flow and what state we want to shift into—solid like an iceberg or ethereal like a mist. Water has many masks, and so does the thousand faces of our emotional lives.

ACE OF CUPS A gift that keeps on giving. Often depicted as the fountain of living water, derived from the Christian iconography of baptism and the mysteries of the Eucharist, the Ace of Cups is a card that announces emotional rebirth, an extraordinary and joyful moment of connection with love and an intimate equalizing where one suddenly feels internally leveled and fulfilled. The allegory of the fountain perfectly described the dynamic of this card. One needs to extend their arms and cup their hands to gather within them the fresh water from its infinite cascade and quench their thirst. One needs to actively open themself to receive love and accept the gift of this flow of positivity in order to be touched by its healing properties and regenerative power. In its reverse, most negative aspects, the card can also speak of our difficulties at receiving strong emotions and denying the love of others.

TWO OF CUPS The law of attraction. If this card has been perceived as the Minor Arcana pendant of the Lovers card, it is because of the unification process the card symbolically proclaimed. Emotions intertwined, forming a solid channel between two entities. This card often reminded me of the mythical origins of "toasting," the traditional custom of joining our glasses together and cheering. The legend tells us that to prevent poisoning, Vikings clattered their drinking vessels together so drops propelled by the shock would land in the opposite cup. Circulation allows for trust to be established, and this card presents the very dynamic in which partnership are formed, polarities attract each other, elements are magnetized, and a bond is found through mutual respect.

THREE OF CUPS Love triangle. In the Three of Cups, times of spirited sensuality and communion are evoked in a colorful way. Feasting with your own circle. Sorority and coven gatherings. Egregore rising. The three vessels call for sibylline meetings in which we join our chalices and look at the moon reflected in the dark wine flowing in them. In addition, the card traditionally celebrates the untraditional. Friendship with benefits, polyamory, illicit love and adultery, arousing moments we spent without guilt, sometimes at the expense of others, to cultivate delight with the one we love. Resonating like a choir of maenads, the Three of Cups glorifies unruly passions, spiritual orgy, and ecstatic excess lived in groups.

FOUR OF CUPS The singing bowls. When the Four of Cups comes to mind, feel the heady vibrations of Tibetan singing bowls ploughing through your body, a hypnotizing resonance that keeps us self-absorbed, turned inward, looking at our own reflection in the mirror within without losing the ability to see what is outside that frame. Can contemplative behaviors always serve us best if they disconnect us from the way we perceive reality? This card signals that we might be too preoccupied by how we emotionally experience the world and don't manage to step out of our own heads. Don't let the way you feel taint your perspectives, otherwise you'll be unaware of the changes and opportunity presented to you.

FIVE OF CUPS Is the cup half full or half empty? With the Five of Cups, we get an opportunity to measure what we've lost, what we have left, and what we once took for granted, highlighting an attitude in which we only give value to things once they are gone or destroyed. Like the other five cards, this one announces a disruption with a negative impact, this time at play in the emotional field. In the pinnacle of sorrows, part of the healing process requires shifting our gears to have faith that sadness is a transitory state. With the Four of Cups, we saw that emotional self-absorbtion could play tricks on the way we perceive our lives. The Five of Cups whisper in our ears that sadness is an alienating experience and urge us to reconnect socially. Opening up to others, bridging back. Our vulnerability, once witnessed by trusted companions, can help us break through this dark cycle and see the glass half full once again.

SIX OF CUPS Once upon a time. The Six of Cups is, to me, the time-traveling card, the DeLorean of tarot, projecting us back into the past, investigating how we built our emotional identity through idealized memories and traumatic experiences. With this card, the fantasy of the golden age lives strong, and sometimes comes to push us to the realization that our gaze is focused on the wrong side of the timeline. We moonwalk through existence, going backward, fixating on the old memories. Alternatively, this card sometimes shows up in moments in which the past bleeds into the present, sometimes a sweet experience, sometimes a sour one. Our history, familiar or cultural, molds us, and we have to understand how it shapes us to counter or appreciate its effect.

SEVEN OF CUPS Delays and rewards. In the Rider-Waite-Smith deck, the Seven of Cups presents a person facing a number of chalices from which ghostly elements have materialized—the wreath of victory, the glowing head of a woman, jewels and pearls, the veiled silhouette of a cryptic figure—all arranged in two rows, and judging by the puzzled body language of the character, we are facing a decision. The Seven of Cups suggests that we need to consider what's available to us and parse our desires against our needs, our fantasies against our goals. In each case, we need to work toward the idea of delayed gratification, because the content of these first cups, accessible by extending the hand, might bite us back, and their rewards might be short-lived. As we learn patience, as we use our imagination and our emotional intelligence to understand where our real fulfillment hides, we can easily designate the cup that will quench our thirst.

EIGHT OF CUPS Moving on. The Eight of Cups is one of the most active cards in the Suit of Cups, demonstrating how we can always compartmentalize or distance ourselves from the heaviness of our emotional stupor. If cups are related to the element of water, this Minor Arcana evokes a drowning, in which we let ourselves be submerged by our feelings and suddenly come to the realization that we need to resurface or face drastic consequences. The Eight of Cups is this first gulp of fresh air that allows one to reactivate the body to swim back to the shore. The mechanical movement provoked by this first breath, fueled by our survival instinct, is what the Eight of Cups is about. A symbolic extirpartion. A physical motion in which we distance ourselves from our own trap, moving toward freedom of mind and a higher perception of ourselves.

NINE OF CUPS Emotional comfort. With the Nine of Cups, we are just here to sit back and enjoy the ride. The card's number is associated with completion, looking back at an experience and learning how to relish what we've learned or gained, what we've overcome. The card speaks about happiness in a simple, honest way. We know what enough means, and we aren't on a never-ending quest for more. The heaviness of the Eight of Cups is replaced by the solidity of the Nine, a feeling of stability and peace restored in which immobility and contentment have replaced the exhausting yearning for "more" or "new."

TEN OF CUPS Oh! What a beautiful card! The Ten of Cups is a complete immersion in love and a burst of true joy. With this Major Arcana, we reach an idyllic state of harmony, a moment in which we bask in the grace of life, a honeymoon period, a moment in which darkness seems like such a distant idea. Part of the beautiful energy linked to this card comes from the way this joyful alignment is experienced to its fullest in the present, an optimistic attitude that lingers in us in an effortless manner.

PAGE OF CUPS The sweet Page of Cups is both shy with words and incredibly imaginative, a gentle soul who tends to idealize situations, communicate best through images and metaphors, and lose themself in daydreams. Incredibly intuitive, he is like a young child who has prophetic abilities, not really shaped yet by the adults around him. A feral poet, he is a fabulist, preferring a good story to a truthful one. His romantic heart and boundless creativity allow him to demonstrate in an artful way the emotional tides moving through him. Close to the troubadour archetype, the Page of Cups has a black belt in longing, and through his carefully crafted poems, finds words that serve to describe universal emotions.

KNIGHT OF CUPS The valiant Knight of Cups is on a mission, the pursuit of an abstraction that might as well be a fantasy. Like Don Quixote de La Mancha, who lives his knight's fantasy disconnected from reality, his heart is in the right place, yet he can sometimes be out of touch. His bravery knows no bounds, and he is sometimes seen as an incarnation of the chivalous spirit, connecting might in action to platonic love and an unbreakable loyalty.

In a less literal sense, this knight often comes to deliver a message in which sentiments of love, friendship, or reconciliation are expressed with great sincerity, heart on the armored sleeve. One should be aware that such an openhearted missive should be treated with utmost respect, and answered with matching honesty.

QUEEN OF CUPS The empathic Queen of Cups, unlike her young page, is sitting in power at the threshold of the two realms she commands. A true figure of compassion, she can read you like an open book, and will ask the right questions at the right time to allow you to open up and confess your troubles. Her gift can be shared universally with the world, and she makes a point by selflessly healing and nurturing the ones around her. Her way feels like a caress, a slow and sensual one. She dwells in beauty, cultivating it through her different forms of expression, and knows how much healing can be provided by fostering sensitivity.

THE KING OF CUPS The King of Cups' heart is as limpid as the crystalline water his chalice holds. His mastery is carefully owned and emerges from the way he rules over his emotional depth without repressing his instincts. With the King of Cups comes an idea of nobility in governance, which is expressed here in his role of maintaining order and being a leader by using creativity, imagination, and empathy. No obstacles resist a good idea, and his capacity to invent and visualize allows him to solve problems. When this king appears in a reading, it might express your moment of achievement and success, a time period in which your drive and capacity to create aligns to transform ambitious ideas into manifested realities.

ACE OF CUPS

TWO OF CUPS

THREE OF CUPS

LEFT

Three golden chalices for this Three of Cups card from the Visconti di Modrone/Cary Yale deck, attributed to Bonifacio Bembo, Milan, Italy, 1428–47.

RIGHT

Mistress card of an Aluette deck, in which the Three of Cups usually represents a voluptuous woman emerging from one of the vessels, 1810–60.

FOUR OF CUPS

LEFT

Royal passementerie for this Four of Cups from an Aluette deck published in Nantes, France, between 1783 and 1803.

RIGHT

Odalisque resting on a leopard pelt surrounded by vines. Four of Cups from a Spanish card deck published by Jose de Martinez, in Madrid, in 1810.

FIVE OF CUPS

LEFT

Five of Cups from the *Tarot Viéville*, 1650s.

RIGHT

A man makes his way along a deserted path, precariously carrying five amphoras. He tries to hold together his carmine trousers while a dog attacks him. A very foolish Five of Cups from the Sola Busca deck, believed to have been created in Ferrara, Italy, toward the end of the fifteenth century.

SIX OF CUPS

LEFT

Six of cups from a British card game published by Rowley & Co in 1772.

RIGHT

Six of Cups from a Marseille-type deck, published by B.P. Grimaud in Paris, 1860–99.

SEVEN OF CUPS

EIGHT OF CUPS

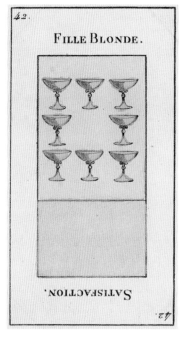

NINE OF CUPS

LEFT

"Victory—Success," Nine of Cups with handwritten cartomantic notes from a Marseille pack modeled after the Arnoult deck, published by B.P. Grimaud, Paris, 1891.

RIGHT

Nine of Cups from a Spanish playing card deck, published in Madrid, Spain, by D. Felipe Ocejo and designed by L. Ruiz and J. Atarriba, 1810–20.

TEN OF CUPS

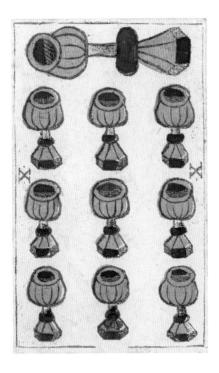

LEFT

Elegant Ten of Cups from a Jean Noblet Tarot deck, published in France in the 1650s.

RIGHT

"The City—Wrath." The fortieth card, a Ten of Cups from the *Grand Jeu de l'Oracle des Dames*, an Etteilla-type divination deck designed by G. Regamey and published in Paris, 1890–1900.

PAGE OF CUPS

ABOVE

The veiled chalice of the Page of Cups from the Jean Dodal Tarot deck, published in Lyon, France, 1701–15.

RIGHT

The gentle Page of Cups from the Visconti di Modrone/Cary Yale Tarot, with his hand gently reaching toward the golden vessel, Milan, Italy, fifteenth century.

KNIGHT OF CUPS

QUEEN OF CUPS

KING OF CUPS

ABOVE

King of Cups from an Italian tarot deck published in Milan by Ferdinando Gumppenberg, 1830–45.

RIGHT

"Blond Man—Man well placed." Angelic-faced King of Cups from the *Grand Jeu de l'Oracle des Dames*, an Etteilla-type divination deck designed by G. Regamey and published in Paris in 1890–1900.

247

THE SUIT OF WANDS

ach of us is born with a box of matches inside us but we can't strike them all by ourselves."
—Laura Esquivel, *Like Water for Chocolate*

Chaud devant! In the realm of the Wands, everything is hot and energetically charged. Beware, these cards will burn your fingertips if you hold them for too long. Call it "life force," "libido," or "drive," the Wands of the Tarot describe this fierce energy that animates our souls, and makes the bags of muscles and bones we are made of magically capable of visionary experience and poetic thinking.

Along with the swords, they form the "active suits" of the tarot, their phallic shape to be taken very literally. Wood—we knock on it to unleash good luck, we use it as a metaphor for masculine sexual desire. In Thailand, wooden phalluses are placed in storefronts or used as talismans to attract auspicious energies and prosperity. There is something very similar in the batons of our decks, as they inherently have the capacity to unveil metamorphosis. The magic wands are synonymous with creativity and invention, they speak about our capacity to create, invent, and manifest.

Associated with the element of fire, the Wands' energy could be interpreted, like Laura Esquivel elegantly describes it, as this phenomenon in which we combust from within. In life and in the tarot, we are but boxes of passionate matches longing for friction, ready to be ignited and be consumed. In this sense, the passionate Wands often open up meditations on our own sacred fire, how to sustain it, how to fan the flames of our inspiration, and what to do if we feel devoured by that incandescent light. The suit of authenticity by excellence, Wands are a universal part of each of us as we shine our own unique glow. The Instinct and the Impulse. The Soulful and the Inextinguishable.

OPPOSITE PAGE

Fire, Giuseppe Arcimboldo, 1566.

ACE OF WANDS The cracking sound of a match as it bursts into flames! The Ace of Wands is the romantic crush, the adrenaline rush, the blast of creative energy igniting the soul. Before, our environment was plunged in darkness. Through the combusted Ace of Wands, light suddenly fills the room. Hurry up, light that candle before the flames get blown away. This particular light is quick, intense, and fragile. Seize the opportunity, hammer while the iron's hot, and use this energy to give shape to what you have in mind.

TWO OF WANDS In the Two of Wands, desire and ambition intersect, creating a first movement forward. With its exemplified energy focused toward one direction, the card evokes the old Chinese saying that a journey of a thousand miles begins with a single step. The Two of Wands is the tipping point of tarot, a moment in which dormant, accumulated energy not only starts to express itself, but creates quantifiable transformations that are objectively visible. That card makes the difference, unleashing the fire, allowing you to push yourself out of your comfort zone, your own foot kicking you in the butt in some absurd-yet-efficient acrobatic move.

THREE OF WANDS What if, while driving a car, we were capable of generating the fuel that nourishes the motor, allowing the car to rise infinitely? Three of Wands suggests that, as we move through situations and deal with the unexpected, our capacity to create, find solutions, and use our imagination expands as it is solicited. For me, this card epitomizes the "New York creative" personality type, or the proverbial expression, "If you want something done, give it to the busiest person you know." Imagination as a muscle whose memory is lasting and ever-growing if it's used regularly.

FOUR OF WANDS The Four of Wands is, to me, the card of the egregore, the imagination of the collective, the artistic entity we become as we gather our talents, ideas, visions, and elbow grease. Energy rising from being brought into unison for long enough has the power to break windows and wine glasses or turn on light bulbs as this abstract power manifests itself. In my imagination, this card is very musical in its analogy; that's the card of the prototypical rock band: guitar, bass, drums, voice—the Fab Four of rock 'n' roll. Although you can use all these instruments independently from one another, together they allow us to enjoy endless nights of dancing, partying, and joyfully consuming our life.

FIVE OF WANDS "Too many cooks in the kitchen!" says the popular adage—and unfortunately for us, the kitchen can be many places at once, an allegory for the workplace, our love life, sometimes for our own head. With the Five of Wands, energetic wires cross and short circuit, canceling out the dynamic flux they carry in a profusion of incandescent sparks that could lead to a fire. The drive animating us is sacred, vigorous, and dangerous. If not distilled through the proper vessels, it might literally backfire. Voices, needs, and priorities have to be equally expressed and heard to be able to harmoniously negotiate their ways.

SIX OF WANDS As usual with the number six, we find a form reconciliation, realignment after the conflicts of the fifth card. Traditionally associated with triumph and success, the Six of Wands is the expression of a shine that allows us to stand out in a crowd, a glow of achievement that makes us charismatic, attractive, or remarkable in the eyes of others. This card is a strange mirror, flattering us and asking us to question whether or not we are comfortable with this attention, and what will happen when the curtains close.

SEVEN OF WANDS Seven in the tarot often comes to speak about inner conflict. As we are warming up with the fire of creative souls, this card can be interpreted as the fear we develop against our own capacity to create. At moments, it feels more comfortable to hide that light inside us rather than share it with others. Timidity, apathy, fear of the judgement of others.... It's a difficult card to negotiate, since it calls out the misuse of our own imagination and its capacity to create the obstacles we set for ourselves. This card questions the validity of the excuses we use and asks us to find out why we won't allow ourselves to carry a project to complete fruition.

EIGHT OF WANDS With the Eight of Wands, energy travels with the rapid pace of a comet. Fast and furiously, actions, events, ideas, and opportunities are jetting past in front of us, leaving us flabbergasted. To its essence, this card tells us to get up to speed with our surroundings, that the reality around us might kick things up a notch and we should be ready to crank up our pace, otherwise we'll get confused and miss our chance. Like a joke landing perfectly, the Eight of Wands also talks about the beauty of timing, and how it is our duty to recognize the ideal moment to move forward with a plan, make a decision, say the sentence that will make a difference in the future.

NINE OF WANDS Glowing embers in the dark of night, the Nine of Wands is this flameless fire that persists in burning everything into ashes. Visually toned down, almost dead, the card describes this inextinguible life force that keeps us alert even in moments of weakness, wounded but undefeated. For me, the card also speaks about initiatic rituals and sacred trials—the baptism of fire—moments that destroy parts of ourselves so we can rise back, phoenix-like, above the ruins of what we once were.

TEN OF WANDS The Ten of Wands is akin to the persistence of vision phenomenon. If we look at a dazzling source of light, its image will print itself in negative on our retina, changing the way we see the world, blinding us. With the Ten of Wands, there is an equal overstimulation, and we lose our grip. Like the straw that breaks the camel's back, we are giving up under the immensity of things we willingly burden ourselves with. Behind this card might lie our irrational need for control and the denial we have of limits. As we fix our eyes straight onto the sun in a sadistic contest with ourselves, we cannot see why we shouldn't sacrifice our well-being because of the false belief that more is more.

PAGE OF WANDS Oh! Page of Wands, you are such a sweet weirdo. Always game for the most bizarre experiments, ever ready for spontaneous adventures. Your excitement, passionate tirades, and tireless motivations makes you a fiery muse. Through your eyes, we see the world in a different way, as a serendipitous land, an incubator for the most absurd necessities.

KNIGHT OF WANDS The fiery charm of the Knight of Wands is hard to resist! Bold and vigorous, this court card's energy is that of a trailblazer, opening paths for others to follow, defining new ways of mapping the world. Their ambition matches their unstoppable determination, and they never back down when they have an idea in mind. As team members, they make great leaders, bringing everyone up to their speed, raising the level of intensity. As partners, they are lusty and passionate, and they make, so I learned, incredible lovers.

QUEEN OF WANDS The exuberant Queen of Wands has always reminded me of Stevie Nicks. A haunting persona, a bohemian vibe, a larger-than-life charisma—she's an absolute art witch. She is the person who always mesmerizes everyone at a party, her vibrant presence gathering everyone's gaze. Naturally intuitive, she is something of a diviner who might finish your sentence or call you on the phone as you were thinking about her.

KING OF WANDS The Solar King of Wands is a radiant genius, a visionary whose unique capacity to create allows him to invent what soon would become our new normal. I called him the *Sui Generis Prince* for his ability to originate from scratch, his brain serving as an alchemical vault transforming the mundane into the purely magical. Kings of Wands define milestones and mark with their inspired visions the before and after of our time.

ACE OF WANDS

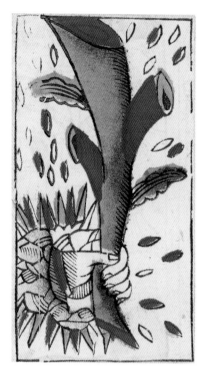

TWO OF WANDS

THREE OF WANDS

Anthropomorphic Three of Wands from a card deck published in Naples, Italy, 1902.

Three of Wands from the late-fifteenth-century Sola Busca deck, Italy.

FOUR OF WANDS

Four of Arrows and Wands from the *Quatre Parties du Monde* playing card deck, published by Daveluy in Bruges, Belgium.

Four of Wands from the Jean Noblet Tarot, France, 1659.

FIVE OF WANDS

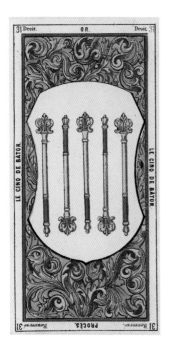

LEFT

"Gold," "Lawsuits." Five of Wands from the *Grand Jeu de l'Oracle des Dames*, designed by G. Regamey, Paris, 1890–1900.

RIGHT

Five of Wands from a Spanish Naipes deck published as an ad for Joseph Bardou & Fils cigarette papers in Manila, Philippines, 1880.

SIX OF WANDS

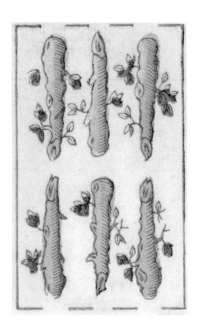

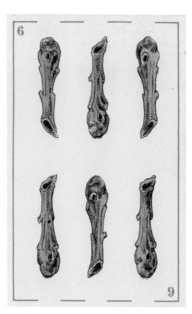

LEFT

Six of Wands from a playing card deck published in France, between 1800 and 1830.

RIGHT

Playing card decks published to advertise Angelical Chocolates, published in Barcelona, Spain, 1880.

SEVEN OF WANDS

EIGHT OF WANDS

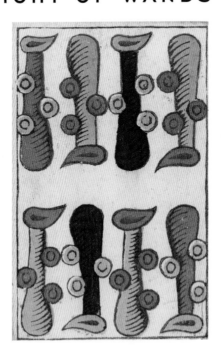

NINE OF WANDS

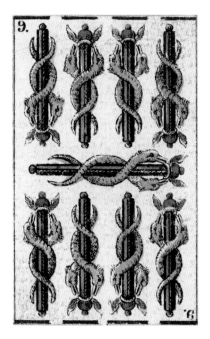

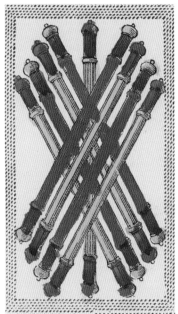

TEN OF WANDS

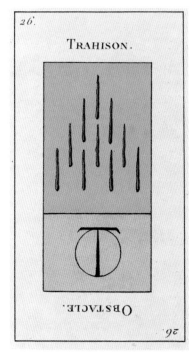

PAGE OF WANDS

LEFT

Page of Wands with flaming "yods," from a double-headed Italian tarot, published by B.P. Grimaud in Paris, 1900–30.

RIGHT

"Kind Stranger," "News." Apollonian page of Wands from the *Grand l'Oracle des Dames*, designed by G. Regmaney and published in Paris, 1890-1900.

KNIGHT OF WANDS

LEFT

Female Knight of Wands riding her horse sidesaddle, from the Visconti di Modrone/ Cary Yale deck, attributed to Bonifacio Bembo, Milan, Italy, 1447–78.

RIGHT

Valiant Knight of Wands with his horse rearing up, from a Spanish card deck published by Jose de Martinez in Madrid in 1810.

QUEEN OF WANDS

REYNE · DE · BATON

KING OF WANDS

22.

HOMME DE CAMPAGNE.

HOMME BON ET SÉVÈRE.

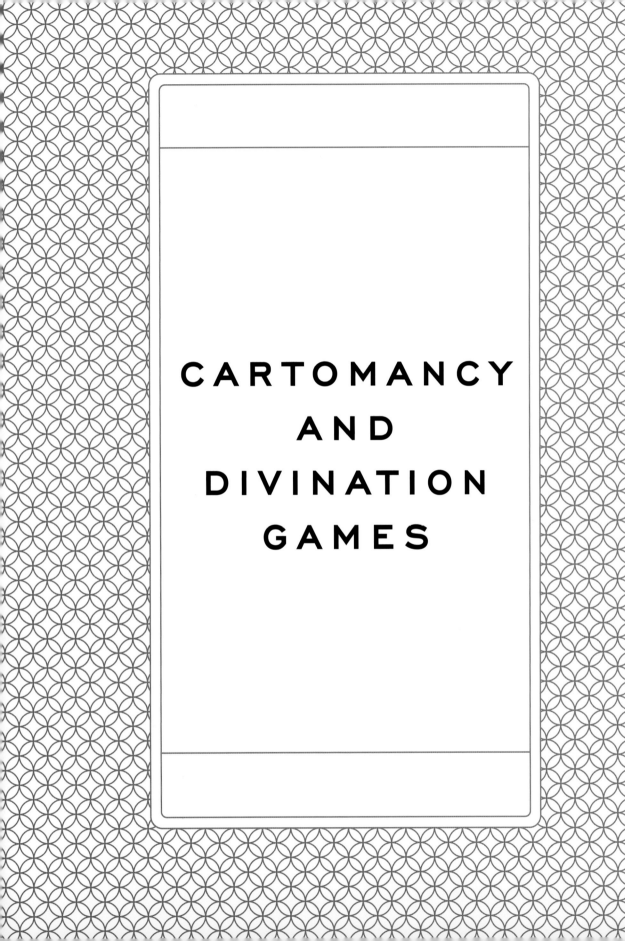

CARTOMANCY
AND
DIVINATION
GAMES

CARTOMANCY

artomancy's history is as fascinating as it is elusive and filled with paradoxes. The act of reading playing cards to find prophetic messages or information was only signaled through times by the accounts of a handful of scholars, poets, and artists, most of them describing it as witnesses rather than as cartomancers themselves. If these studies or mentions give us clues to the fact that there was a repurposed use of regular playing cards as a precognition tool, they also have to be conceived as the visible tip of a folk divination iceberg in which cartomancy as a practice is a vernacular and proteiform tradition, orally transmitted or self-taught, and mostly done privately to avoid persecution. One of the earliest mentions of card divining comes from the game invented by Fernando de la Torre in the form of a poem written in the 1450s. In his "Juego de Naypes," which he dedicated to Mencia Enriquez de Mendoza, countess of Castaneda, the Castilian poet describes in verse the forty-eight cards of an imaginary naipes deck in which each of them evokes a moral value, a symbolical situation, or a famous character drawn from history or mythology. In his text, he explains how this game can be used to "cast lots" (a form of fortune-telling) and understand one's romantic intentions. A century later, card readings, along with dice throwing and bone castings, will be evoked in critical terms by Giovanni Francesco Pico della Mirandola's *De rerum praenotione* (On the Praenotione), one of the most iconic texts against the magical and astrological speculation of the Italian Renaissance.

We have to wait until the eighteenth century and the work of Comte de Mellet, who published an essay in Court de Gébelin's famous *Monde Primitif* encyclopedia titled "Recherches sur les Tarots, et sur la Divination par les Cartes des Tarots," in which he discuss the analogy between suits in tarot and playing cards and their use for divination as well as an actual spread to "consult the fates" (*tirer les sorts* in French). His work will inspire occultist Jean-Baptiste Alliette, aka Etteilla, who owns the title "first-timer" in the history of both tarot and cartomancy, as we'll discuss later on in his own chapter. He is often credited with having accidentally coined the word "cartomancy" and commercialized the first publications and decks dedicated to the practice of this art. Etteilla's work is important because it offered for the first time in history a written account and structural trace of the cartomantic methods. His work will be revisited by many readers for years to come. And yet, a century later, he was profoundly despised by Eliphas Levi, who will use his most acerbic tone to describe him as "a former hairdresser who couldn't speak or spell French correctly." This attitude epitomizes in a strange way the general disdain for cartomancy in nineteenth-century occult cenacles, which often perceived it as vulgar and crass in comparison to their sophisticated visions of the esoteric tarot. Cartomancy is a practice for the misfits, the "fair sex," the outcast, the people, which is why I like it so much.

Methods of reading vary greatly from one area of the world to another. Cartomantic traditions stretched from Morocco to Russia, passing through Mexico, all diverting the local playing card deck for prophecies. In France, the piquet, a playing deck consisting of thirty-two cards (the twos, threes, fours, fives, and sixes are missing), was traditionally used and one of the methods summoned by Mademoiselle Lenormand, according to her autobiography. You might also find thirty-six cards in which the twos or the six cards are added and, of course, divination practiced with the full deck of fifty-two cards. Generally speaking, cards are spread in a tableaux and have their own singular meaning, which evolved depending on the cards they find themself next to.

The following interpretations are the one I have used in the past, cross-referencing different classic methods related to French cartomancy as well as my own intuitive perceptions. They are presented for informational purposes and might surprise some readers who won't find any correspondences linking these meanings to cartomancy's written tradition from the Comte de Mellet or the early Etteilla techniques. One of these actualizations is the suppression of the traditional gender role (Page is for a young man, Queen for a woman) and hair color (Spades as black-haired people, Hearts for the blond-haired), which I personally found outdated and rather disheartening.

OPPOSITE PAGE

"Gypsy Fortune Teller," a collectible card gifted with Dr. D. Jayne's Tonic Vermifuge, a remedy for worms, c. 1880, from the Wellcome Collection, London.

264 — TAROT AND DIVINATION CARDS

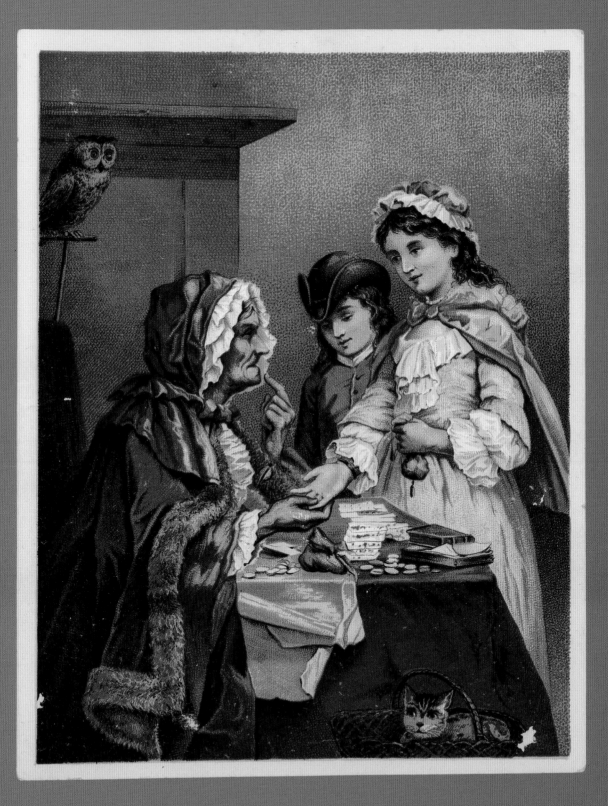

THE SUIT OF DIAMONDS

raditionally, the Suit of Diamonds evokes lands and the pathways between them. Called *Carreau* in France, the Diamonds are sometimes imagined as tiles covering the floor and are by extension frequently linked to the element of Earth. In the eighteenth and nineteenth centuries, these red-squared cards were often associated with rural life, in which people had to sync their rhythm to that of the soil and the season, focusing on agricultural work and earning sustenance from their collaboration with nature. Diamonds are to that extent interpreted as the energy and effort we invoke to cultivate an idea through fruition or produce concrete change. To expand on the pastoral metaphors, Diamonds also conventionally designate travel and paths of communication, like the farmer having to make a weekly transit to the city to sell the fruit of his labor. With the Diamond suit, we are trying to understand what needs to be accomplished in order to "go places."

In French cartomancy, you'll also find another poetic analogy for the Suit of Diamonds, in which they are imagined as arrows. In this case, they are interpreted as standing for projections, swift displacement, and being goal oriented. The French term *Carreau* was indeed the name for the metal quarrel of the crossbow's projectile, and the suit is often appreciated as an allegory for archery, unfolding for each number a metaphor of tensing the bow, aiming for a target, launching the arrow in the air, or reaching the bull's eye.

ACE OF DIAMONDS "Something new under the Sun." A message or a letter, access to new information, an unexpected but positive development. An invitation to reinvent yourself or to rebrand something.

TWO OF DIAMONDS A true collaboration in the professional domain, like a piano duet in which two musicians share a keyboard. Each plays their part, sharing their skill set. The melody emerges from these two layers of sounds becoming one.

THREE OF DIAMONDS Early success. Small but symbolically important financial reward. This card reminds me a lot of the "first dollar" business owners pin behind their counter as a good luck symbol to assure the prosperity of their business.

FOUR OF DIAMONDS A work routine finding its flow, reaching financial stability. The card can also evoke the establishment of a name, a family business or venture whose reputation (good or bad, depending on the neighboring cards) is solidly anchored in the past.

FIVE OF DIAMONDS Tensions between desire and expectation. Material possessiveness. Power madness or greedy behavior. Wanting too much too fast. Uncommunicable desires. Misinformation in the pursuit of wealth. Gossip, biases, and harsh judgements. Possibility of miscommunication or hidden information.

SIX OF DIAMONDS New motivation, movement, and energy. The power to puncture reality and make a difference by taking initiative. Trying without fear. Generosity of spirit.

SEVEN OF DIAMONDS Strike of luck, serendipitous opportunities linked to work. A path cleared and unexpected gains. The rewards of the risk-taker.

EIGHT OF DIAMONDS Journey, travels, relocation in familiar-yet-distant areas. A change of scenery. Outdoor activities, going back to the land. Event planning and bag packing.

NINE OF DIAMONDS Delays and obstacles. A project lagging dangerously behind schedule. Having to navigate emotions like frustration and impatience.

TEN OF DIAMONDS Successful venture, the golden years of one's life. Material wealth and the end of anxiety linked to poverty. This card can also announce a journey in an exotic or faraway land, a place in which one will find oneself lost in translation.

JACK OF DIAMONDS A messenger, a person conveying important information in an objective or subjective fashion. A student, a person who doesn't have much authority yet, will play a key role in a future situation.

QUEEN OF DIAMONDS A "nest-maker" type of personality, who uses her intelligence and power to build financial and material safety. Strong personality who might turn into a she-wolf if that stability is threatened or if she become envious that your grass looks greener.

KING OF DIAMONDS A strong, intelligent, and opinionated person who is a keen leader and can be a business visionary, thinking outside the box and redefining the rules. Hyperactive and hard to pin down. Potentially a workaholic.

ACE OF DIAMONDS

PREVIOUS SPREAD

Eight of Diamonds from an illustrated deck created in Frankfurt, Germany, in the 1840s by Johann Anton Steinberg.

LEFT

Three men playing cards on a barrel. Ace of Diamonds, from the so-called Wallenstein transformed deck, a set of figurative playing cards created in Germany in 1807. The pack, inspired by the Friedrich Schiller trilogy, was illustrated by Christian Wilhelm von Faber du Faur.

RIGHT

A phantom hand drops a letter in a French mailbox, a card from the *Jeu du Petit Sorcier* (Little Witchboy Game), a cartomancy deck published by Grimaud in 1880.

TWO OF DIAMONDS

LEFT

Two of Zucchinis as Two of Diamonds, from a playing deck in which all of the cards in the Diamond suit are represented by fruits and vegetables. Published in Paris in 1650.

RIGHT

Two of Diamonds from a double-headed card deck, published in Paris in 1853 by Nicolas-Marie Gatteaux and Anatole Hulot.

THREE OF DIAMONDS

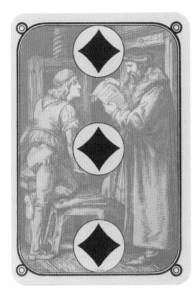

"The Print Shop." Three of Diamonds from the ever-beautiful *Luxus-Spielkarte Vier-Erdteile*, an illustrated card deck depicting the four continents, published by B. Dondorf in Frankfurt, Germany, 1875.

Three of Diamonds from an illustrated card deck designed by Charlotte von Jennison-Walworth, published in Germany in 1808.

FOUR OF DIAMONDS

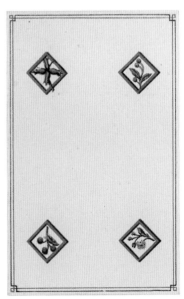

Four of parrots as a Four of Diamonds, in this playing card deck celebrating the reign of French king Louis the Fourteenth in which the entire suit is illustrated with birds. Printed in Paris between 1662 and 1715.

Fruity Four of Diamonds from the so-called Jacquemin Gringonneur deck, a medieval-inspired playing card set, published in Paris in 1864 by Mademoiselle Hautot.

FIVE OF DIAMONDS

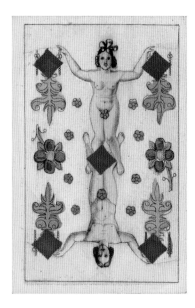

SIX OF DIAMONDS

ABOVE LEFT

Six of Diamonds showing the Avignon Bridge in a medallion topped by a satyr, from a figurative playing card deck illustrated by Charlotte von Jennison-Walworth, 1806.

ABOVE RIGHT

"Pleasurable Outdoor Time," Six of Diamonds from a cartomancy deck published by Pairraux in Bordeaux, France, toward the end of the nineteenth century.

SEVEN OF DIAMONDS

LEFT

Art Nouveau Seven of Diamonds designed by Henri Meunier, published in Brussels, Belgium, in 1900.

RIGHT

A magpie standing on a holly branch. Seven of Diamonds from an illustrated playing card deck, late nineteenth century.

EIGHT OF DIAMONDS

LEFT

Flora, Roman goddess of the flowering plants, from a mythological playing card called *Cartes Héroiques* illustrated by Victor Lange, 1847.

RIGHT

"Countryside road, rural path." Eight of Diamonds from a cartomancy deck published by Pairraux in Bordeaux, France, toward the end of the nineteenth century.

NINE OF DIAMONDS

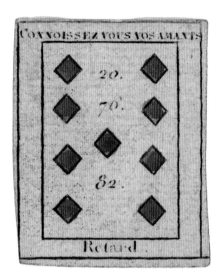

LEFT

LEFT

"Do you know your lovers?—Delay." Nine of Diamonds from a divination deck featuring questions and quotes, created in France between 1770 and 1820.

RIGHT

"Voyage—A Journey." Nine of Diamonds from *Le Livre du Destin* (The Book of Destiny), published by Chartier-Marteau and Boudin and printed by B.P. Grimaud, Paris, c. 1900.

TEN OF DIAMONDS

ABOVE LEFT

Ten of Diamonds showing children riding a cart. This card is from the so-called *Jeu de Jeanne d'Arc*, a transformed playing card deck modeled after Friedrich Schiller's trilogy, designed by Charlotte von Jennison-Walworth and published by Ludwig Ferdinand Huber in 1804.

ABOVE RIGHT

Minerva, Roman goddess of wisdom and trade, from a mythological-themed playing card called *Cartes Héroiques*, illustrated by Victor Lange, 1847.

JACK OF DIAMONDS

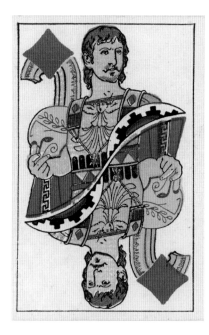

LEFT

Trojan soldier as a Jack of Diamonds for an Antique Greece–inspired playing card deck published by B.P. Grimaud in 1900.

RIGHT

Sylvan, the spirit of the forest, holding a scythe and standing near an agricultural cart. From a mid-seventeenth-century playing card deck printed in Paris.

QUEEN OF DIAMONDS

LEFT

Ceres, Roman goddess of grain crops and fertility as the Queen of Diamonds, from a mid-seventeenth-century playing card deck printed in Paris.

RIGHT

Queen of Diamonds from a medieval-themed playing deck designed by Gaston Quenioux and published in Paris by B.P. Grimaud in 1900.

ABOVE

King of Diamonds from a double-headed card deck, published in Paris in 1853 by Nicolas-Marie Gatteaux and Anatole Hulot.

OPPOSITE PAGE

The mighty King of Diamonds, from a playing card deck in which the four suits represent the four continents. The suit of diamonds is associated with Africa. Published in Germany toward the end of the eighteenth century.

WILLIAM FOX
presents
THEDA BARA
in a photoplay version of
CARMEN
produced by
R.A. WALSH
FOX FILM
CORPORATION

THE SUIT OF SPADES

I n one of the promotional images for Raoul Walsh's 1915 film *Carmen*, Theda Bara, who plays the title role, is depicted doing a cartomancy reading. Opening her signature boggle eyes immensely wide, the Hollywood vamp is stuck in an expression of both fear and surprise as she discovers the last card of her spread is the most sinister of them all, the eminent sign of disastrous prophecy—the Ace of Spades.

In cartomancy, although traditions vary immensely from one culture to another, the Suit of Spades owns an ominous reputation for announcing nefarious serendipity, accidents, pestilence, and everything in between. The Spade is a Vantablack vortex that absorbs any light left in us, possessing us like a deliciously dangerous succubus. But it's not all curses and crimes. The Spades are also linked to law and order, justice systems, authority, politics, martial prowess, and the way we attack or defend in order to survive.

ACE OF SPADES Death and rebirth cycle. Transformation. Radical change and unforeseen obstacles.

TWO OF SPADES Conflict with partners or family members. Verbal arguments, constructive but painful. Betrayal leading to a separation.

THREE OF SPADES Infidelities and love triangles. The straw that broke the camel's back. Nefarious revelations, gossip, and the disclosing of a third party.

FOUR OF SPADES Being stuck, by a disease or a situation. Physical suffering and the body as a painful and inescapable home. Confinement. Impossibility to move or change an outcome. Exhaustion, lethargy, inertia.

FIVE OF SPADES Anger and difficulties of communication, vociferation. Need for removal. Loss and feelings of abandonment, frustration, and grief.

SIX OF SPADES One full circle. The end of a chapter, a happy ending, a natural sense of closure.

SEVEN OF SPADES Misfortune and lack of luck, paying the price for bad decision or short-term thinking. Rebellious behavior and its consequences. Mischievousness.

EIGHT OF SPADES Mental instability, paranoia, and denial. Loss of equilibrium.

NINE OF SPADES Sorrow, feelings of failure, and lack of self-confidence. Disappointment and betrayal.

TEN OF SPADES The winter of the soul. Depressive episodes and lack of desire. Discouragement. Negativity and lack of perspective.

JACK OF SPADES Street-smart, skillful person—often imagined as young—emotionally immature and erratic. A curious, driven person who loves experiments, especially if they are perilous or taboo-breaking. Hidden darkness sublimated in a daredevil spirit.

QUEEN OF SPADES Independent, ambitious person—imagined as a more feminine personality—with many talents, especially rhetorical and anything linked to language. In her darkest iteration, this person would be seen as manipulative. At her best, a great strategist who knows how to persuade and negotiate.

KING OF SPADES A man of power, charismatic and sometimes arrogant. Hungry and voracious for others' energy. Controlling and in control. A shrewd leader, a sharp speaker, and a possessive lover.

ACE OF SPADES

LEFT

Ace of Spades depicting Persephone being ravished by Pluto, the Roman god of the underworld (top) and Charon conducting the souls of the dead on his boat across the River Styx (bottom). From a mythological playing card deck called *Cartes Héroiques*, illustrated by V. or Lange, 1847.

RIGHT

Melancholia—a solitary woman is lost in her thoughts as she gazes longingly at the sea in the moonlight. Ace of Spades from the so-called *Jeu de Jeanne d'Arc*, a transformed playing card deck modeled after Friedrich Schiller, designed by Charlotte von Jennison-Walworth, and published by Ludwig Ferdinand Huber in 1804.

TWO OF SPADES

LEFT

Two men skewered on the other's sword. Two of Spades from a comical playing card deck made in Frankfurt, Germany, 1870–88.

RIGHT

Digger and his shovel. Two of Spades from a *Cartes Barbouillees* deck, engraved by Gottlieb Kissling after Jan Rustem, published in Vilnius, Lithuania, in 1814–15.

THREE OF SPADES

Women weeping on a coffin. Ace of Spades
from the so-called *Jeu de Jeanne d'Arc*,
a transformed playing card deck modeled
after Friedrich Schiller's trilogy, designed
by Charlotte von Jennison-Walworth
and published by Ludwig Ferdinand
Huber in 1804.

FOUR OF SPADES

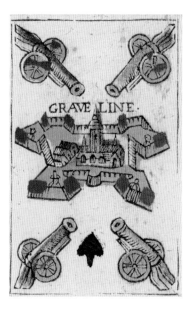

Four of cannons as a Four of Spades, from a
card deck celebrating the military victories
of Louis XIV, King of France, 1735-1751.

An old man walks naked in the snow,
from an illustrated playing card deck, late
ninteenth century.

FIVE OF SPADES

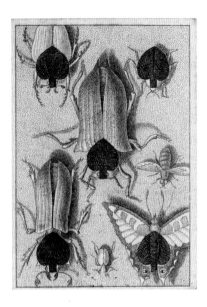

SIX OF SPADES

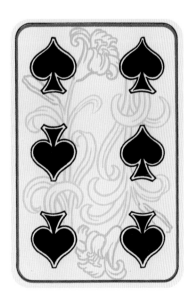

SEVEN OF SPADES

LEFT

Seven of Spades from a photographic deck by Adolphe Bilordeaux, published in Paris in 1865.

RIGHT

"Constancy leads to Good Fortune." Seven of Spades from a divination deck with questions and quotes, published between 1770 and 1820.

EIGHT OF SPADES

LEFT

Devilish Eight of Spades card from a playing deck designed by Célestin Nanteuil, France, c. 1838.

RIGHT

Art Nouveau Eight of Spades designed by Henri Meunier in Brussels, Belgium, published in 1900.

NINE OF SPADES

TEN OF SPADES

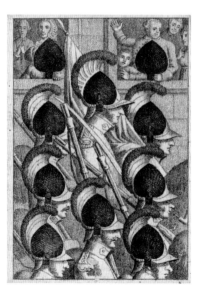

JACK OF SPADES

QUEEN OF SPADES

KING OF SPADES

ABOVE

King of Spades as a tattooed Marquesas Island tribal chief, from a *Jeu Transformée* modeled after the *Jeu de Jeanne Hachette*, published in Darmstadt, Germany, c. 1860.

OPPOSITE PAGE

The vulnerable, almost-naked king loses his crown because of a lobster attack. From an illustrated playing card deck, late nineteenth century.

Coeur pipeur

56 Au ieu de cartes pipeur, au tictac delectable,
Mon coeur se recreé, quand il m'est profitable

ABOVE

An allegory of the cheating heart, from
a deck of cards with mottos, published
in France in the seventeenth century.

286 — TAROT AND DIVINATION CARDS

THE SUIT OF HEARTS

"Sweeter than wine, softer than a summer night." The suit of hearts is in appearance all pink and pleasures, evidently presiding over how we engage socially, sensually, and affectingly with the world. Card after card, the suit demonstrates how we let our emotional intelligence, for the best and sometimes for the worst, define who we are, what we love, and how we love. The classic themes presented in this suit are of course romance, friendship, and family, but should be extended to everything binding us with passion—a hobby, an artistic venture, a vocation. The Suit of Hearts lays the groundwork on which we foster peace and harmony, and on which we establish the spirited monuments to our faith.

Ace of Hearts Joy and a complete renewal in optimism and positive energy. Good news or a new love. A desired pregnancy. A successful idea or happy accident. Beauty, in the sense of the sensory expression of pleasure and grace at once.

Two of Hearts Affection toward a partner, a loving exchange or conversation. A reconciliation or a new relationship in which both parties are equally infatuated. A collaboration, union, or marriage.

Three of Hearts Intense creativity. Fertility. Mating rituals and rites of passage. A child's coming of age into adulthood. A need for independence and freedom. A symbolic blossoming.

Four of Hearts Comfort and concord. The establishment of a relationship over the long term, a motion in which rhythms are finding their cruise speed.

Five of Hearts Sensual, carnal energy and how much or how little control we have over these overwhelming feelings. Desires and pulsions felt toward others. What makes us want to hold, touch, taste, and seek intimacy. Love as a multisensory experience.

Six of Hearts Harmony and bliss. A real sense of peace restored. Faith and courage. A renewed feeling of trust in someone.

Seven of Hearts A crush! A surprise! A coup de théâtre! An eccentric element breaking the routine with a startling affect on your life. Like a carpet pulled out from under your feet, this card is neither positive nor negative; instead, it depends on the querent's ability to deal with the unexpected and surf the wave of serendipity.

Eight of Hearts Family traditions, values, and legacy. The power of filiation. The idea of a social group as a trusted and stable place. Fidelity and friendship. The importance of a name. What belongs and what doesn't.

Nine of Hearts Short-term victory and the need to sustain a positive outcome with aspirations. This card speaks about what dreams are made of and how they fuel our future. If we don't hope and have faith in our passion, we can't truly be accomplished.

Ten of Hearts The apotheosis of the heart! Happy endings and fulfillment, a relationship restored, emotional stability and joyful gatherings.

Jack of Hearts An Apollonian type, the Jack usually symbolizes a bright and slightly idealistic person who revels in their creative talent. But beware, their extroverted nature might hide a sensitive, emotional, insecure heart.

Queen of Hearts Caring and affectionate, the Queen of Hearts usually comes to symbolize a person who feels spontaneously drawn to give and nurture. She is often associated with the Mother archetype. At their best they are kind and thoughtful, at their worst they can be overbearing and invasive.

King of Hearts Protective and generous, the King of Hearts is, like his suit consort, envisioned as the father figure of the cards. A strong-willed leader, yet a clement commander, he can be indulgent in times of crisis. His darker side involves overindulging and a pleasure-oriented sense of priority.

ACE OF HEARTS

TWO OF HEARTS

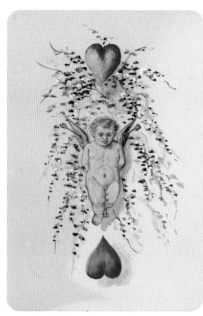

THREE OF HEARTS

ABOVE LEFT

Zephyrs ravishing Psyche. Three of Hearts from a transformed playing card deck, published in France, c. 1815–30.

ABOVE RIGHT

White on red. Three of Hearts from a double-headed card deck, published in Paris in 1853 by Nicolas-Marie Gatteaux and Anatole Hulot.

FOUR OF HEARTS

LEFT

Child's play. Four of Heart from a *Jeu Transformée* modeled after the *Jeu de Jeanne Hachette*, published in Darmstadt, Germany, c. 1860.

RIGHT

An old lady just surprised two lovers embracing, from a card deck created in Frankfurt, Germany, in the 1840s by Johann Anton Steinberg.

FIVE OF HEARTS

SIX OF HEARTS

SEVEN OF HEARTS

LEFT

Musical Seven of Hearts from a German deck created c. 1830s.

RIGHT

"Young Woman, Blond, Sweet" and "Thoughts and feelings of Love" symbolized by the yellow-and-purple flower, a pansy, which in French is associated with longing. Seven of Hearts from a cartomancy deck published by Pairraux in Bordeaux, France, toward the end of the nineteenth century.

EIGHT OF HEARTS

LEFT

A bear hunting a hunter with his rifle. Eight of Hearts from an "Alt-Bayerisch" playing card deck, published in 1757.

RIGHT

Antique vase with grotesque putti. Eight of Hearts from a deck designed by Charlotte von Jennison-Walworth and published in 1808.

NINE OF HEARTS

TEN OF HEARTS

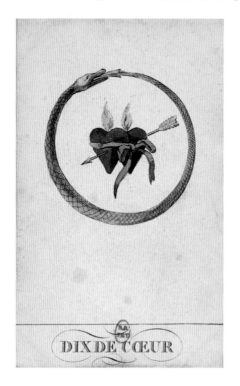

DIX DE CŒUR

ABOVE LEFT

Narren-Karte, or "Fool's Deck," published by C.H. Reuter, Nuremberg, Germany, 1860–70.

ABOVE RIGHT

Flamboyant Jack of Hearts from a medieval-inspired playing card deck designed by Gaston Quenioux and published by Grimaud in 1900.

QUEEN OF HEARTS

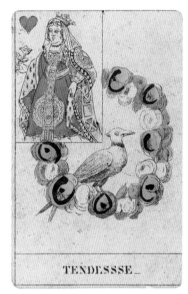

LEFT

The gorgeous Indian Queen for the heart suit of the extraordinary *Luxus-Spielkarte Vier-Erdteile*, an illustrated card deck depicting the four continents, published by B. Dondorf in Frankfurt, Germany, in 1875.

RIGHT

Queen of Hearts/Tenderness card from the *Jeu du Petit Sorcier* (Little Witchboy Game), a cartomancy deck published by Grimaud in 1880.

KING OF HEARTS

LEFT

"Genius of the Arts" instead of a King of Hearts for this playing card deck from the French Revolution era, late eighteenth century. In this deck, Kings have been substituted by *genii*, or geniuses. This deck was modeled after a similar one created by Jaume and Dugourc.

RIGHT

Priam, King of Troy, depicted as the King of Hearts, from a card deck in which every court figure is riding a horse. This playing deck was published by François Deletre in Paris toward the end of the seventeenth century.

THE SUIT OF CLUBS

raditionally, the Suit of Clubs speaks about economic preoccupations and possibilities, from our relationship to money to our capacity to define what's valuable to us. Presenting some literal gain and loss of financial power, the Clubs can also be seen as depicting generosity of spirit and interpersonal connections, how our drive allows us to bond to others. It is as much about business as it is about our desire for association and the yearning to gather with people to create something we deem important around a set of shared values.

ACE OF CLUBS Lucrative venture or career opportunity. An auspicious moment in which your will and desires align. Success in your project. Sudden and temporary financial gain, a bonus, a strange twist of luck.

TWO OF CLUBS A positive exchange or partnership, an alliance at work, a collaboration. The card also signifies a generous act, in which the querent is either giving or being gifted something without expectation of return. For this reason, the two cups address generosity and how freely we can give.

THREE OF CLUBS Expansion and growth. Branching out. Developing a new skill or working with different tools. A raise or a promotion.

FOUR OF CLUBS Reaching or acknowledging stability. Financial prudence and preferring safety to risk-taking.

FIVE OF CLUBS A need to take action to restore an unbalance. Dodging bullets. Quick problem-solving and decision-making. This card, to me, speaks about casual heroism. A whistleblower or someone spontaneously intervening to help a person in danger.

SIX OF CLUBS Ideal group dynamics. Team spirit. Differences being harmonized. Diplomacy.

SEVEN OF CLUBS "The Hamster Wheel." Losing control. Overwhelming activities. Lack of boundaries between life and work. More money, more problems.

EIGHT OF CLUBS Work gestation, the need for perseverance, dynamism, the "marathon" rhythm, paced to last.

NINE OF CLUBS Well-earned success, the light at the end of the tunnel. Optimism and clarity.

TEN OF CLUBS Achievement. Celebration. Graduation. A moment of public recognition.

JACK OF CLUBS Clever, ambitious, and extroverted, the Jack of Clubs' spirit is that of a motivated and proactive intern who takes initiative and ends up making themselves indispensable. They can be competitive and love to play solo, but can make trustworthy friends and are the life of the party.

QUEEN OF CLUBS A kind, grounded person who leads by privileging the communal aspect of ventures and making sure that gains are shared equally among everyone. Hardworking, she silently pulls the strings and might be shy about publicly assuming her role as leader.

KING OF CLUBS Savvy and visionary, the King of Clubs' spirit is the one of a self-made man, a person who is intuitively good at creating their own opportunities and following their business instincts. They can be viewed as eccentrics because of the unique way they perceive the world, but this translates into creativity in the way they manage to solve problems. They are somewhat charismatic, and if they have an influence on others, it's because of their radiant authenticity.

ACE OF CLUBS

PREVIOUS SPREAD

Suite de Trèfle, aquarelle by Lou Benesch, 2018.

LEFT

Ace of Clubs surrounded by vines, from a playing card deck published in Paris between 1791 and 1794.

RIGHT

Ace of Clubs with carnation flowers from a medieval-themed playing deck, designed by Gaston Quenioux and published by Grimaud, Paris, 1900.

TWO OF CLUBS

LEFT

Hebe, Greek goddess of youth, and Cupbearers of the Gods as a Two of Clubs from a transformed deck published in France around 1815.

RIGHT

An intimate encounter as the Two of Clubs from a fruity deck created by Johann Anton Steinberg in Frankfurt, Germany, in the 1840s.

THREE OF CLUBS

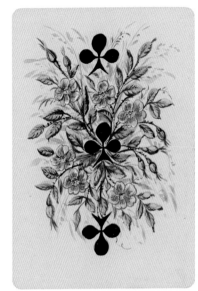

LEFT

"Beginnings of Success," "Birth." Three of Clubs from a cartomancy deck published by Pairraux in Bordeaux, France, toward the end of the nineteenth century.

RIGHT

Pink flowers and triple clubs, from an illustrated playing card deck from the late nineteenth century

---

FOUR OF CLUBS

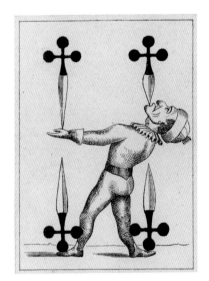

LEFT

Knife juggler balancing blades on his hand and chin. Four of Clubs from a *Jeu Transformée* modeled after the *Jeu de Jeanne Hachette*, published in Darmstadt, Germany, around 1860.

RIGHT

Cheers! Two men sharing a drink. Four of Clubs from a deck designed by Charlotte Jennison-Walworth and published in 1808.

FIVE OF CLUBS

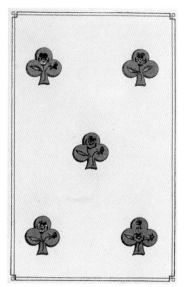

LEFT

The quack doctor. Five of Clubs from a deck designed by Charlotte Jennison-Walworth and published in 1808.

RIGHT

"Pansies." Five of Clubs from the Jacquemin Gringonneur deck, a medieval-inspired playing set published by Mademoiselle Hautot in Paris, 1864.

SIX OF CLUBS

L'Ange des tenebres vaincu par St. Michel

LEFT

"The angel of Darkness subdued by the Archangel Michael." Six of Clubs from a transformed card published in France around 1815.

RIGHT

Two men smoking pipes. Six of Clubs transformed card from the Wallenstein playing card deck, inspired by Friedrich Schiller's trilogy, designed by Christian Wilhelm von Faber du Faur, 1807.

SEVEN OF CLUBS

LEFT

Puss in Boots as the Seven of Clubs for this fairy tale–themed playing card deck, published by Lequart and Mignot in Paris, late nineteenth century.

RIGHT

A green demon pulls the hairs of a man holding a bag of gold depicted on this Seven of Clubs, which came to signify "cursed money." This card is part of the *Jeu du Petit Sorcier* (Little Witchboy Game), a cartomancy deck published by Grimaud in 1880.

EIGHT OF CLUBS

ABOVE LEFT

Entomological Eight of Clubs from the so-called *Jeu de Jeanne d'Arc*, a transformed playing card deck, modeled after Friedrich Schiller, designed by Charlotte von Jennison-Walworth, published by Ludwig Ferdinand Huber in 1804.

ABOVE RIGHT

One card, two heads. Two hats for this Eight of Clubs, published in France in 1850.

NINE OF CLUBS

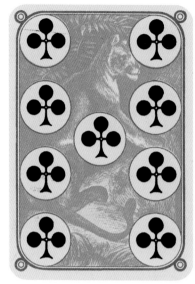

TEN OF CLUBS

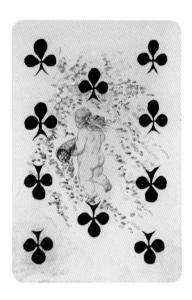

ABOVE LEFT

Horn-blowing triton from a mythological-themed playing card deck called *Cartes Heroiques*, illustrated by Victor Lange, 1847.

ABOVE RIGHT

"Racial Equality" as the Jack of Clubs for this playing card deck from the French Revolution era, late eighteenth century. In this deck, the Jacks represent different progressive concepts linked to equality. This deck was modeled after a similar one created by Jaume and Dugourc.

QUEEN OF CLUBS

ABOVE LEFT

Redhead Queen of Clubs for this Art Nouveau–inspired playing card deck created by Henri Meunier and published in Brussels, Belgium, 1900.

ABOVE RIGHT

"I don't remember/Brown-Haired Woman," Queen of Clubs from a cartomancy deck from the late eighteenth century.

ABOVE LEFT

"Rene of Anjou, the crown of Sicily at his feet." King of Clubs from the so-called *Jeu de Jeanne d'Arc*, a transformed playing card deck modeled after Friedrich Schiller, designed by Charlotte von Jennison-Walworth, published by Ludwig Ferdinand Huber in 1804.

ABOVE RIGHT

Alexander the Great, King of Macedonia, as a King of Clubs. From a photographic deck by Adolphe Bilordeaux, published in Paris in 1865.

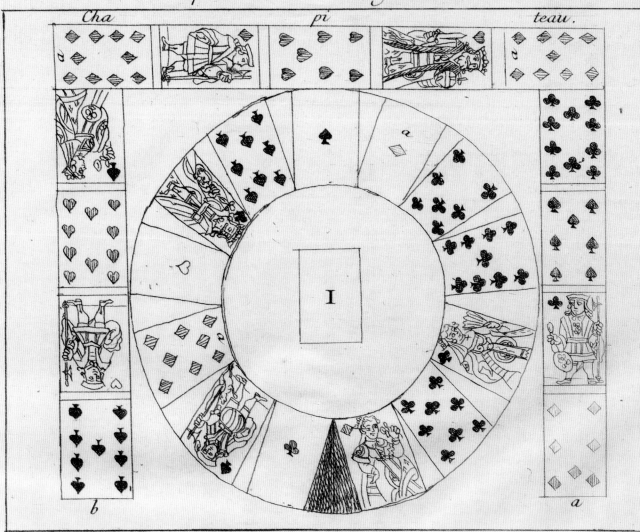

ABOVE

Wheel of Fortune spread by Jean-Baptiste
Alliette, published by Lesclapart, 1770.

ETTEILLA

nighted by Decker, Depaulis, and Dummett as "the First Professional Cartomancer," Jean-Baptiste Alliette is one of the most fascinating enigmas in the history of card divination. Does he deserve this title? As we'll see together, Alliette can justifiably pride himself for many cartomantic coinages and proclaim his authority without blushing, although he was later criticized, if not mocked, by other occultists. Yet, his legacy, hinging together the world of popular cartomancy with the early hours of the esoteric tarot, still impacts the way we read cards today. The systems he theorized were named after his nom de plume, Etteilla, the reversed anagram of his last name. Though we know very little about his early life, his taste for self-invention filters through the several books he wrote, especially their forewords, which describe a life filled with many character shifts.

Born in Paris in 1738, Jean-Baptiste Alliette came from a modest background; he was the son of a caterer father and a seed merchant mother, a profession he himself embraced early on. An amusing legend claims he also was a wigmaker, but this erroneous affirmation was due to the address of one of his residences, in a house owned by a *perruquier*. Alliette married Jeanne Vannier around 1763, who gave him a son, but the couple separated after a few years of marriage, leaving the sorrowful man in some serious financial difficulties. In *A Wicked Pack of Cards*, the "Three Ds"[1] speculate that these times of uncertainty might have kindled Alliette's interest in the occult sciences and the use playing card for prognostics.

Gradually his life shifted back together, and he became a print seller, going to auctions where he traded and sold paper rarities and art etchings. In 1770, he published his first book—*Manière de se recréer avec le jeu de cartes* (Ways to Entertain Oneself with a Pack of Cards), in which he explored cartonomancy, an oracular method of his invention using a classic *Jeu de Piquet*, a method he had been using for sixteen years, and of which, of course, he was a self proclaimed master. In his foreword, cartonomancy is described as both a game and a science that anyone can practice by following simple steps. Although definitely described as a sibylline activity allowing anyone to glimpse into their fate, Alliette is evidently reluctant to call himself a diviner, claiming in some humorous disclaimer that such person should be seen as suspicious.[2]

Often forgotten and never translated, *Manière de se recréer avec le jeu de cartes* is nonetheless a milestone in card-reading history, for it seems to be the first publication to comprehensively systematize a practice that, prior to that publication, only existed as oral folk tradition in which readers had their own ways. It is impossible to know what methods Alliette genuinely created and what he might have acquired from other readers, but his cartonomancy book definitely establishes many of the fundamentals of the craft for centuries to come. If each card has a meaning of its own that can be summarized in a few keywords or concepts, this interpretation might be subject to change according to the position—reversed or upright—of the card and the other cards next to it. Combined together as pairs, they will reveal new sets of information but should also be read in a large grouping or line (what Alliette called the "Coup"). Several diagrams demonstrate how to read the cards or arrange them into a spread. These illustrations also present another detail very clearly: At no point are tarot cards being discussed in this book; Etteilla's method focuses solely on classic, French-suited playing cards.

No matter what, this first foray into card reading was a publishing success that was reprinted several times until Antoine Court de Gébelin published the eighth book of *Le Monde primitif* in 1781. This encyclopedia (which included an influential essay by Comte de Mellet), in which the Protestant pastor famously discusses the tarot as an esoteric compendium of Egytpian hermetic sciences was a turning point for Alliette, who completely reshapes his way of seeing the cards and pretends that he *always knew* that the tarot was, in fact, the Book of Thoth. From that point on, Alliette "rebranded" himself as a savant, so to speak, pushing aside his work aimed for a large audience to embrace the role of an academician of the esoteric. From then on, he responded to the self-appointed title "Professor of Algebra" and, in 1783, two years after Gébelin and Mellet's contribution to the study of tarot, he published *Manière de se récréer avec le jeu de cartes nommées tarots.*

Notoriously difficult to read, both for its mathematical jargon and its spelling mistakes,[3] Alliett's tarot book is yet quite interesting, giving the magus the opportunity to completely rethink his system through a new, Egyptianized lens. In his introduction, the man who now went by Etteilla explains his project of restoring the iconography of the trump cards of the tarot, whose true images were lost over time[4] because of careless printmakers. Etteilla's project is to both reestablish these cards' integrity and translate their profound esoteric meaning. He also narrates with great poetic verve a detailed version of the legend of the Book of Thoth, invented by seventeen magi,[5] including Hermès Trismegistus at their head. Composed of twenty-two golden blades[6] (*lames*) carved with hieroglyphs, the Book was stored in the Temple of "Heat and Fire," near Memphis, Egypt. Etteilla also retraces the genealogy of his Tri Mercure Athotis as a late descendant of Zoroaster, winking at his readers that, because he was too sensitive to name-dropping, he wouldn't bother citing his sources, since he assumes anyone who picks up his volume is an initiate.

Using the metaphor of Genesis, in the way it was introduced by the Comte de Mellet, Etteilla modified the order of the tarot, arguing that he had decoded its sacred numerology, and famously reintroduced the Prudence card, which along with Fortitude, Temperance, and Justice, restored the four set Cardinal Virtues. The Etteilla/Egytpian Tarot was born, an idiosyncratic vessel, in theory presenting a matrix of creation rules by divine arithmetics. At the time, only a couple of cards were actually recreated to illustrate his publication, but Etteilla, a keen businessman and ephemera professional, would retail François Tourcaty's tarot[7] with his book at a time when such decks would be hard to find in the French capital.

After his first tarot book, Etteilla went on to become a sort of celebrity and a prolific esoteric author, writing books on astrology, alchemy, and even palm reading, as well as several updated versions of his Book of Thoth research. Starting in 1788, he founded his own "tarot school," *La Societe des Interprètes du Livre de Thot* (The Book of Thoth Interpreters Society), gathering enough subscribers and students to finance a lavishly printed and complete version of his restored Egyptian tarot, the first ever deck of cards created for divination purposes. His corrected tarot served as a model for the Grand Etteilla/ *Tarot Egyptien*, and its subsequent variations and Etteilla ersatz produced over the years after Etteilla's death in 1791 are still popular to this day, reprinted regularly and reclaimed by modern cartomancers.

Is Etteilla the "First Professional Cartomancer"? It's hard to tell. Although he was a savvy merchant and definitely made a living through his esoteric publications and, later in life, as a teacher, it's hard to know if he was actually reading cards for people during private consultations and doing the actual work of a cartomancer. If he did, he didn't advertise it, which although completely understandable, doesn't fit his personality, as he was always ready to propose his full catalogue and associated price tags, even on card wrappers.

OPPOSITE PAGE

Cartomancer studying his cards arranged in a spread. Frontispiece from the 1770 edition of *Manière de se récréer avec le jeu de cartes.*

ALPHA

TABLEAU

DES LAMES DU LIVRE DE THOT QUI ÉTOIT PLACÉ DANS LE TEMPLE DU FEU A MEMPHIS.

"The blades of the Book of Thoth, placed in the Temple of the Fire of Memphis," printed by Basan and Poignant, Paris, 1788.

GRAND ETTEILLA - BOOK OF THOTH
A late-nineteenth-century version modeled after the original version from 1791.

Etteilla/Questionnant
Eclaircissement/Feu
Appui/Protection
Etteilla/Questionnante
La Prudence/La Pudeur
Mariage/Union
Force Majeure
Mortalité/Néant
Folie

13.

MARIAGE.

UNION.

13.

14.

FORCE MAJEURE.

FORCE MAJEURE.

14.

17.

MORTALITÉ.

NÉANT.

17.

78

FOLIE.

FOLIE.

78

LE PETIT ETTEILLA

In contrast with playing cards repurposed for cartomancy, the *Petit Etteilla* was one of the earliest examples of cards exclusively designed for divination, reprising the correspondences and meaning established in Aillette's first cartomancy book, published in 1770, prior to his foray into tarot. Based on a classic piquet deck (Ace, Seven, Eight, Nine, Ten, Jack, Queen, and King), the deck also includes an extra "blank" card called the Etteilla, which Alliette often placed at a highlighted position in the spread to symbolize the querent. Modest-looking and far removed from the Egyptianized iconography of the Grand Etteilla/Book of Thot published during Alliette's lifetime, the *Petit Etteilla* decks seem to have been anachronistically created after his death to entertain a popular audience.

King of Hearts
Ace of Hearts
Queen of Clubs
Seven of Clubs
Jack of Diamonds
Eight of Diamonds
Queen of Spades
Nine of Spades

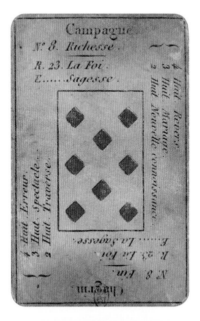

OPPOSITE PAGE

GRAND ETTEILLA / EGYPTIAN TAROT

Reimagined as fully Egyptianized, published in Paris.

Génie
Paix/Intelligence
Béatitude/Ténèbres
Vertu/Douceur
Bonheur/Disgrace
Circonspection/Discours

1   GÉNIE.

L'homme qui consulte.

SAGESSE.

4   INTELLIGENCE.

Les étoiles.

PAIX.

6   TÉNÈBRES.

Le firmament.

CONTENTEMENT. — BÉATITUDE.

8   DOUCEUR.

La femme qui consulte.

VERTU.

11   DISGRACE.

La Force.

BONHEUR.

12   DISCOURS.

La Prudence.

CIRCONSPECTION.

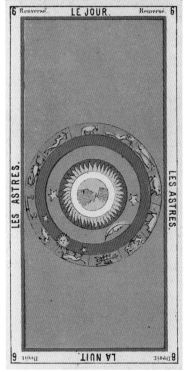

THIS SPREAD

GRAND JEU
DE L'ORACLE
DES DAMES

One of the most iconic Etteilla-inspired decks, created in the late nineteenth century, designed by G. Regamey, and published in Paris.

Propos/ Eau
Voyage / Terre
Le Jour / La Nuit
Appui / Protection
La Tempérance/ Le Peuple
Maladie
Traître/ Faux Devot
Misere/ Prison

MADEMOISELLE LENORMAND

793—Paris is in the midst of the French Revolution; the Reign of Terror, to be specific. Somewhere on rue Tournon, supporters of the revolution, a maid, and an aristocrat, probably disguised to assure their clandestinity, are all waiting in the small salon, staring daggers at each other. Although it sounds like the prologue of a joke, this was a common occurrence at the office of Marie Anne Adelaide Lenormand. Somehow, in the waiting salon of the diviner's establishment, a harrowed crowd that otherwise would jump at each other's throats, patiently holds their fire, waiting for their turn to consult the fortune-teller. Wasn't the most famous cartomancer of all time worth a brief moment of concord?

Born in Alençon in 1772, to a family who traded in fabric, Lenormand was sent at a young age to the Benedictine convent of Monsort[1] to receive an education. According to one of her autobiographies,[2] her prophetic visions began then, as she received a copy of *L'Iliade* (The Illiad), a gift granted by the nuns for her good results in school. One day, mimicking the Oracles of her favorite book, she played the child clairvoyant, canting prophecies like her imaginary Delphi peers as her classmates congregated around her. Quickly, the small gathering attracted the suspicious attention of the Mother Superior, who came to interrupt the unholy performance. According to this story,[3] this is when Lenormand had her first visionary experience and foretold that the abbess would lose her title and reputation, and be imprisoned by the Church. The ominous prediction got Lenormand expelled from the religious order, and, as legend goes, a twist of fate later, she turned against the Mother Superior who was condemned by her hierarchy. Lenormand's first fortune was fulfilled!

Leaving behind bucolic landscapes for the bustling city of Paris, Lenormand became a seamstress and slowly grew her reputation as a cartomancer, reading for customers over the sewing workshop counters. Different accounts describe her as a chubby rural girl with piercing black eyes, always dressed in black. She learned astrology with "celestial mathematician" Bonaventure Guyon,[4] and the story goes that she once had her cranium inspected by phrenologist Franz Joseph Gall, who confirm she had the "clairvoyant bump."[5] As the revolution roared and overthrew the monarchy, the Norman girl had already well established herself as a prophetess, having her own office, a place soon haunted by the "big wigs" of the revolution. Before the age of twenty-two, she predicted Marat's baleful destiny, revealing to him that he would be knifed to death in a bathtub by Charlotte Corday. Robespierre and Saint Just were told of their equally miserable fates. Enamored with the theater, she also befriended the actors and other members of the Comédie-Française,[6] providing them with horoscopes and other colorful prognostics.

In 1794, her life itself took an operatic turn when the Parisienne sibyl was accused of being involved in a coup, plotting to free disgraced Queen Marie Antoinette from prison. Yet, her short trip at La Force penitentiary turned into one of her greatest business opportunities, as Lenormand found herself rubbing elbows with what was left of the Parisian noblesse. Her kind tone and reassuring prophecies gave solace to the former court elite and other marquises in despair. The intra muros' fortunes soon spread beyond the tights walls of La Force. One day, she received a clandestine message from a young woman, a prisoner destined to be guillotined, named Rose-Joséphine de Beauharnais. Was she going to die, she asked? No, retorted Lenormand. Not only would she live, but the widow would remarry a man and be destined to rise back in glory.

Josephine, of course, marries Bonaparte, a Corsican general who will become Napoléon. Once empress, Josephine never forgot the auspicious omen; she tracked down Lenormand and dubbed her spiritual adviser, regularly sending for her to come to the imperial residence, the Château de la Malmaison. With such a prestigious customer vouching for the clinical accuracy of her vision, Lenormand became a living legend. She took immense care to consolidate a well-manicured reputation in the several autobiographical books she published over the years. The prolific cartomancer talks very little about her techniques or her practices, instead focusing in on the intimacy of her séances with her celebrity clientele. Her humorous verve and romanesque tone were only matched by a rather entertaining lack of discretion, as she waited for the death of these historical icons to spill the beans and deliver all the juicy bits of their private affairs. Charming and somehow aloof, her books are sensationalized accounts of her life probably aimed for advertisement, "tell-alls" that would make any of today's ethical readers cringe.

According to these books, she was a traditional cartomancer,[7] reading with a *Jeu de Piquet* of thirty-two cards, which, interestingly enough, is where she was most often represented by the artists who created portraits of her. The famous Jules Champagne lithograph,[8] which seems to have been done posthumously, represents her as a dark sylphid woman with rosy cheeks; French playing cards are on the table, and she holds a Queen of Hearts. So does the epic painting by Josef Danhauser, in which she looks like a hysterical crone, stricken by the nefarious images she foresees for the imperial consorts, nagging the table-cloth on which her cards are spread.

She also seems to have read an Egyptian version of the Etteilla deck[9] and mentioned a deck of tarot as well.[10] Furthermore, Lenormand was famously an exceptional palm reader, and some of her books come with chiromantic illustrations of the famous hands she held in hers. Now here is the trick question: Did Lenormand read Lenormand cards? No, she didn't, and the decks prominently featuring her name were all created after her 1843 death as an attempt to capitalize on her fame. Having never married nor had children, all her belongings were left to her nephew, Alexandre Hugo, who is said to have burned all her belongings, letters, and archives. Yet somehow, in the Bibliothèque nationale, a Marseille deck once in the collection of Paul Marteau is catalogued as bearing "divinatory inscriptions attributed to Mademoiselle Lenormand"—a last relic of the Parisian prophetess? Hard to know.

PREVIOUS SPREAD

Portrait of Mademoiselle Lenormand,
Jules Champagne, 1857.

RIGHT

Napoleon entering as Mademoiselle Lenormand read cards for Josephine in La Malmaison, by Jean François Ribault, 1827. This illustration is from the third volume of *Mémoires historiques et secrets de l'impératrice Joséphine* (Historical and Secret Memories of Empress Joséphine), a book in which Mademoiselle Lenormand also retraces the ominous finals moments of Napoléon, who was exiled on the island of Sainte-Hélène.

FROM THE GAME OF HOPE TO LE PETIT LENORMAND

In the strange saga of the Lenormand divination systems blooming after her death, we probably should begin with the "rebranding" of the Game of Hope. This one-of-a-kind collapsible board game, divided into thirty-six cards, was first developed in 1799 by Johann Kaspar Hechtel, a Nuremberg-based writer and factory owner who would spend part of his career creating this ingenious parlor game. Originally, the cards were to be displayed in a rectangle featuring four rows of nine cards that formed the board, and were played with dice and tokens. Each card was numbered, and depicted a simple central design relating to everyday life—a house, an anchor, a heart, a lion, a cat—flanked by small playing cards in each corner, with German suits on the left and their French equivalent on the right. A couple years after Lenormand's death, the small pack of cards was repurposed as a fortune-telling game[11] in which the central figures were translated into divinatory interpretations. Each element on the cards has to be read literally, sometimes in association with several other cards, a seemingly easy system that still demands a lot of practice but is said to provide crystal-clear messages to the reader. The universality of the illustrations, definitely less cryptic than the tarot, added to its adaptability and helped ensure that it would remain one of the most accessible and popular decks throughout time.

BOTTOM

Das Spiel der Hofnung, The Game of Hope, in what seems to be one of its oldest versions, printed in the mid-nineteenth century in Nuremberg by G. P. J. Bielingand kept at the British Museum.

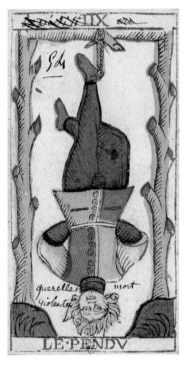

ABOVE

"Quarrels, Violent death," a calamitous handwritten interpretation for this Jean François Tourcaty *Tarot de Marseille*, published between 1734 and 1753. Once in the Paul Marteau collection, this deck, now archived at the Bibliothèque nationale, is described as having been inscribed by the hand of Mademoiselle Lenormand herself.

Die achten Wahrsagekarten des Kartenschlägerin Mlle *Lenormand* (The Eighth Fortune-telling Cards of Card-reader Mlle Lenormand) in Paris, a German version of the *Petit Lenormand*, created between 1875 and 1899 and published by Ensslin & Laiblin, in Reutlingen, Germany. The originality of this deck comes from these enigmatic sigil-like inscriptions, which replace the regular cartomantic values of each card.

The Sun / The Moon / The House / The Key / The Tree / The Coffin / The Bouquet / The Scythe / The Birds / The Bear / The Fox / The Children / The Snake / The Cavalier / The Letter / The Ship

19.
Annonce une longue et heureuse vieillesse mais entourée de nuages elle annonce une maladie même selon les circonstances aussi la mort

HAUTE TOUR.

20.
Annonce une bonne et grande compagnie ou l'on entrera, tout près, elle assure encore une amitié constante mais éloignée, c'est un signe pour de faux amis.

JARDIN.

21.
Près de la personne nous fait craindre un ennemi puissant mais dans l'éloignement nous pouvons compter sur de forts amis.

MONTAGNE.

22.
Entourée de nuages est signe de malheurs mais si cette carte est loin de la personne il y a des voies ou des moyens que nous trouverons pour échapper à un danger.

CHEMINS.

23.
Signifie vol si elle est près on retrouvera l'objet perdu et si elle est éloignée la perte est irréparable

SOURIS.

24.
Signe de joie de bonheur et de concorde.

CŒUR.

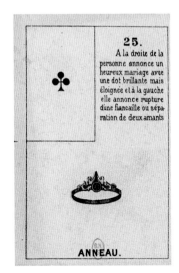

25.
A la droite de la personne annonce un heureux mariage avec une dot brillante mais éloignée et à la gauche elle annonce rupture d'une fiancaille ou séparation de deux amants

ANNEAU.

26.
Communique un secret sa position nous fait juger ce qu'il concerne cependant il faut agir avec circonspection à cet égard.

LIVRE.

FROM LEFT TO RIGHT,
TOP TO BOTTOM

Belgian *Petit Lenormand* published around 1895 by Geûens-Seaux in Bruges, Belgium.

The Tower / The Garden /
The Mountain / The Road /
The Mouse / The Heart /
The Ring / The Book

Le Grand Jeu Lenormand

Published by Grimaud in 1845, two years after Lenormand's death, and conceptualized by "Madame Breteau," a woman who claimed to be one of the famed clairvoyant's students, the *Grand Jeu* is the complete opposite of its *Petit Lenormand* cousin. Impenetrable, maximalist, and esoteric all the way. Each of the fifty-two oversized cards deploy an armada of divinatory elements allowing the most skilled reader a platform for traditional interpretation and intuitive ignitions. Divided into seven vignettes, each card includes a central scene (referred to as *Le Grand Sujet*) associated in uneven groups to the Trojan War, the saga of the Argonauts, alchemical work, or the zodiac personified. Some others are drawn from various mythologies, are genre scenes, or depict the natural world and its fauna. This central medallion is topped by constellations at its centers, allowing for astrological musing. The right-hand corner is adorned by a letter from the Latin alphabet whose shape or sound owns a symbolic significance. A number of them also present geomantic figures, adding yet another antique magical tradition to decipher from.

Wait! It's not over! The bottom of the *Grand Sujet* serves as an opportunity to train your floriographic knowledge with a botanical arrangement borrowing from the allegorical meanings attributed to flowers and plants. On each side of this floral design, two more illustrations representing subjects as diverse as nineteenth-century daily life, Ovid's *Metamorphoses*, heraldry, and geological formations.... Needless to say, the *Grand Jeu* gained a reputation of being the most complex and enigmatic divination card system ever created, a "third eye melter," which might explain why its iconography has been kept untouched, the original and simply beautiful 1845 drawings always the same throughout its different reimpressions. Why would one reinterpret a deck that is, in its essence, so hard to interpret? A good *Grand Jeu* reader must be a polymath and an expert in such a wide array of esoteric traditions as to be able to read the cards. Most of the literature attached to this deck, its iconography and reading techniques, was written in French and, too niche to be translated, became inaccessible as tarot and divination card culture became mainstream. Yet in France, it remained a "professional" staple, seen here and there in the hands of seasoned cartomancers, famously laying on the table of Brassai's iconic photograph *La Voyante* or in Agnès Varda's film *Cléo from 5 to 7*'s unforgettable tarot-reading montage.

The Tortured Victim, "Movement, Displacement, Trials, and Sacrifice."

The Demon, "Force Majeure Case, Blows, Wounds, Disease."

The Consultant King, "Good Man, Protector, Amicable Reunion, Success in One's Venture, Fortune."

Fortune, " Necessity, Fatality, Fortune."

The Milky Way, "Good News, Hope, Commerce, Exchange."

The Woman Consultant, "Wise Woman, Quiet, Secret Words, Sanctuary."

THE HIEROGLYPHIC TAROT OF MADAME DULORA DE LA HAYE

G orgeously Art Nouveau, and with a soft, pastel palette, the *Tarot Hiéroglyphique Egyptién* is a world of its own, presented through only twenty-two cards, which function as both Major and Minor Arcanas. Although each of them is driven by an archetypal value that often finds an equivalent in the tarot, the symbolic message is made rather explicit and sometimes differs from Papus's *Tarot des Bohémiens*, which Dulora quotes as a divinatory model she aimed to simplify.[1] One of the best examples might be *Le Supplicié*—the Tortured Victim—echoing the Hanged Man, yet showing a rather Saint Sebastian–like figure grimacing under the pain of the many arrows piercing his chest. The divinatory meaning attached to this card and written at its top says it involves "Movement, Displacement, Trials, and Sacrifice."

Although it features the word "hieroglyphs" in its name, the deck itself doesn't share the Egyptian-revival sensibilities that were raging in the occult milieu at the time. No veiled Isis or ankh-brandishing deities here: This term should be read as "esoteric keys," illustrations that are more than the sum of their parts and need to be unpacked. Divided into several sections by an ornamental frame, each medallion features verbal or visual indications—adding symbolical layers of interpretations that the novice or seasoned reader would be invited to decipher, such as a letter from the Hebrew alphabet and its equivalent in the Roman one; a zodiac sign or planetary influence associated with the card. . . . right above the main image, a small glyph also connects each card to one of the suits of the Minor Arcanas, augmenting its significance, which varies depending on the adjacent cards.

What about the author, the elusive Madame Dulora de la Haye? It seems she conceptualized the deck within the last hours of the nineteenth century in Le Havre before moving to Paris, and we found no records of the artist who illustrated it. In her introductory text, Madame Dulora describes her effort to democratize cartomancy and tarot reading, creating a minimal deck with a synthetical system so novices would have to understand twenty-two cards and not seventy-eight.

Self-appointed "strongest somnambulist of her time" in one of her many newspaper ads,[2] Madame Dulora was identified as a scholar, a clairvoyant, and a publisher of esoteric books. Some colorful article[3] described how she used her mediumship gifts to help locals identify cadavers and recount stories behind their accidental death. Considered well-versed in everything occult, she seemed to have been a central figure of the Parisian Belle Epoque esoteric scene, where she organized a mystical poetry contest,[4] and authored lavish books in which esoterica and feminist sensibilities intertwined.

Temperance, "Temperance, Economy, Great Results, Profit, Pregnancy."

Thunder, "Disappointments, Accident, Money Loss."

The Moon, "Violent Passion, Hidden Enemies, Dangers, Rupture."

The Consultant, "Man of Authority, Protection, Assured Position."

The Cross, "Happy Relationship, Belief, Intelligence, Life, Health."

Death, "Changes, Inheritance, Death."

The Scale, "Law, Justice, Balance,
Trials, Contestation, Contrariety."

Strength, "Authority, Strength,
Courage, Regained Freedom."

Will, "Will Power, Determination,
Change of Perspective."

Sun, "Maternal Happiness,
Fecund Marriage."

Love, "Enlightenment of the Senses,
Physical Beauty, Involuntary Attraction,
Coquetish Woman."

Earth, "Balance, Harmony, Some
Good Results to Be Expected."

"Large Amount of Money"

"Fidelity, Attachment"

"Flattery"

"Pleasure, Entertainment"

"Hope"

"Reconciliation"

LA SIBYLLE DES SALONS

nce more, the colossal influence of Mademoiselle Lenormand finds echo in *La Sibylle des Salons*, a deck first published 1827, whose name evokes the rather romanesque idea that the Parisian Sibylle, still very much alive, was presumably flipping these very arcanas on the most select guéridons of the capital. If the fifty-two cards in the deck are signed by Mansion, it's been established since they were penned by the genius caricaturist, prince of floral whimsy, and unsettling characters J.J. Grandville, famous for his *Fleurs Animées* (The Flowers Personified), a bizarre-yet-charming compendium of botanicals in which flower women dressed with petals frolic in the wild surrounded by anthropomorphized insects. Each card presents a colorful central vignette, its equivalent in playing card value, and a small banner describing the fortune in one or two words. As you look at these cards, you'll get a slice of everyday Parisian life, with its outdated rituals and comical situations, an inquiry into fashion worn by the burgeoning bourgeoisie, and the ups and downs of an urban dynamic slowly moving toward an industrial revolution. Divided into four groups of ten cards with three additional court cards, each suit seems to have a sensibility of its own, often a stone's throw away from the cartomantic tradition it sometimes borrows from, offering insights and a practical tool box for dealing with nineteenth-century preoccupations.

The heart cards seemed to focus on romantic prospect, family life, friendship, and how the querent can get affected by others emotionally: Receiving a love letter, being stood up by your date in the Jardin du Luxembourg, the hopes of building a life in a rural mansion in the outskirts of the capital or in a fancy apartment on the rue du Louvres. And let's not forget, marriage!

The club suit reflects the hazards and mundane joys of everyday life once we are out of the private sphere, evoked by the heart suit, and more into social perceptions; financial gains and losses, promises kept, and loyalty, but also the fear of enemies or hypocrites. Men counting their piles of coins announced wealth, success, and recognition, victory, even. Yet beware, spite can surface, and villains wrapped in red capes are lurking, ready to provoke you!

The suit of diamonds suggests the realm of expression—what is said, the intention behind words, and the mode of expression. According to the Sibylle, language can heal a friendship and lead to reconciliation; chanting and dancing are an expression of joy. Alas, according to the Sibylle, language can be perverted and isn't always put to its best use. The card Gossip, showing two ladies having a hoot and gawking, informs the querent they might be the subject of malicious talks. Behind the ladies, an exotic bird in a cage, symbolizes the idea that private information might be repeated, exaggerated, parodied.

At last, the ominous spades classically showcase images foretelling dread, pestilence, and conflict. A little girl cries, a dog lying at her feet, realizing her canine companion's demise. The King of Spades, a "Man of Law" according to the card, looks disheveled and corrupted, gesticulating in his robe, presenting himself as a sneaky but heartless Saul Goodman character, without the sense of humor nor the salmon-colored suit found in *Breaking Bad*.

Although some might find the deck quaint and lacking in esoteric depth, it's been an incredibly popular one for more than a century now, republished quite a few times and inspiring many equivalents in Germany and Eastern Europe. Still in print today through Grimaud, untouched and showcasing the vivid illustrations by Grandville, the Sibylle is a little visual treasure of a deck, importing the golden age of parlor divination to our own tabletops. All of the cards in this section are from a Grimaud version of Sibylle published in 1890 and kept at the Bibliothèque nationale de France.

"Mean Woman"

"Gamblers"

"Gossip"

"Chagrin, Tears"

LEFT
"Death"

"A Widow"

"A Town house"

"A Man of Law"

"Marriage"

"Love"

"Thoughts"

"Letter"

"Thoughts"

"Journey"

DAS AUGE GOTTES:
THE EYE OF GOD

Published in Prague by M. Severa's Nachfolger and Anton Kratochvil around the 1860s, the Eye of God epitomizes the democratization of figurative fortune-telling games created and distributed throughout Central and Eastern Europe in the nineteenth century to allow a more popular crowd to playfully consult their fortune with the cards. Along with the Biedermeier and Zigeuner cards, published in Austria by Piatnik, or the German *Kipperkarten*, these decks were not meant to be read intuitively, but visually. Unlike the *Petit Lenormand* or its derivative, they didn't bare a playing card vignette, and no cartomantic knowledge was really necessary in order to decypher them. The reader would spread the cards in groups of six or nine in a rectangular grid and find significance by reading each card and combining them with the ones adjacent to it. The message of the reading, often literal, would capture the pictorial grammar of the ensemble. To help users, each card displayed one word that captured its meaning, in this case translated into Slovak, Hungarian, German, and Polish.

"Marriage"

"Enemy"

"Officer"

Rychtář.   Biro.
Richter.   Sędzia

"Judge"

Neštěstí.   Szerencsetlenség.
Unglück.   Nieszczeście.

"Misfortune"

Touha.   Vágy.
Sehnsucht. Tesknosc.

"Desire"

Věrnost.   Hüség.
Treue.   Wiernosc.

"Fidelity"

Peníze.   Pénz.
Geld.   Sicniadze.

"Wealth"

Milenka.   Kedves.
Geliebte.   Kochanka.

"Sweetheart"

Vdova.   Özvegy.
Willwe.   Wdowa.

"Widow"

Xenadálá radost. Véletlenöröm.
Unverhoffte Freude. Xiespodziana Wicha

"Unexpected Joy"

Dar.   Ajandek.
Geschenk.   Podarunek.

"Gift"

"Widower"

"Message"

"Luck"

"Troubles"

"Death"

"Child"

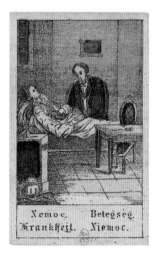

"Malady"

"Lover"

"Grief"

339

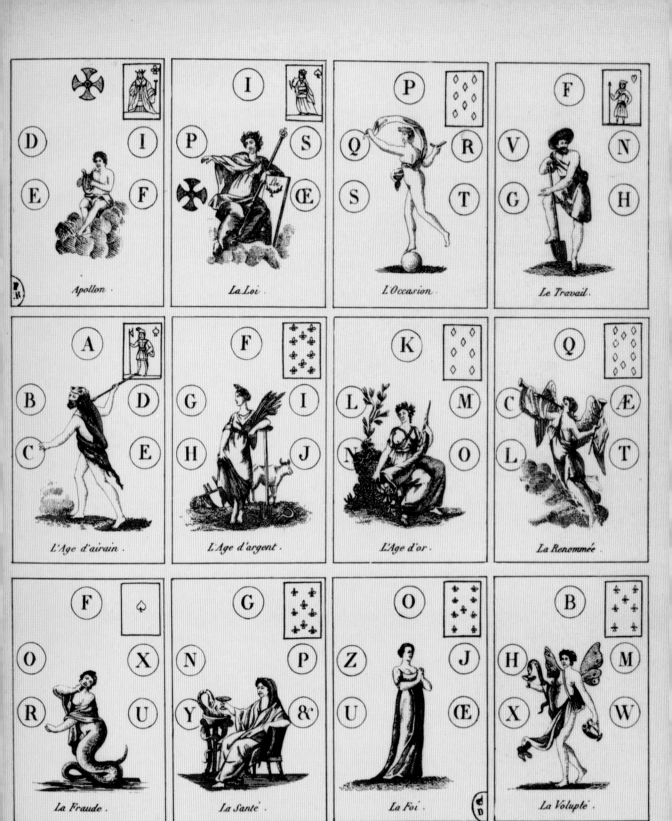

Apollon.

La Loi.

L'Occasion.

Le Travail.

L'Age d'airain.

L'Age d'argent.

L'Age d'or.

La Renommée.

La Fraude.

La Santé.

La Foi.

La Volupté.

JEU DE CARTES DE BONNE AVENTURE
gravé par Bouchard, rue Saint-Christophe, 7, à Paris (époque Restauration).

(BIBLIOTHÈQUE NATIONALE. — ESTAMPES.)

THE ARAB GAME,
OR ARITHMETIC

C an a deck be more mysterious than this one? One unique copy of the *Jeu Arabe* (Arabian Game) remains like a hidden treasure in an obscure corner of Paris's Bibliothèque nationale, seemingly nowhere to be found in other libraries or museum collections, nor on auction records of the past. Once in the collection of Georges Marteau, partner and co-director of the Grimaud card-making firm, this enigmatic set of thirty-two etched cards is as exquisite as it is puzzling. Because it's the sole example left of a mass-produced game and the information about it found in contemporaneous catalogues and books is sparse, this deck raises so many questions. Who was it designed for? Was it created for divination, and if not, was it used for such?

First, let's examine the facts: The *Jeu Arabe* was designed and engraved in Paris around 1820 by Bouchard, a now-forgotten engraver whose print shop was once located on the former Saint Christophe Street. In the cardboard box preserved at the Bibliothèque nationale, a small leaflet describes it as aimed "for children's delight," claiming it was manufactured for educational purposes, while the library label promotes it as an "arithmetic game." Originally the set contained five dice inscribed with letters of the roman alphabet, unfortunately now absent from the collection.

To play the *Jeu Arabe*, participants were given an equal number of cards. One after the other, they would roll the dice, revealing five letters corresponding to one circled on each card. The rest is a bit confusing—cards are lost or gained by participants, but at no point does spelling, creating words, or counting appear to be the goal, somehow minimizing the pedagogic intentions promised by our *jeu*.

In a strange twist of narrative, it appears in the second volume of Henry-René D'Allemagne's treatise on card playing labeled as a fortune-telling deck. D'Allemagne was a historian, archivist, and prolific writer who spent his entire life researching toys and games, and authoring the behemoth-sized *Cartes à Jouer du XIVᵉ au XXᵉ siècle* (Playing Cards from the 14th to the 20th Century), published in 1906. Although some of his theories have been disputed by modern scholars, his research is extraordinarily rich and laid the foundations for modern historical research on cards. Could he be wrong about the *Jeu Arabe*'s purpose? If D'Allemagne was an expert and authority on cards, can we trust him? After all, his oeuvre doesn't explore topics such as cartomancy or hermetic tarot.

OPPOSITE PAGE

"Fortune Telling Card Game, engraved by Bouchard, Saint Christophe Street, 7, Paris (Restoration Era)." Illustrated page from Henry-René d'Allemagne's exhaustive treatise on playing cards—*Les Cartes à Jouer du XIVᵉ au XXᵉ siècle*—published by Hachette in 1906. In two definitive volumes, the author discusses the history and origins of card playing, the different fabrication techniques used by card manufacturers all around Europe, as well as the social aspects of card playing.

As we examine the deck, we can wonder. The small playing card values, presented in the right-hand corner of each of them, are a visual device often used in esoteric playing cards to inform the reader of possible cartomantic connections. In the *Jeu Arabe*, these *Jeu de Piquet* markers surprisingly correspond to nineteenth-century cartomancy indications that at times match the allegorical figure on the card. For example, the traditionally bleak suit of spades presents Fraud, the Lady Beggars, Terror, the Law, Sloth, and Jupiter, all evoking hardship, disquieting behaviors, and the disciplined rulers who might punish them.

The iconographic choices are equally fascinating, introducing a smorgasbord of gods and values derived from several mythological strains of the antique world, but never as a comprehensive group. Some masculine gods, cardinal virtues, a Christian sin, the ages of humanity. . . . All of them are presented in gorgeous anthropomorphized allegorical figures, so profoundly evocative and surrounded by symbolic attributes whose variety feels like someone handpicked them to mimic a set of tarot Major Arcanas. One could easily be reminded of the Wheel of Fortune in the Providence card, the Popess in the Faith card or Mars as the Emperor. If the deck was created as a game, so was the tarot, and its use for fortune-telling corresponds to a vernacular practice, a repurposing of the cards. If history doesn't solve the mysteries surrounding the *Jeu Arabe*, it is undeniable that such a beautiful and inspiring work of art would become an important oracle deck if republished, and it's easy to imagine a battalion of readers and card lovers reviving the glory of this spectacular deck.

La Volupté.

"Voluptuousness"

La Vérité.

"Truth"

La Pudeur.

"Modesty"

La Santé.

"Health"

La Vertu.

"Virtue"

La Félicité.

"Felicity"

La Foi.

"Faith"

La Providence.

"Providence"

Apollon.

"Apollo"

Henri quatre.

"Henry the Fourth"

L'Age d'argent.

"The Silver Age"

Les Mendiantes.

"The Lady Beggars"

Jupiter.

"Jupiter"

La Loi.

"The Law"

La Paresse.

" Sloth"

La Terreur.

"Terror"

L'Occasion.

"Opportunity"

L'Age d'airain.

"The Bronze Age"

"Victory"

"Fraud"

"Mars"

"The Iron Age"

"Necessity"

"Bellonna"

"Fame"

"Friendship"

"Mercury: Change, Expertise,
Displacement, Business."

"Venus: Harmony, Love, Kink,
the Woman."

"Saturn: Old Age, Patience,
Pride, Good Counsel"

"Neptune: Calm,
Solitude, Constance."

LE TAROT ASTROLOGIQUE

isually stunning, the *Tarot Astrologique* is one of my favorite decks for its dark and mute colors tones and its incredible design. It was created by Henri Armengol, more famous for his movie posters and serial novel covers than this one dive into the esoteric.[1] The deck was seemingly introduced by card maker Grimaud in 1927, under the conceptual direction of Georges Muchery, a French astrologer with a pretty romanesque life. One of the rare images left for us to put a face on this name is an elegant Harcourt portrait, showing Muchery as a rather stoic, pursed-lipped, dignified, silver-haired man, probably taken in around the 1960s. Born in 1898,[2] Muchery was apparently initiated into astrology through his mathematics teacher and developed a great curiosity and talent for the subject, as well as chiromancy, for which he became a household name, reading for celebrities and scientists alike—Charles Richet, Édouard Branly, the poetess Colette, American actor Douglas Fairbanks, and even Musidora, the vampiress Irma Vep in Louis Feuillade's *Les Vampires*. In 1927, after miraculously escaping death several times during the First World War, and having gained a reputation as a palm reader and a journalist, he created his own publishing house, Les Éditions du Chariot, and released several esoteric book including *La Synthèse Du Tarot* (The Synthesis Of The Tarot), *Tarot Astrologique* (Astrological Tarot), *Traité d'Astromancie* (Treatise on Astromancy), which lead to this deck.

Unique in its composition, the *Tarot Astrologique* is composed of a set of twelve Major Arcanas representing the twelve planets, split diagonally to show their symbolic signs and their personifications in a Roman statuary style. The Minor Arcanas depict the zodiac signs and present a three-card set for twelve of each of them, following the decanates divisions. If the first card illustrates the sign in a conventional fashion, the two others can stun by their originality, sometimes echoing directly some mythological episode. For example, the Pisces card shows the traditional pair of fish twirling with one another, a swan gliding on water on the 10 degree, and a swampy green man reminiscent of the lakeside Colossus of Rhodes statue of Villa Di Pratolino on the 20 degree. A little white frame in the bottom of each gives planetary values and possible elemental influences, offering even more indication to the reader. At last, three cards correspond to the Ascendant and Ascending/Descending lunar nodes and the Part of Fortune.

The slim pamphlet included in this set is a short-yet-fascinating read. Muchery of course gives some guidelines and keywords to help the novice navigate the peculiar system he invented, yet urges them not to try to memorize these simplistic indications but read with their intuitive flow. The small white book offers several spreads for beginners, a twelve-card wheel, sharing some similarities with the Waite's Celtic Cross, and a seven-cards one to prepare the week ahead. The most intriguing paragraphs are the indications Muchery carefully gives on the appropriate ritual to read his tarot cards in the most auspicious condition. To partake in a *Tarot Astrologique* reading, the reader must orient themself toward the north, wear comfortable, loose clothing, as Muchery explains, "The one who divines can't suffer from any moral or physical discomfort"—while the consultant has to sit facing south. The reader then needs to grab the querent's hands, look at their third eye location, and mentally pronounce these words: "I wish you well and I'll hope you'll leave this place happy and satisfied" for about thirty seconds. Cards are then shuffled by the reader and cut by the querent. Through this well-scripted how-to, we discover that these cards were meant to be read in a professional context and not for oneself. The best reader to read such a deck should be well-versed in astrology and find their way intuitively in the symbolic gravitas of Armengol's virtuoso drawings.

"Ten Taurus: Stop, Jealousy, Transformation."

"Cancer: Inconsistency, Hidden Facts, Chance, the Home."

"Twenty Cancer: Support, Brightening, Violence."

"Twenty Leo: Difficulties, Troubles, Poisoning."

"Virgo: Sterility, Solitude, Reflection, Malady."

"Twenty Virgo: Chance in Love, Beautiful Marriage."

"Ten Libra: Success, Intelligence, Elevation."

"Ten Scorpion: Health, Cunning, End, Renewal."

"Aquarius: Goodness, Fidelity, Reason, Friendship."

"Twenty Pisces: Inercy, Self-Confidence, Continuity."

"Ascending Lunar Node: Luck, Wealth."
"Descending Lunar Node: Torments, Obstacles."

"Part of Fortune: Change, Material Increase."

ADÈLE
MOREAU

CHIROMANCIE

PARIS
5 RUE TOURNON

THE GREAT GAME
OF THE HAND

Adele Moreau was a chiromancer who once operated from the same building as another famous palm reader, "the immortal Madame Lenormand."[1] In her office on rue Tournon she would receive customers daily, but she read hand lines remotely through the newly invented medium of photographs and also allowed people to mail her casts of their palms in plaster. Although not as famous as her cartomancer counterpart, she left us an important palmistry classic, *L'Avenir dévoilé. Chiromancie nouvelle. Études des deux mains* (The Future Unveiled. New Chiromancy. A Study of Both Hands), written in 1869, in which, along with other palm readers such as M. Des Barolles, she helped pioneer the revolutionary idea of examining both hands at once.

Coinciding with the development of now considered questionable disciplines such as physiognomy and phrenology, Moreau's ambition was to elevate palmistry, taking it out of the fairground and legitimizing her practice as a scientific one.[2] Two hands, because the folds, lines, and loops are different on each of them, and according to Moreau, these could determine so much about the temperament, the character of a person, as well as their destiny.

In the late nineteenth century, the famed card maker Grimaud developed the *Grand Jeu de la Main*, inspired by the palm reading system created by Moreau. Each card features a hand whose characteristics differ according to the planet that they are associated with. Seven planets, seven suits, all counting eight cards. All of them are matched with a playing card to add cartomantic significance to the reading and bear some texts, symbols, and written descriptions correlating to the hand, the physical and psychological characteristics of the person associated with it, and other divinatory elements that can be used by the reader.

OPPOSITE PAGE

Portrait of Adèle Moreau, Frontpiece
of her book *L'Avenir dévoilé. Chiromancie
nouvelle. Études des deux mains.*

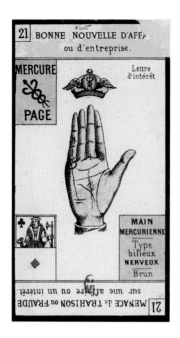

Ten of Mercury: "Mercurial Hand, Bilious type. Nervous. Color Brown color. Success in Business and at Work. Reversed: Small Money Loss on a Deal."

Page of Mercury: "Mercurial Hand, Bilious type. Nervous. Brown color. Good News in Business and at Work. Reversed: Threats of treason or Fraud on a Deal or Money Interests."

Eight of Jupiter: "Jupiterian Hand, Bilious-Sanguine type. Dark Blond color. Visit of a Man of Law. Reversed: Unsuccessful Endeavors with a Man of Law."

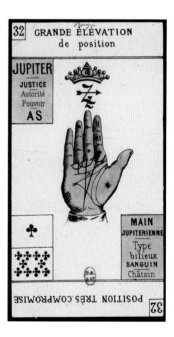

Typical mercurial hand: "Long hand, long and smooth fingers. Closed palm, slightly hard. The Auricular or small finger is the finger of Mercury, often pointy even if the others are rounded. Long thumb, with two equal sections. Accentuated protrusion on the small finger. Queen of Mercury: "Mercurial Hand, Bilious type. Nervous. Brown color. Intelligent and skillful brown-haired woman. Business-oriented.
Reversed: A clever and greedy woman. Menace of being cheated by a self-interested woman."

Ace of Jupiter: "Jupiterian Hand, Bilious-Sanguine type. Dark Blond color. Great Improvement in Situation. Reversed: Very Compromising Position."

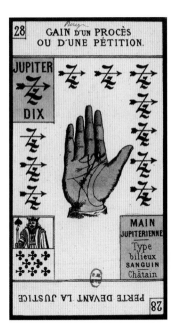

Ten of Jupiter: "Jupiterian Hand, Bilious-Sanguine type. Dark Blond. Victorious in a Trial or a Petition. Reversed: Loss During a Trial."

Nine of Venus: "Venusian Hand, Nervous-Lymphatic type. Blond and Brown color. Small romantic satisfaction. Reversed: Doubt–Worry–Jealousy."

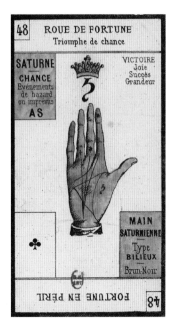

Ace of Saturn: "Saturnean Hand, Bilious type. Brown, Black color. Wheel of Fortune, Triumph in Luck. Reversed: Perilous Luck."

Seven of Venus: "Venusian Hand, Nervous-Lymphatic type. Blond and Brown color. Young Blonde Girl, Soft and Loving. Reversed: Indifference–Standoffish."

Eight of Saturn: "Saturnean Hand, Bilious type. Brown, Black color. Luck either comes or comes back. Reversed: Annoyance and setbacks in a financial deal."

Nine of Sun: "Apollonian or Solar Hand, Harmonious and Artistic type. Blond, Gold color. Wealth Through a Marriage or through the help of a friend. Reversed: Indoor Times."

THE ANTIQUE DESTINY DECK

 riginally published by Maurin around the 1860s, the *Jeu du Destin Antique* presented here is a colored lithographed version created by Grimaud between 1890 and 1910. The Antique Destiny is still in circulation as a collectible today, thanks to two facsimiles published by Éditions Dusserre and Piatnik toward the end of the twentieth century. Its beguiling design, created by an artist unknown to us, still captures the imagination of the contemporary readers longing to time travel to the golden age of parlor divination. At the time, one might imagine that such a deck, manufactured industrially by one of the largest French *maître cartier* (card maker), the *Destin Antique* would be presumably easily available, finding its place in books and stationery stores. Yet, this deck isn't a novelty set. None of these illustrations shares the exaggerated (and often charming) qualities of a popular cartomancy game, created for a more mainstream audience, and in which turnkey auguries would sometimes be featured directly on the cards. Instead, each of the *Destin Antique* thirty-two arcanas presents a cryptic central image with a subtle narrative or psychological dynamic to be interpreted by the reader.

Enclosed in the volutes of a golden baroque frame, this image is topped by two insets: a *Jeu de Piquet* card on the left as well as, on the right hand side, a small vignette depicting either a deity from the Roman pantheon, a zodiacal value, or a figure that some have associated with traditional tarot archetypes. This idiosyncratic mélange, mingling historical figures in period costumes, picturesque scenes from different eras, astrology and cartomancy, constitutes such a unique system, if hardly documented,[1] allows for such depth of interpretation in its practice. The following visual descriptions might offer some help and suggest to our readers some keys of interpretations, but are by no means the one originally suggested as the deck's creation. Their characteristic associations are drawn from the Éditions Dusserre booklet published in 1991,[2] which offers to our knowledge the most concise set of information around the *Destin Antique*.

OPPOSITE PAGE

Seven of Spades—The Squire.
A malicious man is surrounded by a group
of women who seem under his spell.

Queen of Hearts—Taurus.
On a stone terrace, Queen Hildegarde stands, her left hand on her collar, the other one pointing at the ground. Behind her, the entrance of a French garden, delimited by an iron fence, on which wild bushes of red roses grow wild.

Knave of Hearts—Gemini.
Bearing a hatchet, the palatine knight Roland de Roncevaux poses with his legendary sword Durendal in the other hand. The rocky background evokes the Pyrenees mountains in which he meet his death fighting against the Basques.

Ace of Hearts—Cupid.
A young man cradles his *bien aime* with one arm as they both repose, leaning on a fence. Above them, the extremity of a tree curves toward them, as if to offer a bit of shade or protection.

Seven of Hearts—The Mystic.
Surprised by a sound, a young traveler resting on a boulder turns his body in a gesture of vigilance.

Nine of Hearts—Juno.
Twisting his body to find momentum, a farmer sows his field, preparing it for the next season.

Ten of Hearts—Jupiter.
Surrounded by desolation, a contemplative philosopher sits, a scroll unfolding from his hands toward the ground.

King of Clubs—Scorpio.
Coiffed with a Phrygian helmet, Alexander the Great proudly stands with his martial attribute, a shield and a spire.

Queen of Clubs—Leo.
Persian Queen Roxanne and her feathery crown, appearing coy and gentle, one of her hands timidly concealed behind her back.

Knave of Clubs—Virgo.
The impetuous Perdicas, hiding a hand behind his back, his gaze lost in a vision.

Seven of Clubs—The Hermit.
A man gently sculls away in a small boat on a quiet lagoon. A woman, elegantly dressed, holds a red rose in her hand. Behind her sits a basket filled with apples and pears, while a white drape seems to escape the boat, partially dipping in the water.

Eight of Clubs—The Angel.
Having freshly landed, a sailor sits as if he were waiting for something or someone, one hand resting on his heart.

Nine of Clubs—Venus.
In a garden filled with flower bushes, a young peasant woman has been gifted a rose by a court gentleman, who serenades her.

MODERN
TAROT

The Hermit

The Lovers

The Wheel of Fortune

The World

THE BRADY TAROT

"Where Do We Come From? What Are We? Where Are We Going?" This set of interrogations, which is the title of one of my favorite Gauguin paintings, often lingers in my head when I shuffle Emi Brady's extraordinary tarot deck. Inspired by the fauna, the flora, and the geology of North America, the Brady Tarot addresses the trifold question with a simple answer: the wild matrix of the land. The land that bares us, defines us, and will swallow us again once our transitory state comes to an end, dividing our body cells to feed its other protégés. A land that we lost touch with, incapable of understanding the subtlety of its language or its rhythm. A land that I acclimated to so recently myself, after immigrating to the United States around 2011. A land that I slowly learned to comprehend through this tarot's incredible depth. Amid the vast collection of animal-centric packs of cards, Emi's deck is one of a kind, because her visions are at the intersections of the natural sciences and the esoteric. In the Brady Tarot, nature is not anthropomorphized nor mystified; it simply is, powerful in its violent and poetic ways, its singular inner life, in its lush beauty and brutal honesty.

I met Emi many years ago in New York and have very fond memories of a tour she gave me of her campus at Pratt Institute, where she studied printmaking. She showed me around the incredible buildings, telling me stories, pointing at artworks, and introducing me to the famous Pratt cats, all of whom she seemed to have tamed over the years. I marveled at her vast erudition in anything zoological or touching on animal behavior, especially birds, which she knew so well; she was capable of recognizing many aviary songs and feathers. She grew up in Tennessee and spent much time alone in the woods, enjoying the spectacle of the natural world for herself, absorbing that language that seemed so foreign to me.

As we reconnected to talk about her tarot deck, she told me how she left for Colorado and almost abandoned her artistic ambitions to pursue medical ones when her path led her to study to become an ultrasound technician. She described with much glee the fascination of being able to use a device to see what hides in people's bodies. Unfortunately, yet fortunately for us, life decided otherwise. Through the impulse of a tarot reading she gave herself, she rekindled an idea she had held for many years of creating her own set of cards. Once consulted, the tarot's message was very simple. She should not fear deep-diving into her creative endeavors; the medical field wasn't her place yet, but being an artist was. Still on the fence about her big jump, she then had two auspicious and noisy visitations from birds—a great horned owl and two red-tailed hawks—who awkwardly perched in her urban setting as if to indicate that if they were convinced she should be too.

Two years later, she had meticulously carved and hand-colored seventy-nine linocut prints, giving the Brady Tarot the mastered rawness of the card decks of the past. Her deck is a true treasure, both as an absolute artistic achievement and for the immense wealth of knowledge she incorporated into each drawing. Like an hagiographer of a sanctified biodiversity, Emi presents nature in its most intimate aspect, without distortion, with a sense of observation translated in her unique graphic style, joyful and incisive. Predators and their feasts, the secret pacts between species, the sense of humor of otters, mountains goats questing for psychoactive lichens, the fierce love rites of cranes . . . The deck is to be appreciated like you'd explore nature itself, with an open and curious attitude, an invitation to quiet one's mind in order to absorb and connect to each of the stories it contains. Emi also incorporated several indigenous stories, celebrating the wisdom and uninterrupted dialogue that Native Americans keep with the land we occupy. To forward that effort, part of the proceeds of each deck goes toward several associations committed to protecting indigenous heritage and natural preservation. Her project, more than just illustrating a centuries-old divination tool, is to offer a device that allows us to see what hides within our own depths and understand which role and position we have to play in the collective and how we can mend our relationship to the most sacred aspects of the land.

The Hierophant

Death

1 of Feathers

1 of Roots

1 of Arrow

6 of Horns

THE DUST II ONYX

Before elaborating the Dust II Onyx Tarot deck, Courtney Alexander found herself at a crossroad, a sensitive point in which her creation and her spirituality almost overlapped, but not quite. While going to art school to pursue visual marketing, she lived through a personal revelation that she describes as a sort of auto-apocalypse, in which she was living the path of a designer to become an artist. Her practice, she realized, the fruit of her creations, allowed her to connect to the depth of who she was. Slowly coming to terms with the idea that art could be used as a means for self-expression, Courtney found in image making a profound healing tool, enabling her to articulate and manifest "the way she moved through the world," mending back together parts of herself that had been fragmented for years by society's expectations.

Self-described as "Black, fat, queer, and divine," Courtney told me birthing these images, sculptures, and collages enabled her to define her own space, hear her own voice, and sort out what was hers and what was projected onto her. Caught in this introspective process, she started to use oracle cards and tarot intuitively, only to confront the fact that none of these tools were designed with her in mind. The lack of racial diversity in the iconography of tarot decks wasn't a new topic, so few of them featured Black bodies, and the number of sets developed by people of color was even smaller. "The creators are just as important as the creations," she told me. "You cannot mistake the energy of someone and their lived experience, their heritage, bringing forth the nuances that they carry as a culture."

Standing above this void, Courtney designed, if not to say "received," the Dust II Onyx Tarot deck, counteracting the lack of representation in the realm of divination cards, but most importantly, giving to the world a body of work that allows us to contemplate the many meanings of Blackness. Mostly composed of "black on black" portraits created from collage, mixed medias, and painted images, the Dust II Onyx is a dark feast, coagulating the shattered pieces of the African Diaspora, its cultural wealth, and its vivid spiritual legacy. Brought back to a form of opulence and wholeness, the deck mirrors an Afrocentric culture thriving in its complexity, anchoring its roots deeply into the timelessness of our world. The eyes of Nicki Minaj, the sacred visions of Elegba, or the monolithic beauty of Sande masks—Courtney's tarot levels Black culture up in one very high vibration, without novelty, but with a profound sense of respect for what she received from "otherworldly ancestors." An absolute masterpiece, the Dust II Onyx is exactly why this new era of tarot is fascinating to me. Transcending the divination practice, it is an invitation to contemplate what our identities are made of, built upon, and fed with and acknowledge if this is what we choose. And although I'm not a time traveler myself, I sincerely believe that a century from now, the Dust II Onyx will have forged its own tradition, much like the Rider-Waite-Smith Taro did.

KAHN & SELESNICK

ince 2017, Nicholas Kahn and Richard Selesnick, the pluridisciplinary artistic duo famous for their fictional photography and installation work, have created two divination tarot decks—the exquisitely illustrated Carnival of the End of the World Tarot and its photographic cousin, the Tarot of the Drowning World. In the manner of their other work, these impeccable packs of cards weave together apocalyptic moods and forgotten magical folklore with naturalist lyricism and an ecological subtext allegorically presenting the dystopian impact of climate change. Playful, satirical, and slightly morbid, Kahn & Selesnick's body of work presents a tension between past, present, and future, unfolding a narrative that is hard to pinpoint in time and space. All these ingredients serve as a backdrop for both decks, which humorously explore the absurdity of self-inflicted end times.

What is the meaning of reading cards during the age of the Anthropocene? What fate do we build for ourselves as we destroy the planet? Both decks attempt to articulate visual answers to these dramatic questions in their own poetic ways, accompanied by a strange ballet of archetypal figures, inspiring us to reclaim agency on the ecological situation when the idea of a "tomorrow" seems threatened. Inspired by the duo's fascination with historical tarots, the two tarot decks are also populated with cameos from their own artistic influences, from the contemplative attitudes of Caspar David Friedrich's subjects to the composite portrait of Giuseppe Arcimboldo. The maximalist beauty of these cards has won the hearts of card lovers and divination enthusiasts alike, who have found an incredible symbolic depth in their unique revisitation of iconography.

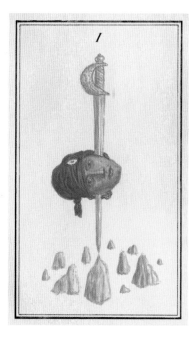

Queen of Pentacles

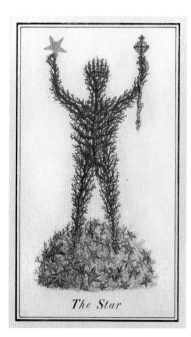

The Star

II

VII

Knave of Cups

Death

The Devil

The Empress

The Fool

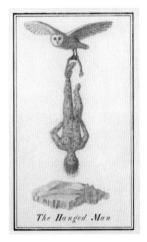

The Hanged Man

The Hierophant

High Priestess

Justice

King of Pentacles

The Moon

II

Strength

V

Queen of Swords

Temperance

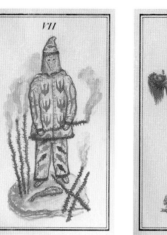

VII

IX

V

Deniers · II

Coupes · IV

Coupes · VIII

Bâtons · VIII

Épées · IX

La Roue de Fortune · X

Tempérance   XIV

La Maison Dieu   XVI

Deniers   VIII

Coupes   Valet

La Force   XI

Le Perdu   XII

Épées   Cavalier

Bâtons   Cavalier

GHETTO TAROT

I
n 2008, Belgian artist Alice Smeets won the prestigious Unicef photography prize for an image she captured in Haiti the year before. A little girl from Cité Soleil, one of most impoverished areas of Port-au-Prince, has just crossed a large puddle filled with detritus, in bare feet, carefully holding up her immaculate dress. She powers through the dirt to reach her destination under the unfazed gaze of two pigs feeding off the garbage in the background. The fierceness and determination of this six-year-old is palpable, moving. Discovering the complexity of Haiti's life beyond the prejudices of poverty, including the great spiritual wealth it relies on, might be one of the many things that inspired Alice to return again and again to the Caribbean island. She later settled in the capital for two years to participate in several community projects, which primarily involved teaching photography to the aspiring local youth.

Alice, who learned tarot intuitively, had the idea of creating a photographic version of the deck she used, the Rider-Waite-Smith, but the timing never felt right. After meeting the artistic collective Atis Rezistans, which operated from the Grand Rue, the project was sparked as a collaboration. Many members of the collective were sculptors, primarily working with recycled material they found around them in the ghetto. They reclaimed the term "ghetto" for themselves, freeing it from its pejorative aspects. Atis Rezistans invites artists to create a sense of community and became an important part of the local cultural life. It organizes the Ghetto Biennale every other year, a spectacle in which creative inspirations are experienced firsthand. As Alice explains: "They immediately jumped on board to create the Ghetto Tarot deck together. Being very spiritual themselves, and working a lot with voodoo symbolism, they immediately understood the spirits of the cards."

The Ghetto Tarot is the perfect jewel created from this collaboration, showcasing Haiti's most precarious areas as a territory for the extraordinary invention of these artists, who harvest from chaos the materia prima of their art. Alice brought Pamela Coleman Smith's vision to life by choosing the prototype of the image; they brought the DIY spirit and creativity, posing as actors in the evocative *tableau vivant* and also creating the props and costumes for each card. Casseus Claudel, disguised as Justice; Andre Eugène, founder of the collective, was portrayed as Death with one of his disquieting sculptures; Herad Blondine posed as the Queen of Wands; Racine Polycarpes as the Magician; Nathalie Amboise depicted the Star; Mario Halito Denis created some of the black silhouettes elements visible in the Moon or Queen of Wands card; and Wesner Bazil, Claudy Chamblin, Jean Robert Palanquet, and more Atis Rezistans members contributed to the Ghetto Tarot!

Proceeds from the sale of this deck are shared equally between the collaborators, and each artist's success provides more opportunities to support the arts and creations in the ghettos of Port-au-Prince. You can support this project by buying the deck via ghettotarot.com.

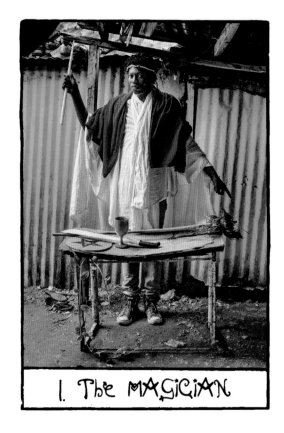

I. The MAGICIAN

II. The High Priestess

III. The EMPRESS

VII. The CHARIOT

XIII DEATH

PAVLOV'S TAROT

he bearded Angel of Temperance pours water from a jar into another with a gregarious smile. Saint Sebastian hangs in reverse from a tree; his body, punctured by arrows, is partially hidden by a shroud. A marble-eyed sibyl, lost in volutes of intoxicating vapors, opens her veil to visions of infinity. In Fyodor Pavlov's Tarot, Hermes invites Eros, and the allegorical characters are seen in the flesh, sensuously incarnated, radiant of humanity, in audacious and serpentine lines so characteristic of his work. It's no surprise that, with such incredible talent and skills, Fyodor's deck, avidly anticipated, blew the roof off its own Kickstarter campaign a handful of hours after its launch. Images such as the Lovers card, shared over and over online, have expanded the symbolic lexicon of the tarot.

Born in Moscow, Fyodor arrived in the United States at the age of thirteen and has since found a home in Washington Heights, where he emerged as a prolific artist, his polymorphic genius allowing him to create illustrations, portraits, and comics. For several years, Fyodor has been keenly chronicling the glorious underworld of the burlesque scene and more recently started apprenticing as a tattoo artist. Oscillating between pre-Raphaelite melancholia and the grandeur of a fin de siècle decadent movement, Pavlov's work is the work of an esthete, always more than the sum of its parts. It took him four years to draw, one by one, in black ink and watercolor, seventy-eight remarkable reimaginations of Pamela Coleman Smith's legacy. A cornucopia of graces, the Pavlov deck feels like an epic in which heroes and splendid figures bask in the generosity of nature itself. More than just being an exquisite work of art, its author, Fyodor Pavlov, who identifies as a trans, bisexual man, challenges the canonical idea of gendered archetypes and their visual representations in the tarot. Historically, tarot calcified into an esoteric system toward the end of the nineteenth century, and so did the masculine/feminine symbolic polarities it presented. Images in earlier decks were not always self-evident, depicting allegorical and often indeterminate characters. Traditionally, if the Devil card bore all sexual attributes, characters like the Star or the World have often been historically represented in far more androgynous fashion.[1]

By giving a beard to the traditionally asexual Temperance angel or choosing to interpret Adam and Eve as a trans duet, alchemically binded in a renewed Garden of Eden for his Lovers card, the figures populating Pavlov's deck dissolve the traditional masculine/feminine binaries contained in the tarot system. Playfully twisting and turning all previous cultural stereotypes about gender, race, and age, Pavlov bends the liminal toward the beautiful, allowing the voluptuous feminine to express and take space, the masculine to be vulnerable, the young to be wise, the old to be celebrated.

By creating such a beautiful tarot deck, Pavlov gives the card-reading community a great gift, a deck celebrating queerness as part of a universal human experience in which the human body in its diversity is shown as an esoteric and poetic vessel longing for wholeness.

· the fool ·

· the high priestess ·

· death ·

· the emperor ·

· the hierophant ·

· the hermit ·

· the chariot ·

· wheel of fortune ·

43 · TECHNETIUM · Tc

UUSI

usi—four letters bundled up together to form what sounds like a magical spell. A term meaning "new" in Finnish and used as a moniker for artist duet Linnea Gits and Peter Dunham. Uusi, a word akin to their work: curiously foreign yet somehow intriguing both visually minimal and elegant.

Created in 2010, Uusi Studio produced several refined poker decks through Kickstarter before falling down into a divination card rabbit hole. This venture blessed us with the stunning Pagan Otherworlds Tarot, the Eros Tarot, Supra, and the Materia Prima, all patiently imagined in the artists' home, lost in the forest of northern Michigan's Upper Peninsula. "Life is worth the meaningful effort, and its reward is one of discovery," says a poetic line in their biography. Each set of cards they create is an invitation to visual and symbolical experimentation, a concept at play at the core of their work, in which traditional craftsmanship and innovative imagery find a perfect balance. Gits and Dunham have an inspired eye, achieving a reconciliation of highbrow and lowbrow, instilling noblesse into simplicity, and, in my opinion, achieving the impossible task of fomenting playfulness without an ounce of childishness.

Whether they are for play, contemplation, or divination, each pack of cards has an energy of its own, imbued with a singular esthetic sensibility that inspired so many readers and proceeded to establish them as cult creators in the exigent world of card enthusiasts. For me, Uusi elegantly demonstrates that visual sophistication can be accessible without having to be dogmatic or elitist. If beauty ignites intuition, their contribution to the modern history of divination cards is inestimable.

THE PAGAN
OTHERWORLDS TAROT

Here is a story: In the past, I used to give tarot classes in my little Brooklyn apartment, and one evening, a student that I had never met before brought this deck for us to see, carefully unwrapping his treasure cards from an indigo silk scarf as if they were made out of crystal. Once spread on the table, it took me a second to realize it was a contemporary work. The visual bliss of this Northern Master color palette turned my head enough that I wrongfully believed these were from another century. Created in 2016 from a series of oil paintings by Linnea Gits, the Pagan Otherworlds cards combine inspirations echoing the gravitas of Hieronymus Bosch's characters, or the quiet exaltation of nature of a William Morris drawing. Even though the deck predominantly kept the traditional structure of the tarot and often visually pays tribute to the work of Pamela Coleman Smith, it has been celebrated for the originality of its art while respecting tarot's traditional symbolism and narrative. The deck includes an extra Major Arcana named the Seeker, emulating the famous illustration from Camille Flammarion's 1888 *Atmosphere: Popular Meteorology* and showing a man puncturing the limits of his world to reach the Empyrean heavens. The deck also features five Lunar cards showing the silvery satellite in its different phases, a set that cartomancers seem to have adopted as indicators of timing as well as waxing/waning flows in the narrative impacting their reading.

The Devil

The Emperor

The High Priestess

Knight of Pentacles

King of Wands

The Materia Prima: An Expression of Matter

"In nature, nothing is lost, nothing is created, everything transforms,"[1] a familiar motto often attributed to eighteenth-century scientist Antoine-Philippe Lavoisier, the father of chemistry, serves as a perfect introduction for Uusi's Materia Prima. This one-of-a-kind deck proposed an esoteric reading of the periodic table, in which each chemical element has been anthropomorphized, psychologized, adorned with symbolic attributes. The black, white, and gold orbs and primordial shapes in which they float allow the cards to connect to one another like the archaic puzzle of nature, in which the basic components interlock to form our body, the land we walk on, the air we breathe, the stars shining above us. To me, the Materia Prima is an alchemical device that allows us to meditate on microcosmic realities and encounter the hidden soul of matter itself.

10 · NEON · Ne

7 · NITROGEN · N

8 · OXYGEN · O

15 · PHOSPHORUS · P

16 · SULFUR · S

47 · SILVER · Ag

THE EROS TAROT, THE GARDEN OF LOVE

Ludo Venerae: Impossible not to fall in love with the saucy glory of this Eros deck, a titillating Marseille-style set created by Uusi in 2017. Don't be fooled by the classic looks of the pip cards: court cards and their trionfi consorts are caught indulging in the Garden of Love. Lips and nipples vibrate in unison in carmine tones. In Eros's land, turgid swords are tightly held in hands. Maenads cavort in the nude waiting for the last judgment. Flocks of pudgy cherubs are seen blowing in trumpets and over the fluid garments of queens, revealing their sensuous forms drawn by a single calligraphed line. Take me there; this place, this deck, is simply irresistible.

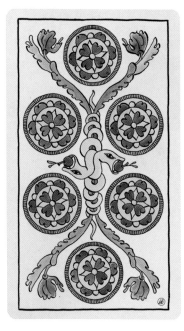

IX

The Hermit

XI

Justice

Knight of Wands

VI

The Lovers

King of Wands

I

The Magician

NOTES

THE FOOL

1. Max Harris, *Sacred Folly: A New History of the Feast of Fool* (Ithaca, NY: Cornell University Press, 2011).

2. The Crocodile trope seems to emerge from Paul Christian's 1870 book *History and Practice of Magic*. In his chapter "The Mysteries of the Pyramids," Christian describes twenty-two Arcana allegedly created by the Egyptians to conceal the "Science of the Will." Although not illustrated, the description of Arcanum 0, called the Crocodile, will serve as a base for Falconnier's *XXII Lames Hermetiques du Tarot Divinatoire*'s Atheist card, which seems to be the earliest one.

3. Oswald Wirth, *Tarot of the Magicians: The Occult Symbols of the Major Arcanas that Inspired Modern Tarot* (Newburyport, MA: Weiser Books, 2012), 149.

4. Paul Foster Case, "The Fool," *The Tarot: A Key to the Wisdom of the Ages* (New York: Penguin, 2006), 31.

THE POPESS AND THE HIGH PRIESTESS

1. Tariro Mzezewa, "Rihanna Reigns with Pope-Inspired Dress at Met Gala," *New York Times*, May 7, 2018.

2. Arthur Edward Waite, *The Pictorial Key to the Tarot*, 1910 (U.S. Games System Inc., republished in 1995), 79.

3. Waite, *The Pictorial Key to the Tarot*, 79.

4. Gertrude Moackley, *The Tarot Cards Painted by Bonifacio Bembo* (New York Public Library, 1966).

5. Sherryl E. Smith, *Is the Visconti-Sforza Popess a Heretic?*, tarot-heritage.com, November 18, 2020.

6. Naomi Ozaniec, *The Watkins Tarot Handbook: The Practical System of Self-Discovery* (New York: Sterling Publishing Company, Inc., 2005), 174.

THE EMPRESS

1. Translation of the second epigram of Michael Maier's *Atalanta Fugens* by Adam Mclean, alchemywebsite.com.

2. Instagram Post, May 31, 2019, @marykgreer

3. Lynn R. LiDonnici, "The Images of Artemis Ephesia and Greco-Roman Worship: A Reconsideration" *The Harvard Theological Review* 85, no. 4 (Oct. 1992): 393.

THE EMPEROR

1. Alejandro Jodorosky and Marianne Costa, *The Way of Tarot, The Spiritual Teacher in the Cards* (Rochester, VT: Destiny Books, 2004), 145.

2. In his *Encyclopedia of Tarot*, Stuart Kaplan postulated that the cards might have been created in Venice. *Encyclopedia of Tarot, Volume I*, U.S. Games Systems, 1978.

3. *Le Tarot des Bohemiens, Le Plus Ancien Livre Du Monde, À L'Usage Exclusif des Initiés*, Papus, 1911, Hector et Henri Durville, Paris, p.10.

4. *Tarot of the Magicians*, 71.

THE POPE – THE HEIROPHANT

1. Antoine Court de Gébelin, "The Vth represents the chief of Hierophants, or the Great Priest," *Le Monde Primitif (. . .)* (Paris, 1773–82), translation by the author, 370.

2. S.L. McGregor Mathers, *The Tarot: A Short Treatise on Reading Cards* (Weiser Books: first published in 1888, republished in 1993), 15.

THE HANGED MAN

1. Historically, Pietro della Vigna is not believed to have hanged himself; it is more likely that he succumbed from torture. Yet the rumors persisted that he had commited suicide, adding to the whiff of dishonor upon his name.

2. Eliphas Levi, *Dogme et Rituel de la Haute Magie*, 1856 (Unicursal: 2018), 523.

THE DEVIL

1. Levi, *Dogme et Rituel de la Haute Magie*, 422.

2. Paul Huson, *Mystical Origins of the Tarot* (Rochester, VT: Destiny Books, 2004), 125.

THE MINOR ARCANA

1. Rachel Pollack, *78 Degrees to Wisdom, Part II: Minor Arcana and Readings* (The Aquarian Press, 1983), 12.

ETTEILLA

1. Ronald Decker, Thierry Depaulis, and Michael Dummett, *A Wicked Pack of Cards: The Origins of the Occult Tarot* (Duckworth, 2002), 77.

2. Etteilla, *Manière de se récréer avec le jeu de cartes nommées tarots* (Amsterdam : BNF, 1783), 9.

3. Eliphas Levi, as well as Jean Baptiste Millet-Saint-Pierre in the little biography he dedicated to Etteilla, make notes that more or less attest to the fact that this text was tainted by wild grammar and orthography.

4. Etteilla, *Manière de se récréer avec le jeu de cartes nommées tarots* (Amsterdam : BNF, 1783), 7.

5. Etteilla, *Manière de se récréer*, 9.

6. The term *blades* is still used in French to this day to refer to tarot cards.

7. Decker, *A Wicked Pack of Cards*, 90.

MADEMOISELLE LENORMAND

1. Dicta Dimitriadis, *Voyante de Louis XVI à Louis-Philippe* (Paris: Éditions L'Harmattan, 1999), 22.

2. Dimitriadis, *Voyante de Louis*, 23.

3. Dimitriadis, *Voyante de Louis*, 23.

4. Dimitriadis, *Voyante de Louis*, 42.

5. Dimitriadis, *Voyante de Louis*, 44.

6. Dimitriadis, *Voyante de Louis*, 62.

7. "I took a *Jeu de Piquet*, with 32 cards. I cut it three times. I spread them eight by eight, and took special attention in examining the extremities of my tableau." Mlle. Lenormand, *Les oracles sibyllins, ou la suite des souvenirs prophétiques* (Paris: BNF, 1817), 150.

8. Illustration by Jule Champagne in Frank B. Goodrich, *The Court of Napoleon: Or, Society Under the First Empire* (New York: Derby & Jackson: 1857), New York Public Library.

9. Louis De Bois, *De Mlle Le Normand et de ses deux biographies récemment publiées*, Paris, Chez France,, 1843).

10. In her autobiographical account, she points out some anonymous mockers of things sacred: "I could [dropped word?] why one would pass judgement on the teeth of Saint Amable, the eye of Basilic, the ardent mirror of Archimede, but for pity's sake, leave us the Tarot." *Les Souvenirs prophétiques d'une sibylle sur les causes secrètes de son arrestation, le 11 décembre 1809*, Mlle M.-A. Le Normand, 1814, Paris, Bibliothèque nationale de France, iii.

11. This correlation was first highlighted by Detlef Hoffmann and Erika Kroppenstedt in *Wahrsagekarten: Ein Beitrag zur Geschichte des Okkultismus*, quoted in Decker, Depaulis, and Dummett, *A Wicked Pack of Cards* (Bristol Classical Press, 1996).

THE HIEROGLYPHIC TAROT OF MADAME DULORA DE LA HAYE

1. Madame Dulora de La Haye, *Le Tarot Hieroglyphique*, deck booklet, 1897, 1.

2. Morning of February 7, 1910, Paris, Bibliothèque nationale de France.

3. "Le Noyé de Southampton," *Le Travailleur Normand*, October 11, 1910, Rouen, France, Bibliothèque nationale de France.

4. La Petite Presse, October 10, 1900, Paris, Bibliothèque nationale de France.

LE TAROT ASTROLOGIQUE

1. Armengol also created a portrait of Muchery in a woodcut for his book *La Synthese du Tarot* published in 1927.

2. For more information, you should definitely visit g-muchery.com, a Website rich in information made available by his children.

LE GRAND JEU DE LA MAIN / THE GREAT GAME OF THE HAND

1. Moreau reclaims herself as one of her students. *L'Avenir dévoilé. Chiromancie nouvelle. Études des deux mains* (Paris: Adele Moreau, 1869), 5.

2. Le physionomiste Lavater reconnaissait le caractère d'un individu à l'ensemble des traits du visage. Gall, Spurzheim, Idgiès, Castle et d'autres encore ont tiré de la phrénologie des certitudes en faveur de l'éducation. La chiromancie, unie à ces deux sciences, apporte au dix-neuvième siècle sa part de conseils et de lumières."

LE JEU DU DESTIN ANTIQUE: THE ANTIQUE DESTINY DECK

1. The 1986 Piatnik Edition features a booklet written by J.F. Simon in 1944, which mostly covers traditional cartomancy interpretations and combinations but doesn't give any information on the decks rich iconography.

2. Images of the 1991 booklet of the Dusserre edition were kindly provided to me by collector and cartomancer extraordinaire Ian Laycock.

PAVLOV'S TAROT

1. In the 1650 Viéville, for example, the World card represents a Christ-like figure who, although naked, doesn't present nipples nor breasts, ombilic nor genitalia. So is the long-haired figure in the early eighteenth-century Jean Dodal Tarot. In the François Isnard published in the late 1700s, the character on the Star card is equally ambiguous.

THE MATERIA PRIMA: AN EXPRESSION OF MATTER

1. Although apocryphal, this quote is inspired by a short paragraph of Lavoisier's *Elementary Treatise on Chemistry*, published in 1789, in which he describes the conversion of mass as matter change state.

SELECTED BIBLIOGRAPHY

BOOKS

Adams, Peter Mark. *The Game of Saturn: Decoding the Sola-Busca Tarrochi*. Scarlet Imprint, 2018.

Depaulis, Thierry. *Tarot, Jeu et Magie*. Paris: Bibliothèque Nationale,1984.

Dummett, Michael, and Ronald Decker. *A History of the Occult Tarot*. London: Duckworth, 2013.

Dummett, Michael, Ronald Decker, and Thierry Depaulis. *A Wicked Pack of Cards: Origins of the Occult Tarot*. London: Duckworth, 2002.

Farley, Helen. *A Cultural History of Tarot: From Entertainment to Esotericism*. London: Bloomsbury Academic, 2019.

Hundley, Jessica. *Tarot: The Library of Esoterica*. Köln: Taschen, 2020.

Huson, Paul. *Mystical Origins of the Tarot*. Rochester, New York: Destiny Books, 2009.

Jodorowsky, Alejandro, and Marianne Costa. *The Way of Tarot*. Rochester, New York: Destiny Books, 2009.

Kaplan, Stuart R. *The Encyclopedia of Tarot*. New York: US Games Systems Inc., 1978.

Kaplan, Stuart, Mary K. Greer, Elizabeth Foley O'Connor, and Melinda Boyd Parsons. *Pamela Colman Smith: The Untold Story*. Stamford, Connecticut: US Games Systems Inc., 2018.

Nadolny, Isabelle. *Histoire du tarot: Origines, Iconographie, Symbolisme*. Escalquens, France: Trajectoire, 2018.

Nichols, Sallie. *Jung and Tarot: An Archetypal Journey*. York Beach, Maine: Weiser Books,1984.

O'Neill, Robert V. *Tarot Symbolism*. Lima, Ohio: Fairway Press, 1968.

Place, Robert. *The Tarot: History, Symbolism, and Divination*. New York: TarcherPerigee, 2007.

Pollack, Rachel. *78 Degrees of Wisdom: A Book of Tarot*. York Beach, Maine: Weiser Books, 2007.

Talbot, Jude. *Fabuleuses cartes à jouer: Le monde en miniature*. Paris: Gallimard, 2018.

WEBSITES

Mary K. Greer's Tarot Blog: https://marykgreer.com/

Sherryl E. Smith's Tarot Heritage: https://tarot-heritage.com/

Le Tarot Cultural Association, presided by Andrea Vitali: http://www.letarot.it/index.aspx?lng=ENG

OPPOSITE PAGE

The Moon, from the Pagan Otherworlds
Tarot, Uusi, 2016.

The Moon

I · HYDROGEN · H

ACKNOWLEDGMENTS

First and foremost, and since this book was written during the COVID-19 lockdown, I want to share my gratitude to the invisible librarians and archivists who digitized and made accessible via libraries and museums' online collections so many of the primary sources, texts, and cards that served me for this book. Allowing many researchers to continue their work at institutions that were closed, these essential workers of the cultural world were invaluable allies during my research. A big thanks as well to Rodolphe Lachat, Amelie Retorre, Lucille Kroenlein, and Benjamin Brard, and the Cernunnos/Abrams team for their patience and support during this process. This book would not exist without their dedication. Many regards to my friends, students, and family for their support and encouragement, especially my parents, Janou and Michel, and Adrienne Simone, Chloe Sugden, and Amy Slonacker.

Thanks to all the participating artists, collectors, and tarot specialists who generously gave me their time; Brandie Knight and Brandon Hodge; Meredith Grave; Eugene Vinitski and McClosky Antiques.

Finally, a special bow to my dear Joanna Ebenstein and Judy Ebenstein for giving me the birthday gift of a lifetime and a tarot reading that changed everything.

This book is dedicated to Spencer Lamm, my King of Hearts.

OPPOSITE PAGE
Hydrogen, Materia Prima deck, Uusi, 2020.

CREDITS

BIOGRAPHY

French-born Laetitia Barbier is an independent scholar and curator, as well as a professional tarot reader and teacher. She earned a bachelor's degree in art history at the Sorbonne in Paris. Barbier has worked with Morbid Anatomy as the programming director and head librarian since 2012. Her work has been featured in *Atlas Obscura*, *Vice*, and in *Death: A Graveside Companion* (Thames & Hudson) and she recently authored *Jesus Now: Art + Pop Culture*, an examination of portraits of Christ in Contemporary Art (Cernunnos / Abrams books). She shares her love for tarot and obscure fortune telling decks and techniques through her Instagram account @laetitia.cartomancy - You can reach her at www.laetitiacartomancy.com

T A R O T
AND DIVINATION CARDS

Text: Laetitia Barbier
Cernunnos logo design: Mark Ryden
Book design: Benjamin Brard

ISBN: 978-1-4197-5637-5
eISBN: 978-1-64700-388-3

Printed and bound in China
10 9 8 7 6 5 4

Abrams books are available at special discounts when purchased in quantity for premiums and promotions as well as fundraising or educational use. Special editions can also be created to specification. For details, contact specialsales@abramsbooks.com or the address below.

Abrams® is a registered trademark of Harry N. Abrams, Inc.

ABRAMS The Art of Books
195 Broadway, New York, NY 10007
abramsbooks.com